The Shewing

of

Julian of Norwich

Middle English Texts

General Editor

Russell A. Peck
University of Rochester

Advisory Board

Rita Copeland
University of Texas

Thomas G. Hahn
University of Rochester

Lisa Kiser
Ohio State University

Alan Lupack
University of Rochester

Thomas Seiler
Western Michigan University

R. A. Shoaf
University of Florida

Bonnie Wheeler
Southern Methodist University

The Middle English Texts Series is designed for classroom use. Its goal is to make available to teachers and students texts which occupy an important place in the literary and cultural canon but which have not been readily available in student editions. The series does not include those authors such as Chaucer, Gower, Langland, the Pearl-poet, or Malory, whose English works are normally in print in good student editions. The focus is, instead, upon Middle English literature adjacent to those authors that teachers need in compiling the syllabuses they wish to teach. The editions maintain the linguistic integrity of the original work but within the parameters of modern reading conventions. The texts are printed in the modern alphabet and follow the practices of modern capitalization and punctuation. Manuscript abbreviations are expanded, and u/v and j/i spellings are regularized according to modern orthography. Hard words, difficult phrases, and unusual idioms are glossed on the page, either in the right margin or at the foot of the page. Textual notes appear at the end of the text, along with a glossary. The editions include short introductions on the history of the work, its merits and points of topical interest, and also include briefly annotated bibliographies.

The Shewings

of

Julian of Norwich

Edited by
Georgia Ronan Crampton

Published for TEAMS
(The Consortium for the Teaching of the Middle Ages)
in Association with the University of Rochester

by

Medieval Institute Publications

WESTERN MICHIGAN UNIVERSITY

Kalamazoo, Michigan – 1994

Library of Congress Cataloging-in-Publication Data

Julian of Norwich, b. 1343
    [Revelations of divine love]
    The shewings of Julian of Norwich / edited by Georgia Ronan
Crampton.
        p. cm. -- (Middle English texts)
    Middle English printed in the modern alphabet with modern
capitalization and punctuation.
    Includes bibliographical references.
    ISBN 1-879288-45-1
    1. Devotional literature, English (Middle) 2. Love--Religious
aspects--Christianity--Prayer-books and devotions--English (Middle)
3. Private revelations--Prayer-books and devotions--English (Middle)
4. Julian, of Norwich, b. 1343. I. Crampton, Georgia Ronan.
II. Title. III. Series: Middle English texts (Kalamazoo, Mich.)
BV4831.J8 1994
242--dc20   94-27758
                                                 CIP

ISBN 1-879288-45-1

Printed in the United States of America

Cover design by Elizabeth King

For my mother, my sisters, my brother

"Mayflower Regina, think of us"

                        Somehow,
reading or read to, she'd spiralled
up within tall towers
of learning, steeples of discourse.
Bells in her spirit
rang new changes.

Contents

Acknowledgments

Calogrenant, knight and story teller in the *Yvain* of Chrétien de Troyes, asks for both ears and hearts of listeners because although the word comes to the ear like wind, it does not pause unless the heart is alert to grasp and enclose it. Many of Julian of Norwich's readers give the impression in their writings that her book has reached both ear and heart. I am more indebted to their commentary than the notes in this edition can indicate.

I am grateful to the British Library for permission to publish Sloane MS 2499 and extracts from Sloane MS 3705 and Additional MS 37790. Readings from MS Paris Fonds anglais 40 appear with the kind permission of the Bibliothèque Nationale, Département des Manuscrits. The help of librarians and staff at the British Library, the Bibliothèque Nationale, the Library of Congress, the Princeton Index of Christian Art, Mount Angel Abbey Library in Oregon, and the Branford Price Millar Library of Portland State University is appreciated. At Portland State Jennifer Bowers, Evelyn Crowell, Sharon Elteto, Janet K. Wright, and Robert C. Westover have given particular help. I thank Lorraine Duncan and her staff of the Portland State University Faculty Resource Center for both skill and kindness in its exercise.

At Cambridge and Norwich, Judah Bierman found answers to questions I should have thought to ask during my own visit to Julian's territory. At Norwich, the Cathedral's Secretary and the Julian Centre, All Hallows, helped him. Christine Rose, Rose Ronan Halpern, and Susan Mosedale found particular sources. Julia Turner first called my attention to Luce Irigaray's "La Mystérique" and its relevance to Julian's book. Canon Michael McLean of Norwich, Dame Gertrude Brown, O.S.B., of Stanbrook Abbey, and Hywel W. Owen graciously responded to questions. I value the care Russell A. Peck, Alan Lupack, and Karen Saupe have given to this edition. Their judgment and skill have improved it greatly. And thanks are due to the National Endowment for the Humanities for support in preparing the revised and corrected edition of this volume.

Among my family, there are earlier readers of Julian than I. They have encouraged me. My greatest debt is, as always, to John A. Crampton. His patience throughout the length of my preoccupation with *The Shewings*, if not invariable, was nevertheless generous and largely sustaining. An early draft of the introduction had the benefit of his characteristic lucidity.

The Shewings of Julian of Norwich

Introduction

The Shewings of Julian of Norwich tells of an intense experience that took place within a few days and nights of May, 1373, in Norwich. The book is a first-person account of a young woman's visions. They came, she tells us, when she was thirty and a half years old, after seven days and nights of illness. At the very point of death — her curate holds a crucifix before her eyes to comfort her, and she is aware that her mother, thinking her dead, has moved to close her eyes — she received fifteen "shewings," to be confirmed the next day in a sixteenth. Health restored, she lived on into old age, almost certainly as an anchorite.

Two accounts of the showings, or revelations, as Julian also calls them, one much longer than the other, survive. She apparently wrote a first, short narrative soon after the 1373 illness, and a second, six-fold longer, twenty years later: "For twenty yeres after the tyme of the shewing, save three monethis [months], I had techyng inwardly" (lines 1865–66). Much of the short text reads as if it were immediately, spontaneously, recounted. An authorial consciousness as well as a bolder and a more elaborated theology mark the long text.

Julian's showings comprise visual images, words that emerge in her mind fully articulated, and spiritual events without sensuous representation, either visual or verbal. She carefully reports not only the content of her experiences, but also their modes of perception: "All this was shewid by thre, that is to sey, be bodily sight, and by word formyd in my understonding, and be gostly sight. But the gostly sight — I cannot ne may not shew it as hopinly ne as fully as I wolde" [All this was shown in three ways, that is to say, by bodily sight, by words formed in my mind, and by spiritual sight. But I cannot nor may not show the spiritual sight as openly nor as fully as I would wish to do] (lines 340–43; see also 2974–79). And again, "Than He, without voice and openyng of lippis [lips], formys [forms] in my soule these words: *Herewith is the fend* [fiend] *overcome*" (lines 500–01; see also 2829–30). Most of the visual showings center upon Christ's suffering during the crucifixion:

> I saw His swete face as it was drye and blodeles with pale deyeng, and sithen more
> pale, dede, langoring, and than turnid more dede into blew, and sithen more browne

blew, as the flesh turnyd more depe dede. For His passion shewid to me most propirly in His blissid face, and namly in His lippis. There I saw these four colowres, tho that were aforn freshe, redy, and likyng to my sigte. This was a swemful chonge to sene, this depe deyeng, and also the nose clange and dryed, to my sigte, and the swete body was brown and blak, al turnyd oute of faire lifely colowr of Hymselfe on to drye deyeng. For that same tyme that our Lord and blissid Savior deyid upon the Rode, it was a dry, harre wynde and wonder colde, as to my sigte. [I saw His sweet face when it was dry and bloodless in its pale dying, and after, as it became even paler, more death-like, languishing, and then it turned more deathly into blue, and after, a more brownish blue, as the flesh turned more deeply into death. For His passion showed itself to me most in His blessed face, and especially in His lips. There I saw these four colors, in those lips that before were fresh, red, and pleasant in my eyes. This was a grievous change to see, this deep dying, and also the nose shriveled and dried in my sight, and the sweet body was brown and black, completely turned from His own fair, life-like color on into this dry dying. For at the time that our Lord and blessed Saviour died upon the Cross, there was a dry, harsh wind, and it seemed to me terribly cold.] (lines 589–99)

Not all of the visual showings are of Christ. Secular images whose meanings unfold in Julian's understanding, sometimes after years of reflection, sometimes immediately, are a striking feature of the showings. An often-quoted example is the hazel nut cosmos: "Also in this He shewed a littil thing, the quantitye of an hesil nutt [hazel nut] in the palme of my hand; and it was round as a balle. I lokid there upon with eye of my understondyng and thowte, What may this be? And it was generally answered thus: *It is all that is made*" (lines 148–51).

Julian accepts her experience as answering previous, but forgotten, petitions to have bodily sight of the Crucifixion and to undergo in youth a severe illness in order to be "purged be [by] the mercy of God and after lyven [live] more to the worshippe of God because of that sekenesse" (lines 60–61). But between the prayers and the May of their granting, "These two desires foresaid passid fro [from] my minde" (line 70). She also had asked to receive what she calls three "wounds," true contrition, compassion, and "willfull longing to God" (line 69); this third petition "dwelled with me continually" (lines 70–71).

If *The Shewings* did no more than recount these events in the fashion that it does, the book would merit attention for the particularity and verve of its prose, as a vivid spiritual document, and as an early autobiographical fragment in the vernacular. But what makes it more deeply significant is that, especially in her longer version, Julian incorporates in no simply appended way but in an evolving integration the results of a long concentration upon the visions. Reflective passages support the narrative of the visions with a circling, complex, always reasoned consideration of the doctrinal and devotional implications twenty years of thinking about them have yielded. For Julian, the showings reach deeply into what it means to be a human being, which for her is to be a creature created by God living in Christendom.

Her discussions include the nature of the Trinity, God, and most especially Christ; the nature of sin; the relation of the individual soul to God, to neighbor, and to self; the roles of providence and chance; the process of prayer; the salvic roles of nature and grace, and a theology of creation. The church and the sacraments are accorded a respectful, summary, mention. Through her exploration of these topics, Julian offers to our regard her world. It is one in which pain, illness, sin, desolating loneliness, and numbing stupidity occur, but one in which, because every human creature in it is suffused with the presence of God, all things are, finally, and also in an underlying deep and present reality, "well." Her world is not an open one and surely not an open-ended one. It is not a world that is being fabricated, or improvised, or written into existence through the endeavors of successive human generations. But although a totalization, not of human making, the world is not recalcitrant or static; rather it is shot through with interchanging energies. It is, in Julian's word, a "werkyng," and also "sekir" [secure] space and time in which people — all that is within them — are "kept," saved, cherished, and loved. It is a world whose potential, bent, and reality, even unfelt and unseen, is joy. A fundamental vocabulary of plain words — *werkyng, sekir, kepyng,* and *lyking* (pleasure) — reiterates directly this sense of how things are.

The writing, while idiomatic and pungent, is marked throughout by the description of abstractions in terms of their properties, by succinct statements couched as formal definitions, by rigorous distinctions, by negative clarification, by enumerated analytical classification; by some conspicuous meticulousness in disposal of prepositions (see lines 2181–84 and 3114–15), and by a vocabularly that recalls not only the Bible (especially John and Paul), but also learned discourse. Some examples to which she repeatedly has recourse include the can-may-will division of possibility, action and suffering as binary categories, the contrast of creator to creature, and the use of *substance* in its technical, philosophical sense. This intellectuality has led most scholars to conclude that the writer could not have been illiterate and that she probably knew Latin, at the least well enough to read the Latin Bible, a conclusion that would be unexceptional except that it contradicts her flat assertion that the revelation came to a "simple creature that cowde [knew] no letter" (line 41).

A number of explanations of how this is to be interpreted have been offered: It may be an instance of *captatio benevolentiae*, a modesty topos, that could be accepted at face value only by those unfamiliar with the convention of such disclaimers; it may mean that, like the German mystic Mechthild of Magdeburg whose similar profession indicated ignorance of Latin but not of German, Julian was literate in the vernacular only; or, it may mean that the visions did come to her when she was unlettered, but that before composing the longer account she became literate.[1]

To be taken into account is Julian's residence in a town, large by medieval standards in England, with a number of institutions of learning.[2] It claimed a noted grammar school. At the great cathedral, the priory gave instruction both to monks and to young men destined for the diocesan clergy. Late fourteenth-century Norfolk still drew scholars from the continent. Julian's contemporary, Peter of Candia, the scholar who became the controversial Pope Alexander V, traveled to England to study at Norwich as well as at Oxford. The four mendicant orders maintained Norwich convents which prepared candidates in philosophy and theology before they went on to Cambridge or Oxford. Scholars from the orders, most of whom lived within a mile or two of one another, held disputations, although these probably were not open to women auditors.[3] In such a place, the quality of the sermons must have been enviable, and an eager listener might well absorb both advanced ideas and the formulations that would most economically express them. As a late twentieth-century person might speak of the mirror stage in child development without reading Piaget, a fourteenth-century person lacking formal education might grasp theological issues and terms.

The fact is that it is very difficult to judge confidently the degree to which a listener might become learned in a late medieval milieu.[4] Even the twentieth-century

---

[1] Among those endorsing the first suggestion are Fathers Edmund Colledge and James Walsh (C&W, I, 47); among those proposing the second, Riehle, p. 29, and the third, von Nolcken, p. 103. The evidence for Julian's learning is most formidably assembled in the 1978 edition of Colledge and Walsh, I, 43–59, and notes throughout, cited here as C&W. See also J. A. W. Bennett, pp. 322–34. A gathering of evidence which leans toward keeping the question open appears in Pelphrey (1982), pp. 18–28. Competence in Latin was an accepted fourteenth-century meaning of literacy.

[2] Medieval England did not have the populous urban centers of the continent. London's population was about 35,000. Evidence points to Norwich's relative size and importance at the close of the Anglo-Saxon period. In 1066, the population was something over 10,000. Population fell dramatically in the fourteenth century because of the plague. Estimates given for Julian's lifetime range around 6,000. At times in the Middle Ages it was the second most populous city in England; at other times, York and Lincoln outpaced Norwich. For basic information on medieval Norwich see James Campbell, "Norwich," *The Atlas of Historic Towns* II, 1–25.

[3] For the educational situation in Norwich, see William J. Courtenay, *Schools and Scholars in Fourteenth-Century England* (Princeton: Princeton University Press, 1987), pp. 106–11.

[4] For a brief overview of "cultural diglossia," the scope of interactions between orality and literacy in the Middle Ages, see Walter J. Ong, "Orality, Literacy, and Medieval Textualization," *NLH* 16 (1984), 1–12.

mix of oral and written, authorial and scribal, may become complex. Consider only Ferdinand de Saussure's *Course in General Linguistics* or a *Paris Review* interview. Lacan writes that his subsequently published lecture, "The agency of the letter in the unconscious or reason since Freud," is inserted "at a point somewhere between writing [l'écrit] and speech — it will be half-way between the two." Lacan then footnotes, "The lecture took place on 9 May, 1957, in the Amphithéâtre Descartes of the Sorbonne, and the discussion was continued afterwards over drinks."[5] Evidently he considers the final writing to owe something to this pendant, surely oral, occasion. Weighty and plausible, the evidence that Julian was literate in both Latin and English is not conclusive.

Interest centers upon the statement not only for its bearings upon the issue of the late medieval interplay of orality and literacy but also because this is one of the rare facts Julian offers about herself that does not issue directly from the few hours of the visions, their occasion and context. We know little or nothing of her life with certainty. Even the identification of the book's author with the anchoress who in the late fourteenth century occupied a cell at St. Julian's church in Norwich, though secure from reasonable challenge, depends not upon internal evidence but upon a manuscript rubric. Of a neighboring, younger religious seeker, Margery Kempe of Lynn, we know family, Christian and married names, status of father and husband, number of children, business ventures, travel itineraries, and the gist of encounters with many persons, clerical and lay, including Julian herself (see Appendix B). Saint Augustine addresses his *Confessions* (a book Julian may have known — see note to line 918–19), to God, but exposes to incidental audiences a David Copperfieldian abundance: names of mother, father, son, and various friends and associates; education and reading; marriage negotiations, and professional conditions in two cities. Of the English solitary of the generation preceding Julian, Richard Rolle, we have many anecdotes, including how he dropped out of Oxford at the age of eighteen and embarked on his hermit's career in a garment fashioned from his father's rainhood and two tunics of his sister, prompting her to cry out, "My brother is mad!"

But Julian models no emblematic anecdote and offers few facts. Least of all self-dramatizing, neither is she forthcoming. Some of the sparse externals — that her mother was present at her bedside and that a child accompanied the priest on his sick call — as well as her defiant sense of her own daring in presuming as a woman to speak up with authority (see Appendix A) are even pared away in the later version of the *Shewings*. A curate, anonymous others in her sick room, and "a certeyn

---

[5] *Psychanalyse et sciences de l'homme*, 1958; rpt. *Écrits: A Selection*, trans. Alan Sheridan (New York: W. W. Norton, and Tavistock, 1977), pp. 146, 176, note 3.

creature that I lovid" (line 1167) survive into the revision, the last to make the point that one ought to be interested in what is general, not in who is particular. A charmingly illuminated cat in the modern Julian of Norwich Cathedral window is extra-textual, no doubt prompted by the thirteenth-century *Ancrene Riwle* whose author warned his recluses against owning a cow as a too cumbrous and worldly responsibility, but did allow a cat: "Ge mine leoue sustrene ne schule ye habben nan beast bute cat ane." [You, my dear sisters, should have no beast, except for one cat.][6]

Nonetheless, the book projects a strong sense of a particular, intensely-lived life, of a distinctive personality coupling a benign, open temperament with a discriminating mind, energetic, ardent and focused, working hard. This working, and reworking, strains the outline of the showings, as becomes especially clear when comparing short and long versions. The visionary events which continued "shewing be process ful faire and sekirly ich folowand other" [showing by a fair and certain progression each following the other] (lines 2741–42) are sliced into to form envelopes accommodating the probing of their significance. B. A. Windeatt has described the long version's "structure of exploration and enquiry" as resulting from "the pressure of meditation" that pushes the narrative framework "outwards from within" (*Art,* pp. 57, 60).

This pressure makes it seem that the frequent enumerations are not so much sets of conclusions as a way of securing a hold upon exigent issues. "It *nedyth* me to wetyn it" [I *needed* to know], Julian will write (line 1788; emphasis mine). Explanation and exploration resolve in sudden concisions: "And Hymselfe werkith it; then it is" (lines 2142–43); "He is here alone with us all; that is to sey, only for us, He is here" (lines 3283–84); "For in the beholding of God we fall not; in the beholding of selfe we stond not; and both these ben soth" [are true] (lines 3335–36); "I have seid as I saw as trewly as I can" (line 2976). She quite deliberately thinks of her later version not only as a book but also as a project, a process, drawing to conclusion with an enigmatic proviso: "This booke is begunne be Gods gift and His grace, but it is not yet performid, as to my syte" (lines 3391–92). The reader may find the want of biographical fact and domestic context well compensated by the close view she offers of her mind in the intimacies of its acts of apprehension. Still, a vita can be posited. Julian's dating of the visions, research on the anchoritic life in England and upon the East Anglia of the late fourteenth and early fifteenth century, and a few documents —

---

[6] *The English Text of the Ancrene Riwle*, ed. from B.M. Cotton MS Cleopatra C.vi by E. J. Dobson, EETS 267 (London: Oxford University Press, 1972), p. 305. The author's concern about the inherent distractions of cows may not have been too solicitous. In 1416, the prioress of Carrow Abbey, where Julian may have been a nun, brought the prior of the cathedral and another monk to court for driving cattle off from the convent's pastures to their own grazing lands (Tanner, p. 159).

wills, the visit of Margery Kempe, and a rubric in the short version's manuscript — allow educated guesses.

Putting together the May, 1373, date for the visions and Julian's statement that she was then thirty and a half, we get a birthdate of late 1342. The first will to mention her as an anchoress appears in a testament dated 1394. Surely enclosed then, it is entirely likely that she was an anchoress much earlier. It has been assumed that the company at her bedside means that she was not a recluse at the time of the visions, but the visitors' presence could indicate that a solitary's life might be less rigid than enclosure ceremonies suggest or that the regime was relaxed in emergencies. The manuscript heading of the shorter version states that she was still living in 1413:

> There es a visioun schewed be the goodenes of god to a devoute womann, and hir Name es Julyan that is recluse atte Norwyche and yitt ys onn lyfe. Anno d(omi)ni mill(esi)mo CCCCxiij; In the whilke visyoun er fulle many comfortabylle wordes and gretly styrrande to alle thaye that desyres to be crystes looverse. [Here is a vision shown by the goodness of God to a devout woman, and her name is Julian, who is a recluse a Norwich and still is alive, the year of our Lord 1413; in which vision are many comforting words, greatly moving to all those who desire to be lovers of Christ.] (BL MS Additional 37790, fol. 97r.)

The last bequest naming Julian comes in 1416 from Isabel Ufford, countess of Suffolk, included among numerous gifts to religious and religious houses: "Item jeo devyse a Julian recluz a Norwich 20s" [Item: I bequeath to Julian, recluse at Norwich, twenty shillings]. However, bequests to an unnamed anchoress at St. Julian's continued until 1429, so it is possible that the writer lived until that date.[7]

Although fourteenth-century England offered a diversity of religious callings, options for women were narrow, and the anchoritic way of life was the only one that more women than men chose. It was officially recognized from the twelfth century; then a paper trail of enclosure rituals, ecclesiastical regulations, documents of support, and a virtual genre of advice-to-solitaries literature begins. But the anchoritic choice was never really common. In anchoritism's most flourishing century, the fourteenth, there were 214 anchorites in England to about 35,000 other religious, secular and regular.[8] To be an anchorite was to choose a more severe and idiosyn-

---

[7] Tanner, p. 200, note 29. The quotation from the will of Isabel Ufford is from C&W, I, 34.

[8] Warren, pp. 19–20, and Josiah Cox Russell, "The Clerical Population of Medieval England," *Traditio* 2 (1944), 179. But see John Hatcher, *Plague, Population and the English Economy 1348–1530,* Studies in Economic and Social History (London: Macmillan Press, 1977), pp. 13–15 and pp. 75–76, note 3, for a criticism of Russell's use of the 1377 poll tax returns

cratic, but also a more initially accessible, path than that of communal life in orders where dowries were required. The solitary calling drew lay people, the poor as well as the aristocratic; priests, canons, and friars who moved into seclusion from roles of social service; and monks and nuns who stepped beyond the regular community pattern into a more deeply contemplative solitary life.[9]

Most male anchorites were clerics, but since no record was taken of the previous status of nuns, records do not show how many women recluses were professed religious. Although Margery Kempe gives Julian the title of "dame," customary for nuns, none of the wills naming her identifies her in that way. Nonetheless, it has been supposed that Julian may have been a nun. If so, her most likely community would have been Benedictine. A Benedictine convent, Carrow Abbey, stands about a mile from St. Julian's parish church and held its advowson (i.e., the right to nominate its rector). Certainly Carrow Abbey later supported other anchorites, and, whether or not Julian was a nun there, it is among Benedictine communities of nuns that the *Shewings* reappeared in the seventeeth century. Whether she was indeed a nun, however, remains disputed.[10]

Unlike hermits, solitaries who moved about, most anchorites vowed stability. After enclosure they remained, normally for life, in the same restricted quarters, most

---

as a basis for population estimates. Most details in this summary of anchoritic life come from Warren. For anchorites in Norwich specifically, see the lively essay by F. I. Dunn, "Hermits, Anchorites and Recluses: A Study with Reference to Medieval Norwich," in Frank Dale Sayer, ed., *Julian and her Norwich: Commemorative Essays and Handbook to the Exhibition "Revelations of Divine Love,"* pp. 18–26.

[9] The rule of St. Benedict, which in the sixth century set the pattern for medieval monastic life, envisioned a distinct calling for stricter seclusion. The rule's text opens with a classification of monks. The first, cenobites, belong to the monastery, serving under rule and abbot. "Second, there are the anchorites or hermits, who have come through the test of living in a monastery for a long time, and have passed beyond the first fervor of monastic life. . . . They have built up their strength and go from the battle line in the ranks of their brothers to the single combat of the desert. Self-reliant now, without the support of another, they are ready with God's help to grapple single-handed with the vices of body and mind" (*The Rule of St. Benedict in English,* ed. Timothy Fry, O.S.B., and others [Collegeville, Minn.: The Liturgical Press, 1981], p. 20). Anchoritism as a succession to the desert hermits, in turn thought of as successors to the early martyrs as the most heroic witnesses to faith, is a common medieval theme.

[10] A case for the probability that Julian was a professed nun is given by D. S. H., A Benedictine of Stanbrook, "Dame Julian of Norwich," *Clergy Review* 44 n.s. (1959), 707–09; for a strong dissent, see Sister Benedicta Ward, "Julian the Solitary," in *Julian Reconsidered* by Kenneth Leech and Sister Benedicta (Oxford: SLG Press, 1988), pp. 13–29.

attached to a church or convent. Whether Julian made a formal vow of seclusion cannot be said; Norwich diocesan registers do not have complete records of formal commitments (Tanner, p. 61). Julian very likely took her name from St. Julian's, the Norwich parish where a church had existed since Saxon times and which had an anchorhold. The prescribed size for a solitary's cell was twelve square feet. In actuality, sizes varied from place to place, some modestly spacious, others severely cramped. Some sites provided for more than one recluse, such as that for the three sisters for whom the *Ancrene Riwle* was written. An anchorhold found at Compton in Surrey allowed barely room to turn around, measuring six feet, eight inches, by four feet, four inches, plus a loft (Warren, p. 32). According to Canon Michael McLean, former rector of St. Julian's, the dimensions of Julian's cell, probably built against the church's south side, were almost certainly smaller than the site that visitors see in the present building, reconstructed after the bombing of June 27, 1942. Though most opinion accepts the present site, Canon McLean observes that at least two ancient maps show a cell in different positions alongside the churchyard wall. It had been assumed that Julian's cell was destroyed at the time of the dissolution in 1539, but it is now believed that the structure, which may have been of timber on stone foundations, simply fell into ruins after the Reformation.[11]

Regulations for reclusoria prescribed arrangments beyond size of the quarters. Cells were to have three windows, the first opening to the church to allow the recluse to hear Mass, receive the Sacrament, and speak with a confessor; the second for delivery of necessities; the third, for light, was to be covered so as to be translucent, but not distracting. Julian's window into the church did not allow much view of the altar; the tabernacle housing the Blessed Sacrament, which then hung in front of the altar rather than being recessed upon it, was, however, fully visible.[12] A priest-recluse might have an altar in his cell. Gardens were allowed, certainly a possibility at St. Julian's.

Enclosure rituals for the neophyte recluse included a mass with prayers for the dead; the anchorite was henceforth to be one dead to the world. But in fact enclosure could not preclude ties between anchorites and their communities, ties both practical

---

[11] Letter of 19 February, 1992.

[12] Robert H. Flood, *A Description of St. Julian's Church, Norwich, and an Account of Dame Julian's Connection with It* (Norwich: Wherry Press, c. 1936), p. 44. This book opens with a report of St. Julian's structure which Flood studied before the 1942 bombing. I owe access to this out-of-print book to Professor Judah Bierman of Portland State University. The British Library gives the date 1937 for the book. The 1936 date comes from a frontispiece sketch of the church.

and spiritual. Bishops were responsible to see to it that the life was not assumed carelessly and that the anchorite would have lifetime support. Servants, and no doubt volunteers, fetched and carried. The *Ancrene Riwle* recommends that in order to have time for prayer, anchoresses keep maidservants (p. 311). Julian apparently had two servants, for John Plumpton, a Norwich citizen, in 1415 willed forty pence to Julian herself and twelve pence each to her serving maid and to Alice, her former maid (C&W, I, 33–34). Anchorites counseled visitors. Margery Kempe sometime in 1415 sought and received the counsel of "an ankres in the same cyte whych hyte Dame Ielyan" [an anchoress in the same city (i.e., Norwich) who is called Dame Julian].[13] Priests who took up seclusion might continue duty as confessors; Margery Kempe counted an anchorite of Lynn as her "principal gostly fadyr" (pp. 43–44). Letters of advice warn anchorites that they are not to gossip or get a name for themselves as school mistresses, though they might perhaps oversee a servant's instruction of children. On the other hand, the anchorite might be the one requiring instruction. When Emma Stapleton, daughter of Sir Miles Stapleton, became an anchoress at Norwich's Carmelite friary in 1421, five persons, including the prior and sub-prior, were appointed advisers.[14] Probably most recluses passed some time in secondary occupations; needlework was commended to women; men might be copyists or priests (Warren, p. 42). We know that Julian, like Rolle and like another contemporary recluse, the Monk of Farne, with or without scribal help, wrote.

Still, the center and reason for being of reclusive life was contemplative prayer. Ann K. Warren's fact-filled study of anchorites and their patrons in medieval England reports the bequests and grants from middle class, noble, and royal patrons establishing that lay people and religious alike valued these contemplatives whose lives so differed from their own. She writes of the intangible, but central communal role of anchorites:

> Encouraged, applauded, and supported by society and church, they undertook their solitary life by encamping in the heart of the community. Enclosed and yet exposed, hidden and yet visible, shadows behind the curtains of their access windows, medieval English anchorites were daily reminders of the proper focus of Christian

---

[13] *The Book of Margery Kempe,* ed. Sanford B. Meech and Hope Emily Allen, EETS o.s. 212 (London: Oxford University Press, 1940), p. 42. The date of the visit is uncertain. I follow the Meech and Allen chronology, p. xlix.

[14] Clay, *Hermits,* p. 137. See note 1167 on the possibility that Julian might have known Emma Stapleton as a child.

existence. Martyr, *viator,* penitent, ascetic, mystic, *miles Christi* — the recluse was all of these. (p. 7)

Julian had no immediate, local model for her calling. Although more hermits and anchorites lived in Norwich between the last third of the fourteenth century and the Reformation (which effectively put a pause, for some time, to anchoritism as a recognized religious life) than in any other town in England, none is recorded there between 1312–13, long before her birth, when local records mention two, and her emergence in 1373. During her lifetime, the number of anchorites within the city increased to some ten (Tanner, p. 58).

Julian's Norwich was a vigorous place. Its solitaries formed one element of a mixed, thriving religious life to which both the older church institutions and the new popular avenues of devotion contributed. Norwich had been a cathedral city at least since 1103, its priory and church planned on a scale to match the older cathedrals — a priory for sixty Benedictine monks, a fourteen-bay nave for the church.[15] The scholarly founding bishop, Herbert Losinga, who was responsble for the new cathedral's ambitious scale, also immediately set about the collection of a library, and when fire almost entirely destroyed that collection during a conflict with citizens in 1272, the cathedral set about at once with the labor of copying to replace standard works and profited, too, from the bequests of its own monks and former monks. At the time of dissolution of the monasteries under Henry VIII the collection probably numbered 1,350 books.[16] Nor was the cathedral library Norwich's only one. The Austin friars, whose house was directly across from St. Julian's parish church, had a library from which Julian herself conceivably could have borrowed. The library was considerable,

---

[15] There is some confusion about when the see moved definitely from Thetford to Norwich. For the early history of the cathedral, see Barbara Dodwell, "The Foundation of Norwich Cathedral," *Transactions of the Royal Historical Society,* 5th series, 7 (1957), 1–18.

[16] See H. C. Beeching and Montague R. James, "The Library of the Cathedral Church of Norwich," *Norfolk Archaeology* 19, Part I (1915–17), 67–116, with Addenda in Part II, 174; N. R. Ker, "Medieval Manuscripts from Norwich Cathedral Priory," *Books, Collectors and Libraries: Studies in the Medieval Heritage*, ed. Andrew G. Watson (London: Hambledon Presss, 1985), pp. 243–72, and N. R. Ker, ed., *Medieval Libraries of Great Britain: A List of Surviving Books*, 2nd ed. (London: Royal Historical Society, 1964), pp. 135–40. Dean Beeching's essay shows that the founder's interests in the library ranged widely and keenly. Among Bishop Herbert Losinga's surviving epistles is one asking the Abbot of Fécamp for Suetonius, who was not available in England, and another scolding a young monk for wasting time copying martyrologies, psalters, and breviaries when he should have been writing out Augustine or learning his grammar (p. 68).

we may infer, because a fifteenth-century Norwich donor (a lay woman) provided it with a new building. An Augustinian regulation exists stipulating that books were not to be taken from the library unless there were duplicates, which implies that if there were, they might be borrowed (C&W, I, 39–40).[17]

The fire of 1272 shows that Norwich townspeople did not always feel themselves at one with their cathedral, but possession of the see stimulated and focused cultural, as well as religious, life. It was chiefly the cathedral that patronized the artists who shaped the great period of East Anglian art. This was coming to its end at the time of Julian's birth, but as she was growing up, that art, as well as the masonry of castle, cathedral, and city wall and the wind-swept, sea-near marshlands, pastures, and rivers, made up what she would have seen about her. How rich the art could be can be estimated from what remains of such luxurious manuscripts as the Ormesby and Gorleston psalters. Embroidery, metal work, painting, sculpture, illumination, stained glass — all contributed to the splendor of the cathedral. Norfolk, as the late St. Omer psalter demonstrates, also had lay patrons. Artists from the continent worked throughout the region, supplementing a high level of local craftsmanship. Parish churches too were impressively adorned with illuminated glass, altar pieces and screens, carved fonts, and statues. The large number of surviving wooden rood screens carved with figures of saints, which in Julian's time would still be brightly painted, indicates that they were to be seen in nearly every parish church.[18]

Norman P. Tanner's study documents the vitality of the varied constituents of this religious world in later medieval Norwich. They included not only the cathedral and its priory, but also some fifty parish churches, more per capita than for any other English town — four were within a half mile of Julian's anchorhold — five places of worship attached to the cathedral priory, and eighteen religious houses or hospitals within or just without the city walls as well as anchorholds and the individual chapels of some private citizens. Craft guilds and religious confraternities increasingly sponsored religious activities, including plays. Norwich was the only place in England where communities resembling the continental beguinages developed, somewhat after Julian's lifetime (Tanner, pp. 64–66).

---

[17] A library list at Christ Church, Canterbury, shows that the library lent outside the community, even to lay persons; see James Westfall Thompson, "English Libraries in the Fourteenth and Fifteenth Centuries," *The Medieval Library*, 1939 (rpt. New York: Hafner, 1965), p. 375.

[18] W. W. Williamson, "Saints on Norfolk Rood-Screens and Pulpits," *Norfolk Archaeology* 31 (1955–57), 299–346. *Medieval Art in East Anglia 1300–1520*, ed. Peter Lasko and N. J. Morgan, gives a survey and pictures many objects.

Introduction

The medieval city, enclosed by the river Wensum and its three-mile city wall constructed between 1297 and 1377, centered about the castle and the cathedral close, but as a weaving, leather, and trading center, Norwich also looked to the sea and cultivated flourishing contacts with the Rhineland. It shared fully in the desperately eventful political life and human damage of the last half of the fourteenth century. The plague came upon the town three times, the first a drastic sweep in 1349, when Julian would have been six, and again in 1361 and 1369. When Julian was thirty-eight, the Peasant Uprising of 1381 spread throughout East Anglia. One episode involved her putative convent, Carrow Abbey. Rioters advanced upon it and, threatening violence, obtained from the prioress deeds and court rolls which they afterwards burnt at Norwich in the presence of the rebel leader, Geoffrey Litster (or Lister), who had gained the city.[19] The astonishing mix of secular and religious, ecclesiastical and martial, brutal and refined is instantiated vividly in the account of how the rebels were suppressed. The bishop, Henry Despenser, led forces opposing the rebels. When Litster was defeated the bishop personally shrove him and then presided at the execution — hanging, drawing, and quartering. The bishop expressed gratitude for the victory, according to a plausible tradition, not only with a mass but also with the donation to the cathedral of a wonderful retable with five panels, centered upon a poignant crucifixion scene.[20] The date of its donation, 1381, makes it impossible that the scene could have affected Julian's vision of the crucifixion in 1373 (and her description in no way resembles the retable panel), but if she were not yet enclosed when the gift was made, she might have seen it. Julian's cell was three quarters of a mile from the cathedral; before her death, she had a closer neighbor, the execution place for Lollards, whose repression included, for the first time under Henry IV, burning. Allusions to politics of the times — to what a twentieth century Norwich cathedral dean has characterized a "violent, insecure, ambitious and lively society" — sometimes have been read into Julian's work, but, if there, they are indirect.[21] She indicates her social bond in two more general ways, ways that issue directly from her

---

[19] Edgar Powell, *The Rising in East Anglia in 1381* (Cambridge: Cambridge University Press, 1896), p. 32. The Dictionary of National Biography (DNB) gives the rebel leader's Christian name as John. Powell discusses the confusion of names, both first and last, pp. 26–27.

[20] The painting is described by A. H. R. Martindale in *Medieval Art in East Anglia 1300–1520*, pp. 36–37. Martindale writes that the story that the altarpiece was commissioned as a thank-offering for the suppression of the revolt is comparatively modern, but that the style is right for the late fourteenth century. The retable bears the Despenser arms.

[21] The Very Rev. Alan Webster, Dean of Norwich, "Julian of Norwich," *Expository Times* 84 (1972–73), 229.

inner life: most expansively, by her understanding and reporting of her visions as being intended for all her fellow Christians; second, by her decorous acceptance of the church's teachings, even when her visions refuse corroboration of some doctrine.

Broadening the context beyond Norwich, we may see Julian as a part of that epoch when the vernacular re-emerged as a literary language. Chaucer, Gower, Langland, the author of the *Cloud of Unknowing* and Walter Hilton were all writing. The Gawain poet, with whom Julian shares an insistent motif of courtesy, was her earlier contemporary.[22] Her life overlaps with that of Richard Rolle of Hampole (1300–1349) at one end and with Margery Kempe (born c. 1373) at the other. It has been supposed that she may have read, or even used as a model of rhetoric, Chaucer's translation of Boethius (C&W, I, 45–47) or have read or been read by the spiritual writers who were her contemporaries. But with the exception of Margery Kempe, certain evidence that Julian knew of any of them or their works, or they anything of her or hers, is lacking. Margery Kempe apparently knew Julian only as a spiritual counselor, not an author, significant because the younger woman does record names of spiritual writers whose works were read to her.

We may see Julian in another context, as the late successor of the Rhineland mystics of a century and a half before, many of them women, whose writings, sometimes in a vernacular, constituted a literary phenomenon as well as a contribution to spiritual renewal in their own times. Largely because of feminist scholars' interest, some selections of medieval women's religious writing have appeared in English translations, but few of their manuscripts are known to have been in England in time for Julian to have profited from them directly.[23]

---

[22] R. A. Shoaf, in "God's 'Malyse': Metaphor and Conversion in *Patience*," *Journal of Medieval and Renaissance Studies,* 11:2 (1981), 274–77, brings Julian's theme of God's courtesy, one of her "dominant tropologies," into relation with the Gawain poet's *Patience*.

[23] For its introductions and bibliographies as well as samplings from texts, see *Medieval Women's Visionary Literature*, ed. Elizabeth Alvilda Petroff. This anthology gives chapter 51 of Julian's long text. Careful readers of Julian have come to different conclusions about continental influence. Sister Anna Maria Reynolds, in "Some Literary Influences in the *Revelations* of Julian of Norwich (c. 1342–post 1416)," *Leeds Studies in English* 7 (1952), 18–28, notes resemblances to Meister Eckhart, but decides that points of contact with St. Catherine of Siena and St. Bridget, Julian's contemporaries, and the earlier St. Gertrude and Mechtild von Hackeborn are lacking. Latin copies of St. Bridget's work circulated in England before the saint's death in 1373, and the Middle English version of Mechtild's *Liber specialis gratiae, The Booke of Gostlye Grace*, and Latin abridgments just could have been in Norfolk towards the very end of Julian's life. The Middle English Mechtild (the *Maulde boke)* was bequeathed by Alianora Roos of York to Dame Joan Courtenay in 1438. Four Latin abridgments were in England in the later fifteenth century;

Introduction

If, apart from the Bible, we do not know exactly what Julian read, neither do we know who in her own time or the next generations read her. Some Middle English spiritual texts directly address an immediate audience. Aelred wrote a guide to reclusive life for his own sister. *The Ancrene Riwle,* written for three enclosed sisters of the same family, quickly spread beyond them to others. The *Cloud of Unknowing* author writes for a young monk undertaking a strict solitary life. Hilton wrote for an anchoress, his "ghostly sister in Jesus Christ," and forty-seven extant manuscripts of the *Scale of Perfection* show how generally others found that treatise useful.[24] Julian did not do this, did not direct her *Shewings* to a special reader or readers. She took the showings as given generally for all, and she wrote to all, to her "even Cristene." But, in the short run, the very lack of evidence indicates that she reached very few. In a study of Julian's influence and that of Richard Rolle on the Middle English lyric, Mary A. Knowlton concludes, in effect, that she had none.[25] Lateral contamination indicates that both short and long texts were in circulation by 1413 when Julian, if we trust the short text's introduction, "yitt ys onn lyfe," but between this date and the mid-seventeenth century, there is silence.

Julian's first readers about whom we have any definite information appear in the mid-seventeenth century in two small exile houses of English Benedictine nuns, one at Cambrai, in Northern France, the other its daughter house in Paris. There women of recusant families followed their vocations until the French Revolution drove them back to re-establish in England. (Stanbrook Abbey descends from Cambrai; St. Mary's Abbey at Colwich, Stafford, from Paris.) There, they pursued lives of prayer and

---

there may have been others, earlier, not now extant. This information is from Theresa Halligan's introduction to *The Booke* (Toronto: Pontifical Institute of Mediaeval Studies, Studies and Texts 46, 1979). Like Julian, Mechtild refers to the motherhood of God (p. 353), but differences in their works are what is most immediately striking. Halligan concludes that Julian's work "owes nothing to her predecessors overseas" (p. 59). Riehle believes that what Julian got from continental mysticism was models that gave "a decisive impetus for her literary initiative and her mystical experiences" (p. 30). A difficulty in speculating about sources, as Brant Pelphrey has nicely said, is that Julian seems to have been influenced by whatever theology one is reading oneself. He remarks, not as sources for Julian, resemblances to her ideas in Greek orthodox theology.

[24] I leave aside the question of whether these textually-embedded audiences are partly or wholly fictional. It seems reasonable to assume that the authors wrote for historically existing persons but also expected further reading of their work.

[25] *The Influence of Richard Rolle and of Julian of Norwich on the Middle English Lyrics* (The Hague: Mouton, 1973).

from these communities can be directly linked to Julian's work. The first is that of Margaret Gascoigne (d. 1637), a Cambrai author who quoted Julian in her own writing; the second, that of Barbara Constable, a productive scribe who made her profession at Cambrai in 1640, and wrote a selection from Julian appearing in an anthology of religious writings and translations of Father David Augustine Baker, spiritual director at Cambrai from 1624 to 1633; and, more tentatively, the third, that of Anne Clementine Cary (1615–1671), founder of the Paris convent, who may have been the scribe of one of the complete manuscripts, that one edited here. The first scrap of Julian's long text that we have out of these houses is Margaret Gascoigne's quotation: "Thou hast saide, O Lorde, to a deere childe of thine, Lette me alone my deare worthy childe, intende to me, I am inough to thee, reioice in thy Sauiour and Saluation (this was spoken to Iulian the Ankress of norw[ich], as appeareth by the booke of her reuelations)." [You have said, Oh Lord, to a dear child of yours, Let me alone, my precious child and listen to me; I am enough for you. Rejoice in your Savior and salvation (this was spoken to Julian, the anchoress of Norwich, as appears from the book of her revelations.)][26]

Father Baker translated several late medieval spiritual writers, both continental and English, for the benefit of the convent. He had worked at the library of Sir Robert Cotton, the antiquarian whose library harbored the unique copies of *Beowulf* and the Gawain poet, and from France appealed to him for help for his charges: "Their lives being contemplative the comon bookes of ye worlde are not for their purpose, and litle or nothing is in thes daies printed in English that is proper for them. There were manie English bookes in olde time whereof thoughe they have some, yet they want manie. And thereupon I am in their behallfe become an humble suitor vnto you, to bestowe on them such bookes as you please, either manuscript or printed being in English, conteining contemplation Saints lives or other devotions. Hampooles [i.e., Richard Rolle's] workes are proper for them. I wishe I had Hilltons Scala perfectionis in latein; it woulde helpe the vnderstanding of the English; and some of them vnderstande latein" (Spearritt, pp. 291–92). Possibly this appeal is responsible for

---

[26] MS Colwich Abbey 18, as quoted by C&W, I, 16. The quotation is from Julian's chapter 36, lines 1238–39. C&W traces some of the familial and religious connections among the houses that must be responsible for our having the long text's manuscripts (I, 10–18). See also Placid Spearritt, "The Survival of Mediaeval Spirituality among the Exiled English Black Monks," *American Benedictine Review*, 25:3 (1974), 287–309. For the early history of the exile convents, see *In A Great Tradition: Tribute to Dame Laurentia McLachlan* by The Benedictines of Stanbrook (New York: Harper & Bros., 1956), pp. 3–45. For the life and work of Father Baker, see, in addition to the DNB, T. A. Birrell, "English Catholic Mystics in Non-Catholic Circles," *The Downside Review*, 94 (1976), 61–64.

our having Julian's long version; and it is also possible that her manuscripts were among the "some" books that the nuns had already among them.

The first printed text of Julian, the 1670 edition by Father Hugh (Serenus) Cressy, is also associated with these exile houses. He was briefly chaplain at Paris (1651–52), and his text is taken from one of the manuscripts most probably produced either there or at Cambrai.[27] Library catalogues of the continental foundations refer to at least one other Julian manuscript that cannot be any of the extant manuscripts containing the long text. Though some detail is tantalizingly missing, the association of the long text's preservation with Cambrai and Paris seems certain. This cannot be said of the short text, which came to light in 1909, although it also for a time was in the possession of a recusant family with connections at Cambrai and Paris (C&W, I, 10–12).

The 1670 Cressy edition broke the obscurity which had surrounded Julian, but *The Shewings* has not been at all well known until this century.[28] Cressy was reprinted

---

[27] The family of Mother Clementine Cary was closely linked with Father Cressy, who had been, before his conversion and ordination, a member of the circle of her better known brother, Lucius Cary, Lord Falkland, one subject of Ben Jonson's famous elegy, "To the Immortall Memorie, and Friendship of that Noble Paire, Sir Lucius Cary, and Sir H. Morison." For a brief note on Anne Clementine Cary, see "Cary, Anne Clementina, O.S.B.," in Joseph Gillow, *A Literary and Biographical History, or Bibliographical Dictionary of the English Catholics from the Breach with Rome, in 1534, to the Present Time*, 5 vols. (London, 1885–1902; rpt. New York: Burt Franklin, 1961), I, 417. Cressy's edition is dedicated to their mother. Cressy's career is outlined in the DNB and briefly sketched in C&W, I, 12–13.

[28] T. A. Birrell, in "English Catholic Mystics in Non-Catholic Circles," 60–81, 99–117, and 213–31, recovers several episodes in the reception of Julian as well as of other English mystics. Her book was, for instance, in the library at Fruitlands, Bronson Alcott's short-lived Utopian community (1843); Thoreau selected it as one of two hundred titles picked from the 800-volume collection for publication in a bibliographical piece in the April, 1843, *Dial*. The book's presence at Fruitlands is remotely due to Pierre Poiret (1646–1719), a French Protestant mystic and scholar whose ecumenical bibliography of mystical writings (*Bibliotheca Mysticorum Selecta*, 1708) lists Julian with the annotation, "*Anglice. Theodacticae, profundae, ecstaticae*" [English. Taught by God, profound, ecstatic]. Cressy's edition was known in special quarters. Julian in fact figured in some of the polemical exchanges between between Roman Catholics and Anglicans in the Restoration. Bishop Edward Stillingfleet (1635–99), a Restoration Anglican divine, counted the *Shewings* a score against his adversaries: "Have we any mother Juliana's among us? or do we publish to the world the Fanatick Revelations of distempered brains, as Mr. Cressy hath very lately done . . . ? We have, we thank God, other ways of employing our devout retirements, than in reading such fopperies as these are" (quoted by Birrell, p. 78, whose essay is devoted chiefly to episodes of more hospitable reception in non-Catholic circles of medieval

in 1843, in 1864, and again in 1902. New work from manuscripts came in 1877 with Henry Collins's modernization of the British Library's Sloane 2499 (S1), that long text which possibly is in the hand of Anne Clementine Cary. However, it was Grace Warrack's 1901 version of S1, with its sympathetic, informed introduction, which introduced most early twentieth-century readers to Julian. Dean W. R. Inge's *Studies of English Mystics* of 1906 (where, among others, a young T. S. Eliot read of her; see note to chapter 27), based upon a lecture series of 1905, spread her name, and Evelyn Underhill's works on mysticism and her now often-quoted characterization of Julian as the "first English woman of letters" in the *Cambridge Medieval History* (1932; VII, 807) brought Julian to the attention of readers interested in either religion or literature or, most particularly, their combination. When the short manuscript surfaced a modernization by Dundas Harford came out almost immediately (1911). Nonetheless, not until the seventies have editions of the manuscripts, rather than versions or modernizations, been published. Marion Glasscoe's edition of S1 appeared in 1976, and Frances Beer's text of the short version in 1978. That was the year, too, of the Colledge and Walsh two-volume edition including both texts, a comprehensive introduction, and a critical apparatus that provides a basis for other students of Julian.

The successive medieval volumes in the Oxford History of English Literature plot the acceleration of interest in Julian. When E. K. Chambers wrote *English Literature at the Close of the Middle Ages,* published in 1945, he did not once refer to her; H. S. Bennett's *Chaucer and the Fifteenth Century,* published in 1947, gives her one reference in passing. But J. A. W. Bennett's *Middle English Literature,* completed by Douglas Gray, published in 1986, gives Julian a dozen dense pages. To be sure, from the turn of the century forward, the evidence is that Julian's audience of few was in one way or another extremely fit: William Butler Yeats, Charles Williams, Aldous Huxley, T. S. Eliot, Thomas Merton, Denise Levertov, Iris Murdoch, and Dorothy Day are on record among that audience.[29] Even before the appearance of editions

---

and later Catholic mystic writings). The Anglican community of All Hallows now cares for the Julian shrine at St. Julian's parish church, and since 1980 Julian has had a feast in the Anglican calendar (May 8).

[29] For Yeats and Williams, see Birrell, pp. 223–24 and 227. For Merton, see an entry in *Conjectures of a Guilty Bystander* (Garden City, N.Y.: Image Books, 1968), pp. 211–12. For Denise Levertov, see "On a Theme from Julian's Chapter XX" and "The Showings: Lady Julian of Norwich, 1342–1416," in *Breathing the Water* (New York: New Directions, 1987), pp. 68–69 and 75–78. For Murdoch, see details of Anne's vision in *Nuns and Soldiers* (New York: Viking, 1981), 288–94. For Dorothy Day, see "Correspondence and Interviews," *14th Century English Mystics Newsletter* 1.4 (1975), n.p.

of the manuscripts, the dedication of the reconstructed parish church of St. Julian in 1953 and the 1973 sixth centenary of the showings occasioned celebratory and scholarly publication. Fittingly, Julian's contemporary audience includes those who use her book as she probably had assumed it might be used; towards the close of the eighties, 150 Julian groups in Great Britain were meeting for prayer and spiritual companionship (Jantzen, p. 12).

Some early commentary on Julian raised the question of her visionary experience's validity, although without the confident vigor of Bishop Stillingfleet (see p. 17, note 28). The topic was usually pursued by a consideration of how her account corresponds to paradigms established either in psychology or in mysticism's secondary literature. This discussion has dwindled perhaps because although the importance of the question is undeniable, answering it is impossible. The question of her orthodoxy has been taken up, usually, but not always, resolved in agreement with Julian's own statements of her adherence to church teaching. Source study for particular motifs, ideas, and locutions of *The Shewings* has been another topic of Julian criticism. A rewarding recent line of inquiry focuses on Julian's religious thought pursued not only through its sources but also as a subject in itself. The once largely overlooked development in the long text of the theme of Christ as mother is coming to be seen in Julian not as ornamental, but as a doctrinal exploration of range and force. Interest in mysticism in general and feminist scholars' work to recover women's voices from earlier times have been a stimulus. Literary study that goes beyond praise and quotation has advanced in the work of Stone, Windeatt, Glasscoe's 1983 essay, and the assembling of rhetorical figures and notes upon them in the Colledge and Walsh 1978 edition. Many essays not primarily on style offer valuable remarks about it. More work is in progress on prose style, but most has not reached publication stage. Detail of conclusions will certainly be affected by which manuscript authors choose for close study.

The Manuscripts

The short version exists in one manuscript, the mid-fifteenth century Amherst manuscript, now BL Additional 37790 (A). A handsome vellum book, its selections from late medieval religious writers include Richard Rolle and translations from John Ruysbroek, Henry Suso, and St. Bridget as well as the shorter *Shewings*. The idea that Julian's short text may be, like other items in the volume, an abstract from longer work has never been seriously pursued, and there is no constraining reason to believe that it is (Beer, p. 10, and pp. 22–23). Francis Blomefield, the eighteenth-century historian of Norfolk, had known of this manuscript as his account of St. Julian's parish shows: "In 1393, Lady *Julian* was *Ankeress* here, was a strict *Recluse*, and had

2 Servants to attend her in her old Age, Ao [anno] 1443. This Woman in those Days, was esteemed, one of the greatest Holyness. The Rev. Mr. *Francis Peck,* Author of the Antiquities of *Stanford*, had an old Vellum Mss. 36 4to [quarto] Pages of which, contain'd an Account of the Visions &c. of this Woman, which begins thus"; Blomefield then goes on to quote with fair accuracy the heading of the short text (given above).[30] A Leicestershire antiquarian and rector at Godeby by Melton, the Rev. Mr. Peck died in 1743; his books were sold at auction in 1758. The manuscript vanished from record, to appear in Sotheby's 1910 sale of the Amherst library. There, the British Museum acquired it. The manuscript bears the bookplate of Lord Amherst and a number of names are inscribed upon it, none permitting more than guesses about provenance. The hand is anglicana formata with textura used for emphasis. The dialect is a mixture, and northern, not the Norfolk forms one might expect, are predominant (C&W, I, 28–32, and Beer, pp. 14–20).

Of the long version, three complete manuscripts and two manuscripts with excerpts exist. No manuscript of the complete long text is earlier than the seventeeth century, the two most important of about 1650. In addition, there is the 1670 Cressy printed edition, closely related to, almost certainly directly taken from, one of these manuscripts, Paris, BN MS fonds anglais 40 (P).

This manuscript is a small, beautiful paper book of 175 leaves (fol. 23 is repeated), written in a legible calligraphic hand with italic and bastard elements. Fathers Colledge and Walsh describe the hand as "certainly of the seventeenth century, probably c. 1650," engaged in a "sedulous but unskilled and unconvincing imitation ... of a hand of c. 1500" (C&W, I, 7). Still the hand is clear and pleasing, and along with blue initials at chapter openings, red paraphs and running titles, and occasional phrasal rubrication, it adds to the attractiveness, as well as the legibility, of the book. A later hand has written above the opening, "icy commence le premier chapitre." The manuscript has been skillfully mended; in 1946, according to a note on the flyleaf. The book contains only Julian's long text. Previous editors regard it as the earliest of the long manuscripts.

Like P, BL MS Sloane 2499 (S1) contains only Julian's long text. S1 is a large, paper manuscript of 57 leaves, possibly cropped, now 229 by 369 mm. The hand is an efficient, sometimes sprawling, sometimes compressed, cursive hand of c. 1650. According to Fathers Colledge and Walsh the hand resembles, but cannot be certainly said to be, the hand of Anne Clementine Cary. Marginal annotation, mostly glosses on words obsolete by the seventeenth century, and *nota bene* initials show the

---

[30] *The History of the City and County of Norwich*, vol. 2 of *An Essay Towards a Topographical History of the County of Norfolk* (1739–75; Norwich, 1745), p. 546. The improbable 1443 may come from reading *i* as *l*, easily done.

manuscript to have had considerable use. Ink has soaked through so as to make for some loss of legibility, and lamination has not halted deterioration. Fortunately, Paris and Sloane manuscripts correspond sufficiently so that in almost all cases each can supply readings for the other. The third manuscript, BL MS Sloane 3705 (S2), is clearly a copy, in a fine eighteenth-century hand, of S1, a copy with many modernized spellings, some glossing and other annotation, usually repetition of key phrases, and many *nota bene* signs. Both S1 and S2 have chapter headings giving brief summaries of the forthcoming chapter; P lacks this feature, which is probably a scribal or editorial contribution. (*Shewings* has been chosen for this edition's title because it is Julian's more frequent term in the body of the text; *revelations* occurs more frequently only in the chapter headings.) The earlier manuscripts, P and S1, differ sufficiently to make it unlikely their common ancestor is immediate.

The two manuscripts containing selections of Julian have their own interest, but do not help to determine relationships among texts or to establish readings. Westminster Library Cathedral Treasury 4 (W), which came to light in 1955, is a short book of 67 leaves made up of excerpts from Walter Hilton's *Scale of Perfection*, commentaries on two psalms, variously ascribed, usually to Hilton, and excerpts from Julian. Inclusion of the passage on the motherhood of Christ establishes that selections are from the long text. In some respects closer to the Sloane texts than to P, W includes a brief passage which does not appear in them, but does in P. It may be from a common ancestor, or the scribe may have worked from more than one manuscript. N. R. Ker dated the hand c. 1500; in any case, it is more than a century earlier than the hands of those manuscripts of the complete long text that we now possess.[31] Writing without a break, the redactor chooses material thematically without regard for or mention of his or her sources. Neither Julian's visions nor, by and large, her more concrete images have interested the anthologizer. Selections are from the first, second, ninth, tenth, fourteenth, and fifteenth showings (chapters 4–7, 10, 22–24, 41–44, 53–56, 59–61, and 63–64 of the present text). Cuts are frequent, but there is only slight rearrangment from the sequence as it comes to us in P and S1. Differences in dialect which must have existed between the earliest manuscripts of Julian and of Hilton have been smoothed to a Southeast Midlands of the London area.

MS St. Joseph's College, Upholland, Lancashire (U) is a 127-folio collection of spiritual writings and translations, most of them firmly identified as those of Augustine Baker, and it is reasonable to assume, but not certain, that excerpts from

---

[31] N. R. Ker, *Medieval Manuscripts in British Libraries: London* (Oxford: Clarendon Press, 1969), pp. 418–19. Complete information on the manuscript appears in a translation by Fathers Walsh and Colledge, *Of the Knowledge of Ourselves and of God: A Fifteenth-Century Spiritual Florilegium,* pp. v–xix.

Julian, which were written by Barbara Constable — from the longer text's chapters 26–28, 30, and 32 — are also his.[32] How the book came to Upholland is not clear. The language is very much modernized, more so than the Cressy printed edition or P, from either of which it may derive.

For an edition of the long text, only P or S1 could be seriously considered because of the clear derivation of S2 from S1 and the dependence of Cressy on P. Because of the lateness of the long texts, it is unrewarding to speculate about the dialect of their model; we do not quite know the localized language of Julian, though the short text's northern flavor gives us at least a puzzle about it. More thoroughly modernized than S1, P also contains some deliberate and odd archaizing (C&W, I, 7–8). It has many instances of a more expansive phrasing than in S1. Largely because of this, for their 1978 edition Fathers Colledge and Walsh chose P. They believe that the Sloane scribe in cutting words considered superfluous has destroyed rhetorical patterning integral to Julian's thought (C&W, I, 26). Marion Glasscoe has argued that the greater conservatism of S1 in language and its very lack of concern for appearances may make it a more reliable copy text than the carefully worked over, more modernized P.[33]

The Sloane scribe may indeed have shortened the copy text, trimming a rhetorical finish that is rightly Julian's. But it is also possible that the Paris scribe amplified. For this edition, S1 has been chosen as being closer to the fourteenth-century vocabulary of the author. If S1 is coherent at all, as it usually is, I have used it. When a word is partially illegible in Sloane, I have used the whole word from Paris, not merely the occluded letters. I have followed the conventions of this series in expanding contractions, including the ampersand, much used by the S1 scribe, and changing letters to modern equivalents. Punctuation and paragraphing are editorial, although manuscript cues have been regarded, if not always followed. In several instances the S1 scribe omits *n* or final *r* after the vowel *e*, which suggests that she was working from a Middle English manuscript and simply misses signs of abbreviation. I have identified these omissions in the Notes, along with readings from P. The S1 scribe

---

[32] For an account of this manuscript, see H. W. Owen, "Another Augustine Baker Manuscript," *Dr. L. Reypens-Album*, ed. Albert Ampe, S.J. (Antwerp: Uitgave Van Het Ruusbroec-Genootschap, 1964), pp. 269–80. Parts of an edition of the manuscript by Dr. Owen, including the Julian section, are now in print. For the Julian extract, see H. W. Owen, "The Upholland Anthology: An Augustine Baker Manuscript," *The Downside Review* 107 (October 1989), 274–92.

[33] "Visions and Revisions: A Further Look at the Manuscripts of Julian of Norwich," *Studies in Bibliography* 42 (1989), 103–20.

often uses capitalization in interesting ways. I have followed the policy of the Middle English Text series of capitalizing names for the deity and second and third person pronouns referring to the divinity. The scribe capitalizes irregularly Heaven, Hell, and Holy Church; I have uniformly capitalized these terms. She also capitalizes *Moder* and *Moderhede* quite regularly in chapters 57–63, and in these chapters I have followed her capitalization of those terms (see note to Chapter LVII). In a few other places I have followed the scribe's erratic capitalization of Child and Devil. Manuscript chapterization is regularized and positioned as it appears in the manuscript, usually directly after the chapter synopsis, but centered Roman chapter numbers are intruded. Words that Julian hears in the visions or understands as given to her are italicized, although they are not set off in S1, as they tend to be, by rubrication, in P. Apart from these alterations, this is a conservative text. In this I follow the decisions of Glasscoe and Colledge and Walsh, who give examples of respectful treatment of the manuscripts.

Wording of particular interest which appears only in the short text is reported selectively in notes. Two longer passages from the short text (A) are given in the appendices.

Select Bibliography

Manuscripts

Long Text

London, British Library MS Sloane 2499.

London, British Library MS Sloane 3705.

Paris, Bibliothèque Nationale MS Fonds anglais 40.

Short Text

London, British Library MS Additional 37790, fols. 97–115.

Selections

London, Westminster Cathedral Treasury MS 4, fols. 72v–112v.

Upholland, Lancashire, The Upholland Anthology, fols. 114r–117v.

Editions

Long Text

Cressy, H. [Hugh/ Serenus], ed. *XVI Revelations of Divine Love, Shewed to a Devout Servant of our Lord, called Mother Juliana, an Anchorete of Norwich: Who lived in the Dayes of King Edward the Third.* London, 1670; rpt. 1843, 1864, and 1902, with prefaces by, respectively, G. H. Parker, I. T. Hecker, and George Tyrrell. [Based upon the Paris manuscript.]

Glasscoe, Marion, ed. *Julian of Norwich, A Revelation of Love.* Exeter Medieval English Texts. Exeter: University of Exeter Press, 1976; rev. ed., 1986. [Based upon Sloane 2499. Introduction and glossary.]

Colledge, Edmund, and James Walsh, eds. *A Book of Showings to the Anchoress Julian of Norwich.* 2 vols. Studies and Texts 35. Toronto: Pontifical Institute of Mediaeval Studies, 1978. [Based upon the Paris manuscript; both long and short texts with a full apparatus. Introduction includes a full description of the manuscripts, discussion of scribes and owners, an account of linguistic characteristics of the manuscripts, a summary of what is known about biography, and an essay on Julian's intellectual formation. Appendix of rhetorical figures, index of scriptural citations, and glossary.]

Short text

Beer, Frances, ed. *Julian of Norwich's Revelations of Divine Love: The Shorter Version, ed. from BL Add. MS 37790.* Middle English Texts 8. Heidelberg: Carl Winter, 1978. [Extensive introduction and notes.]

Colledge and Walsh, see above.

Selections

Owen, Hywel W., ed. "An Edition of the Upholland Anthology." B.A. dissertation Liverpool, 1962.

Select Bibliography

———— and Luke Bell. "The Upholland Anthology: An Augustine Baker Manuscript," *The Downside Review* 107 (1989), 274–92, the first installment of three successive issues printing extracts of the manuscript.

Modernizations and translations

Long Text

Collins, Henry, ed. and trans. *Revelations of Divine Love, Shewed to a Devout Anchoress, by Name Mother Julian of Norwich.* London: Thomas Richardson and Sons, 1877.

Warrack, Grace, ed. *Revelations of Divine Love, Recorded by Julian, Anchoress at Norwich, Anno Domini 1373: A Version from the MS. in the British Museum.* London: Methuen and Co., 1901, frequently rpt.

Hudleston, Roger, ed. *Revelations of Divine Love, Shewed to a Devout Ankress, by Name Julian of Norwich.* London: Burns and Oates, 1927; 2nd ed. Westminster, Maryland: The Newman Press, 1952.

Wolters, Clifton, trans. *Julian of Norwich: Revelations of Divine Love.* Harmondsworth, England: Penguin Books, 1966.

Del Mastro, M. L., trans. *Juliana of Norwich: Revelations of Divine Love.* Garden City, N.Y.: Image Books/Doubleday, 1977. [Introduction includes brief accounts of Richard Rolle, the author of *The Cloud of Unknowing*, Walter Hilton, and Margery Kempe, pp. 46–74.]

Colledge, Edmund, and James Walsh, trans. *Julian of Norwich: Showings.* The Classics of Western Spirituality. New York: Paulist Press, 1978. Pp. 175–343. [Contains both long and short texts. Introduction of 104 pages, preface by Jean Leclercq, topical index.]

Short Text

Harford, Dundas, ed. and trans. *Comfortable Words for Christ's Lovers, Being the Visions and Voices Vouchsafed to Lady Julian, Recluse at Norwich in 1373.* London: H. R. Allenson, 1911. Rpt. 1912, and, in 1925, under the title *The Shewings of Lady Julian Recluse at Norwich, 1373.*

Reynolds, Anna Maria, ed. and trans. *A Shewing of God's Love: The Shorter Version of Sixteen Revelations of Divine Love by Julian of Norwich*. Edited and partially modernized from the fifteenth-century manuscript. London: Longmans, Green and Co., 1958.

Colledge, Edmund, and James Walsh, trans. *Julian of Norwich: Showings*. The Classics of Western Spirituality. New York: Paulist Press, 1978. Pp. 125–170. [Contains also the long text.]

Selections

Walsh, James, and Eric Colledge, trans. *Of the Knowledge of Ourselves and of God: A Fifteenth–Century Spiritual Florilegium*. Fleur de Lys Series of Spiritual Classics. London: A. R. Mowbray, 1961. [Modernization of Westminster Cathedral Treasury MS 4.]

Bibliography

Sawyer, Michael E. *A Bibliographical Index of Five English Mystics: Richard Rolle, Julian of Norwich, the Author of The Cloud of Unknowing, Walter Hilton, Margery Kempe*. Bibliographica Tripotampolitana 10. Pittsburgh: Clifford E. Barbour Library, Pittsburgh Theological Seminary, 1978. Pp. 53–68.

Lagorio, Valerie M. and Ritamary Bradley. *The Fourteenth-Century English Mystics: A Comprehensive Annotated Bibliography*. New York: Garland Publishing, 1981. Pp. 105–26.

Studies

Allchin, A. M. "Julian of Norwich and the Continuity of Tradition." In *Julian: Woman of Our Day*, ed. Robert Llewelyn (London: Darton, Longman and Todd, 1985), pp. 27–40. First published in *The Medieval Mystical Tradition in England*, ed. Marion Glasscoe. Exeter: University of Exeter Press, 1980.

Baker, Denise Nowakowski. *Julian of Norwich's Showings: From Vision to Book*. Princeton, N. J.: Princeton University Press, 1994. [Sets forth intellectual frames of reference potentially available to Julian; examines the transformation of the short text, primarily devotional, into a theologically sophisticated longer version; illustrates the recursive, interlace structure of the longer text.]

A Benedictine of Stanbrook (D. S. H.). "Dame Julian of Norwich." *Clergy Review* n.s. 44 (1959), 705–20.

Bennett, J. A. W. *Middle English Literature*, ed. and completed by Douglas Gray. Oxford History of English Literature (Oxford: Clarendon Press, 1986), pp. 322–34.

Bhattacharji, Santha. "Independence of Thought in Julian of Norwich." *Word and Spirit* 11 (1989), 79–92.

Børresen, Kari E. "Christ notre mère, la Théologie de Julienne de Norwich." *Mitteilungen und Forschungsbeitrage der Cusanus-Gesellschaft* 13 (1978), 320–29.

Bradley, Ritamary. "Christ, the Teacher, in Julian's *Showings*: The Biblical and Patristic Traditions." In *The Medieval Mystical Tradition in England: Papers Read at Dartington Hall, July 1982*, ed. Marion Glasscoe (Exeter: University of Exeter Press, 1982), pp. 127–42.

——. "The Goodness of God: A Julian Study." In *Langland, The Mystics and The Medieval English Religious Tradition: Essays in Honour of S. S. Hussey*, ed. Helen Phillips (Cambridge: D. S. Brewer/Boydell and Brewer, 1990), pp. 85–95.

——. *Julian's Way: A Practical Commentary on Julian of Norwich*. London: Harper Collins Religious/ Harper Collins Publishers, 1992. [Clarifies difficulties of the long text and supplies theological background; thematic rather than sequential organization; attention to recurrent images (see especially pp. 123–34 and pp. 202–11). Intended in part as guide to spiritual understanding.]

——. "The Motherhood Theme in Julian of Norwich." *14th-Century English Mystics Newsletter* 2.4 (1976), 25–30.

Chambers, P. Franklin. *Juliana of Norwich: An Introductory Appreciation and An Interpretive Anthology*. London: Victor Gollancz, 1955. [Expanded from the author's commemoration address at the Norwich Council of Christian Congregations on the eve of the dedication on May 8, 1953, of the reconstructed parish church of St. Julian's, the introduction includes rarely cited references to Julian from earlier readers and notice of literary use of her book; an anthology of translated selections grouped under the heads "experiential," "evangelical," and "mystical" and a gathering of "One Hundred Aphorisms" follow.]

Clark, J. P. H. "'Fiducia' in Julian of Norwich." *The Downside Review* 99 (1981), 97–108; 214–29.

———. "Nature, Grace and the Trinity in Julian of Norwich." *The Downside Review* 100 (1982), 203–20.

Colledge, Edmund, and James Walsh. "Editing Julian of Norwich's *Revelations*: A Progress Report." *Mediaeval Studies* 38 (1976), 404–27.

del Mastro, M. L. "Juliana of Norwich: Parable of the Lord and Servant — Radical Orthodoxy." *Mystics Quarterly* 14 (1988), 84–93. [Sets out in outline form five points of divergence in Julian's writing from "popular understanding" of the church's teaching, and notes orthodox precedents in John, Paul, and Augustine.]

Ellis, Roger. "Revelation and the Life of Faith: The Vision of Julian of Norwich." *Christian* 6 (1980), 61–71.

Evasdaughter, Elizabeth N. "Julian of Norwich." In *Medieval, Renaissance and Enlightenment Women Philosophers A.D. 500–1600*, Vol. II of *A History of Women Philosophers*, ed. Mary Ellen Waithe. Dordrecht, The Netherlands: Kluwer Academic Publishers, 1989, pp. 191–222. [Argues that an orderly discourse on knowledge supports the description of Christ's revelations to Julian, that Julian knew the epistemological issues of her day and took positions upon them, assuming, with Aristotle and Aquinas, that sensory images and concepts are informative of reality. Julian stressed the possibility of knowing God, to the degree that she gives the impression of answering the opposite proposition. Her statements on the identity of the human soul and the substance of God are applied so as to sustain ordinary Christians against depression and unwarranted guilt. Comparisons with Aquinas, Augustine, Duns Scotus, William of Occam, and the author of the *Cloud of Unknowing* clarify the discussion.]

Gilchrist, Jay. "Unfolding Enfolding Love in Julian of Norwich's *Revelations*." *14th-Century English Mystics Newsletter* 9 (1983), 67–88. [Sequential summary and explanation of Julian's theology includes the "great deed" of chapter 32 and the "godly will" which never assents to sin of chapter 37.]

Select Bibliography

Glasscoe, Marion. "Means of Showing: An Approach to Reading Julian of Norwich." *Spätmittelalterliche Geistliche Literatur in der Nationalsprache*, ed. James Hogg, *Analecta Cartusiana* 106 (Salzburg, 1983), 155–77.

———. "Visions and Revisions: A Further Look at the Manuscripts of Julian of Norwich." *Studies in Bibliography* 42 (1989), 103–20. [A discussion of problems in editorial choices and an argument for preferring Sloane 2499 for its greater sense of religious experience as a dynamic reality and for its greater closeness to Julian's fourteenth-century vocabulary and syntax.]

Grayson, Janet. "The Eschatological Adam's Kirtle." *Mystics Quarterly* 11 (1985), 153–60.

Hanshell, Deryck. "A Crux in the Interpretation of Dame Julian." *The Downside Review,* 92 (1974), 77–91.

Heimmel, Jennifer P. *"God Is Our Mother": Julian of Norwich and the Medieval Image of Christian Feminine Divinity*. Salzburg: Institut für Anglistik und Amerikanistik, Universität Salzburg, 1982. [Thoroughly treats theme of the motherhood of God, detailing Julian's use of the complete maternal cycle — enclosure and growth in the womb, labor and giving birth, suckling, feeding, washing, healing, and care and education of the older child; includes a gathering of Middle English references to the motherhood of God as well as those in early sources; offers remarks on Julian's prose style.]

Homier, Donald F. "The Function of Rhetoric in Julian of Norwich's *Revelations of Divine Love.*" *14th-Century English Mystics Newsletter* 7 (1981), 162–78.

Inge, William Ralph. "The *Ancren Riwle* and Julian of Norwich." In *Studies of English Mystics*: St. Margaret's Lectures, 1905. 1906; rpt. Freeport, N.Y.: Books for Libraries Press, 1969. Pp. 38–79. [The lecture that helped to introduce Julian to an early twentieth-century audience.]

Jacoff, Rachel. "God as Mother: Julian of Norwich's Theology of Love." *Denver Quarterly* 18.4 (Winter 1984), 134–39.

Jantzen, Grace M. *Julian of Norwich: Mystic and Theologian*. 1987; New York: Paulist Press, 1988. [Theological treatment preceded by biographical and sociological background.]

Johnson, Lynn Staley. "The Trope of the Scribe and the Question of Literary Authority in the Works of Julian of Norwich and Margery Kempe." *Speculum* 66 (1991), 820–38.

Lawlor, John. "A Note on the *Revelations of Julian of Norwich*." *Review of English Studies*, n.s. 2 (1951), 255–58.

Lichtmann, Maria R. "'I desyrede a bodylye syght': Julian of Norwich and the Body." *Mystics Quarterly* 17 (1991), 12–19.

Llewelyn, Robert, ed. *Julian: Woman of Our Day*. London: Darton, Longman and Todd, 1985. [An anthology focused on Julian's current relevance introduced by a former rector of St. Julian's parish, Michael McLean of Norwich Cathedral, with essays by the editor, A. M. Allchin, Ritamary Bradley, Richard Harries, Kenneth Leech, Elizabeth Ruth Obbard, Anna Maria Reynolds, and John Swanson. Essays by Allchin, Bradley, and Reynolds previously printed.]

McNamer, Sarah. "The Exploratory Image: God as Mother in Julian of Norwich's *Revelations of Divine Love*." *Mystics Quarterly* 15 (1989), 21–28.

Mary Paul, Sister. *All Shall Be Well: Julian of Norwich and the Compassion of God*. Fairacres Publication 53. Oxford: SLG Press, 1976.

Molinari, Paul. *Julian of Norwich: The Teaching of a 14th Century English Mystic*. New York: The Arden Library, 1958; rpt. London: Longmans, Green, 1979. [Compares Julian's account with theological paradigms for contemplative prayer and mystic experience; gives attention to the theme of God as mother in the course of a full-length study of Julian's contributions.]

Nolcken, Christina von. "Julian of Norwich." In *Middle English Prose*, ed. A. S. G. Edwards (New Brunswick, N.J: Rutgers University Press, 1984), pp. 97–108. [Succinct account of what is known about Julian and of the work upon her texts; brief remarks on prose style; points out the need for more stylistic studies of Middle English prose to establish context for Julian.]

Nuth, Joan M. *Wisdom's Daughter: The Theology of Julian of Norwich*. New York: Crossroad, 1991. [An explication of the theology of the *Shewings* with a view to offering a paradigm for contemporary women theologians.]

Owen, H. W. "Another Augustine Baker Manuscript." In *Dr. L. Reypens-Album*, ed. Alb[ert] Ampe (Antwerp: Uitgave Van Het Ruusbroec-Genootschap, 1964), pp. 269–80.

Panichelli, Debra Scott. "Finding God in the Memory: Julian and the Loss of the Visions." *The Downside Review* 104 (1986), 299–317.

Pelphrey, Brant. *Christ Our Mother: Julian of Norwich*. Volume 7 of *The Way of the Christian Mystics*, ed. Noel Dermot O'Donoghue. Wilmington, Delaware: Michael Glazier, 1989. [Written with the general reader in mind and with a pastoral orientation, this book goes over much the same ground as the 1982 book by the same author. A useful new feature is a sequential outline of the showings with their contents classified under sub-headings (e.g., corporeal visions, lessons, teachings, locutions), pp. 79–91.]

——. *Love Was His Meaning: The Theology and Mysticism of Julian of Norwich*. Salzburg Studies in English Literature 92.4. Salzburg: Institut für Anglistik und Amerikanistik, Universität Salzburg, 1982. [Treats the interpenetrating development of three areas of Christian theology throughout the *Shewings*: the doctrine of the Trinity, or the nature of the inner being of God; the doctrine of incarnation and atonement, or the nature of God in relation to humanity; and life in the Holy Spirit or the nature of human response to God. Stresses that Julian understands the relationship of the divine to the human as ontological, a matter of being rather than of feeling. Thorough consideration of views that have been thought engimatic or unusual, such as the deed that will make all things well, the absence of wrath in God, sin, the motherhood of God, and human "sensuality" and "substance."]

Peters, Brad. "The Reality of Evil within the Mystic Vision of Julian of Norwich." *Mystics Quarterly* 13 (1987), 195–202.

Reynolds, Anna Maria. "Julian of Norwich: Woman of Hope." *Mystics Quarterly* 10 (1984), 118–25. [Extracts twelve statements from the parable of the lord and servant (chapter 51) which constitute a "concise and accurate summary of Salvation History," furnishing a basis for Christian hope.]

——. "Some Literary Influences in the *Revelations* of Julian of Norwich (c. 1342–post 1416)." *Leeds Studies in English* 7 (1952), 18–28.

Riehle, Wolfgang. *The Middle English Mystics*. Trans. Bernard Standring from *Studien zur englischen Mystik des Mittelalters*, 1977. London: Routledge & Kegan Paul, 1981. [Examines the special vocabulary of the Middle English mystics, Rolle, the author of the *Cloud of Unknowing*, Walter Hilton, and Margery Kempe as well as Julian, with attention to words such as *ground, feeling, homely, courteous, naked*, and *enjoy* that carry theological shadings not immediately evident; notes patristic and scholastic precedents and compares continental mystics' writings throughout. Extensive bibliography.]

Robertson, Elizabeth. "Medieval Medical Views of Women and Female Spirituality in the *Ancrene Wisse* and Julian of Norwich's *Showings.*" In *Feminist Approaches to the Body in Medieval Literature*. Ed. Linda Lomperis and Sarah Stanbury. Philadelphia: University of Pennsylvania Press, 1993. Pp. 142–67. [Discusses Julian of Norwich's view of the body and her descriptions of blood in the course of an argument that medieval medical theory conditions the focus on blood, tears, and erotic imagery that figures in accounts of female spirituality both by men and by women; outlines dominant traditions of relevant medieval medical commentary.]

Sayer, Frank Dale, ed. *Julian and Her Norwich: Commemorative Essays and Handbook to the Exhibition "Revelations of Divine Love."* Norwich: Julian of Norwich 1973 Celebration Committee, 1973. [A gathering of essays for the 600th anniversary observance of the visions. Several contributors have ties with and knowledge of the local context of the work. See especially F. I. Dunn, "Hermits, Anchorites and Recluses: A Study with Reference to Medieval Norwich," pp. 18–27.]

Sprung, Andrew. " 'We nevyr shall come out of hym': Enclosure and Immanence in Julian of Norwich's *Book of Showings*." *Mystics Quarterly* 19 (1993), 47–62.

Stone, Robert Karl. *Middle English Prose Style: Margery Kempe and Julian of Norwich*. The Hague: Mouton, 1970.

Tugwell, Simon. "Julian of Norwich as a Speculative Theologian." *14th-Century English Mystics Newsletter* 9 (1983), 199–209.

Underhill, Evelyn. "Julian of Norwich." In *The Essentials of Mysticism and Other Essays* (London: J. M. Dent, 1920), pp. 183–98. [Influential essay representative of Underhill's interest in Julian.]

Select Bibliography

Vinje, Patricia Mary. *An Understanding of Love According to the Anchoress Julian of Norwich*. Salzburg Studies in English Literature. Salzburg: Institut für Anglistik und Americanistik, Universität Salzburg, 1983. [Julian as an allegorical writer.]

Walsh, James. "God's Homely Loving: St. John and Julian of Norwich on the Divine Indwelling." *The Month*, n.s. 19 (1958), 164–72.

[Ward], Benedicta. "Julian the Solitary." In *Julian Reconsidered* by Kenneth Leech and Benedicta Ward (Oxford: SLG Press, 1988). Pp. 11–35. [Suggestions on Julian's personal background based on what is said, and not said, in the *Shewings*.]

Watkin, E. I. *On Julian of Norwich, and In Defence of Margery Kempe*. Exeter Medieval English Texts and Studies. rev. ed. Exeter: University of Exeter, 1979. [Combines a 1933 essay on Julian of Norwich, pp. 1–33, with a 1953 essay on Margery Kempe. Offers a concise exposition of Julian's theology; includes an argument that Julian must have been from the north because of language forms in the manuscripts.]

Watson, Nicholas. "The Composition of Julian of Norwich's *Revelation of Love*." *Speculum* 68 (1993), 637–83. [Challenges received view that the short text was written shortly after the visionary events it reports.]

Wilson, R. M. "Three Middle English Mystics." *Essays and Studies* n.s. 9 (1956), 87–112. [Proposes that the fourteenth century efflorescence of English mystical literature is to a degree more apparent than real because before the development of vernacular religious prose in the fourteenth century unless mystics were sufficiently literate to write in Latin they were perforce silent; discusses the prose style of Julian, Richard Rolle, and Margery Kempe.]

Windeatt, B. A. "The Art of Mystical Loving: Julian of Norwich." In *The Medieval Mystical Tradition in England*, ed. Marion Glasscoe (Exeter: University of Exeter Press, 1980), pp. 55–71. [Argues that Julian's urgent search for understanding of her original visionary experience results in the long text's structure of exploration in which she layers interpretive commentary into a narrative skeleton; suggests that patterns of contemporary dream vision poems, in particular *Piers Plowman* and *Pearl*, offer illuminating structural correlatives.]

——. "Julian of Norwich and her Audience." *Review of English Studies*, n.s. 28 (1977), 1–17. [A careful examination of differences between short and long texts.]

Wright, Robert E. "The 'Boke Performyd': Affective Technique and Reader Response in the *Showings* of Julian of Norwich." *Christianity & Literature* 36.4 (1987), 13–32.

Related and Background Studies

Birrell, T. A. "English Catholic Mystics in Non-Catholic Circles." *The Downside Review* 94 (1976), 60–81, 99–117, and 213–31. [Includes Julian in a ranging study of the reception, from the 17th century forward, of early Catholic mystic writings.]

Bynum, Caroline Walker. *Holy Feast and Holy Fast: The Religious Significance of Food to Medieval Women.* Berkeley: University of California Press, 1987.

———. "Jesus as Mother and Abbot as Mother: Some Themes in Twelfth-Century Cistercian Writing," *Harvard Theological Review* 70 (1977), 257–84, as expanded in *Jesus as Mother: Studies in the Spirituality of the High Middle Ages* (Berkeley: University of California Press, 1982), pp. 110–169.

Cabassut, André. "Une Dévotion médiévale peu connue: La Dévotion à 'Jésus notre mère'." *Revue d'ascétique et de mystique* 25 (1949), 234–45.

Campbell, James, "Norwich." In *The Atlas of Historic Towns*, ed. M. D. Lobel (London, Scolar Press, and Baltimore: Johns Hopkins University Press, 1975), II, 1–25 plus maps.

Clay, Rotha M. "Further Studies on Medieval Recluses." *Journal of the British Archaeological Association*, 3rd series, 16 (1953), 74–86.

———. *The Hermits and Anchorites of England.* London: Methuen, 1914.

Griffiths, Jeremy, and Derek Pearsall, eds. *Book Production and Publishing in Britain 1375–1475.* Cambridge: Cambridge University Press, 1989. [Although there is no evidence as to how Julian's manuscripts first reached an audience, this collection of essays brings together current research on publishing in her time; see especially the introduction by Pearsall, A. I. Doyle, "Publication by Members of the Religious Orders," pp. 109–23, and Vincent Gillespie, "Vernacular Books of Religion," pp. 317–344.]

Irigaray, Luce. "La Mystérique." In *Speculum of the Other Woman*, trans. Gillian C. Gill (Ithaca: Cornell University Press, 1985), pp. 191–202. *Speculum de l'autre femme* first published in 1974. [The feminist theoretician's reflective meditation upon mystic experience.]

Leclercq, H. "Reclus." *Dictionnaire d'archéologie chrétienne et de liturgie*. Tome 14, Part 2. Ed. Fernand Cabrol et H. Leclercq (Paris, 1948), cols. 2149–59.

McLaughlin, Eleanor. "'Christ My Mother': Feminine Naming and Metaphor in Medieval Spirituality." *Nashotah Review* 15 (Fall 1975), 228–48.

Medieval Art in East Anglia 1300–1520. Ed. P[eter] Lasko and N.J. Morgan, Norwich: Jarrold & Sons, 1973; London: Thames & Hudson, 1974.

Petroff, Elizabeth Alvilda. "The Visionary Tradition in Women's Writings: Dialogue and Autobiography," Introduction to *Medieval Women's Visionary Literature*, ed. Elizabeth Alvilda Petroff (New York: Oxford University Press, 1986), pp. 3–59.

Rahner, Karl. *Visions and Prophecies*. Trans. Charles Henkey and Richard Strachan. New York: Herder and Herder, 1963. [Roman Catholic theologian briefly covers the possibility, theological significance, and psychological problems of private revelations and visions, and gives some criteria for deciding whether visions are genuine.]

Spearritt, Placid. "The Survival of Mediaeval Spirituality among the Exiled English Black Monks." *American Benedictine Review* 25 (1974), 287–309. [Interesting for its observation of the communities where manuscripts of Julian's long text appeared in the seventeenth century.]

Tanner, Norman P. *The Church in Late Medieval Norwich 1370–1532*. Studies and Texts 66. Toronto: Pontifical Institute of Mediaeval Studies, 1984. [Evidence from wills supports a thorough study of both official and popular religious life in Julian's city in her period up to the eve of the Reformation.]

Wallace, David. "Mystics and Followers in Siena and East Anglia: A Study in Taxonomy, Class and Cultural Mediation." In *The Medieval Mystical Tradition in England: Papers read at Dartington Hall, July, 1984*, ed. Marion Glasscoe (Cambridge: D. S. Brewer / Boydell and Brewer, 1984), pp. 169–91. [Comparison and contrast of the local receptions of the writings of St. Catherine of Siena and of Margery Kempe gives context for Julian, mentioned in passing.]

Warren, Ann K. *Anchorites and Their Patrons in Medieval England.* Berkeley: University of California Press, 1985. [Richly-documented study of anchorites in medieval England; includes statistics on anchoritic population from the twelfth century to 1539, with distribution of reclusoria sites and known recluses by localities, sex, and previous status when known; discusses relationships of bishops to recluses, and support levels for recluses from different classes of patrons; extensive bibliography and a bibliographical appendix of the thirteen English anchoritic rules written from the eleventh through the fourteenth centuries.]

The Shewings of Julian of Norwich

I

Revelations to one who could not read a letter. Anno Domini 1373.

A Particular of the Chapters.

The first chapter, off the noumber of the Revelations particularly.

This is a Revelation of love that Jesus Christ, our endless blisse, made in
sixteen Sheweings or Revelations particular. Off the which, the first is of His
pretious coroning with thornys; and therewith was comprehended and specifyed
the Trinite with the incarnation, and unite betwix God and man soule, with many
5   faire sheweings of endless wisedome and teacheing of love, in which all the
sheweings that follow be grounded and onyd. The second is the discolloureing of
His faire face in tokenyng of His deareworthy passion. The third is that our Lord
God, almighty wisedome, all love, right as verily as He hath made every thing
that is, also verily He doith and workeith all thing that is done. The fourth is the
10   scourgeing of His tender body with plentious sheddyng of His blood. The fifth is
that the fend is overcome by the pretious passion of Christe. The sixth is the
worshippfull thankeing of our Lord God, with which He rewardeth His blissed
servants in Hevyn. The seventh is often feeleing of wele and wo. Feleing of wele
is gracious touching and lightening, with trew sekirness of endless joy. The
15   feleing of wo is temptation be heavyness and irkehede of our fleshly liveing, with
ghostly understanding that we arn kept also sekirly in love in wo as in wele be

2 Off, Of. **3 pretious . . . thornys,** precious crowning with thorns. **5 sheweings,** revelations.
6 onyd, joined, made one; **discolloureing,** discoloring. **7 deareworthy,** precious, excellent.
11 fend, fiend. **12 worshippfull,** honorable; **blissed,** blessed. **13 wele,** well-being, joy; **wo,**
woe. **14 sekirness,** sureness, certainty. **15 be,** by; **irkehede,** irritation. **16 ghostly,** spiritual;
arn, are; **also sekirly,** as securely.

37

the godeness of God. The eighth is the last paynes of Christ and His cruelle
dyeing. The ninth is of the likeing which is in the blissefull Trinite of the herde
passion of Christe and His rewfull dyeing, in which joy and likeing He will wee
20 be solacid and myrthid with Him till whan we come to the fullhede in Heavyn.
The tenth is our Lord Jesus shewith in love His blissefull herte even cloven on
two enjoyand. The eleventh is an hey, ghostly sheweing of His deareworthy
moder. The twelfth is that our Lord is most worthy being. The thirteenth is that
our Lord God wil we have gret regard to all the deeds that He hath done in the
25 gret nobleth of all things makyng and of the excellency of man makeyng, which
is above all His workes, and of the pretious asseth that He hath made for man
synne, turneing all our blame into endlesse worshippe; where also our Lord
seith, *Behold and see, for be the same mightie wisedome and goodnesse I shall
make wele all that is not wele, and thou shalt see it.* And in this He will we keepe
30 us in the feith and trowthe of Holy Church, not willing to wete His privityes
now, but as it longyth to us in this life. The fourteenth is that our Lord is
ground of our beseekeing. Herein were seene two properties: that one is rightfull
prayer, that other is sekir truste, which He will both be alike large, and thus our
prayers likyth Him, and He of His goodnesse fullfilleth it. The fifteenth, that we
35 shall sodenly be taken from al our peyne and from all our wo, and, of His
goodnesse, we shall come up aboven where we shall have our Lord Jesus to our
mede and be fullfilled of joy and blisse in Hevyn. The sixteenth is that the
blissefull Trinite, our Maker, in Christe Jesus our Saviour, endlessely wonyth in
our soule worshipfully reuland and geveand all things, us mightily and wisely
40 saveand and keepeand for love; and we shall not be overcome of our enemy.

17 **cruelle**, cruel. 18 **likeing**, pleasure, gratification; **of the herde**, because of the hard.
19 **rewfull**, rueful; **will**, desires. 20 **solacid and myrthid**, comforted and made happy; **whan**,
when; **fullhede**, fulfillment, fullness. 21–22 **His blissefull . . . enjoyand**, His blessed heart,
joyful even as it is cloven in two. 22–23 **hey . . . moder**, high spiritual vision of His
precious mother. 25 **gret nobleth of all things makyng**, great nobility of all things in their
creation; **man makeyng**, man's making, i.e., the human constitution. 26 **pretious asseth**,
precious satisfaction (see note); **man**, man's. 28 **be**, by. 30 **feith and trowthe**, faith and
truth; **wete His privityes**, know His secrets. 31 **longyth**, belongs, is appropriate for. 32
ground, foundation; **beseekeing**, beseeching. 33 **sekir**, sure; **large**, generous. 34 **likyth Him**,
are pleasing to Him. 37 **mede**, mead, reward. 38 **wonyth**, dwells. 39 **reuland and geveand**,
ruling and giving. 40 **saveand and keepeand**, saving and keeping.

II

The second chapter. Of the tyme of these revelations, and how shee asked three petitions.

These Revelations were shewed to a simple creature that cowde no letter the yeere of our Lord 1373, the eighth day of May, which creature desired afore three gifts of God. The first was mende of His passion. The second was bodily seke-nesse in youth at thirty yeeres of age. The third was to have of Gods gift three
45   wounds. As in the first methought I had sume feleing in the passion of Christe, but yet I desired more be the grace of God. Methought I would have beene that time with Mary Magdalen and with other that were Crists lovers, and therefore I desired a bodily sight wherein I might have more knowledge of the bodily peynes of our Saviour, and of the compassion our Lady and of all His trew lovers
50   that seene that time His peynes, for I would be one of them and suffer with Him. Other sight ner sheweing of God desired I never none till the soule was departid fro the body. The cause of this petition was that after the sheweing I should have the more trew minde in the passion of Christe.

The second came to my mynde with contrition frely desireing that sekenesse
55   so herde as to deth that I might in that sekeness underfongyn alle my rites of Holy Church, myselfe weening that I should dye, and that all creatures might suppose the same that seyen me, for I would have no manner comfort of eardtly life. In this sekenesse I desired to have all manier peynes bodily and ghostly that I should have if I should dye, with all the dreds and tempests of the fends, except
60   the outpassing of the soule. And this I ment for I would be purged be the mercy of God and after lyven more to the worshippe of God because of that sekenesse; and that for the more speede in my deth, for I desired to be soone with my God.

These two desires of the passion and the sekenesse I desired with a condition, seying thus: "Lord, thou wotith what I would, if it be Thy will that I have it, and
65   if it be not Thy will, good Lord, be not displeased, for I will nought, but as Thou wilt." For the third, by the grace of God and teachyng of Holy Church, I con-ceived a mighty desire to receive three wounds in my life; that is to sey, the

41 cowde no letter, knew no letters, could not read; or, possibly, did not know Latin. **43 mende of,** attention to, understanding, realization. **43–44 sekenesse,** sickness. **45 me-thought,** it seemed to me; **sume feleing in,** some feeling of. **46 be,** by. **50 seene,** saw; **peynes,** pains. **51 ner,** nor. **52 fro,** from. **53 trew minde in,** true understanding of. **54–55 sekenesse so herde as to deth,** a deathly sickness. **55 underfongyn,** receive. **56 weneing,** supposing. **57 seyen,** saw; **eardtly,** earthly. **58 ghostly,** spiritual. **59 fends,** fiends. **61 lyven,** live; **worshippe,** honor. **64 wotith,** know.

wound of very contrition, the wound of kinde compassion, and the wound of willfull longing to God. And all this last petition I asked without any condition.
70 These two desires foresaid passid fro my minde, and the third dwelled with me continually.

III

Of the sekenese opteyned of God be petition. Third chapter.

And when I was thirty yers old and halfe, God sent me a bodely sekeness in which I lay three dayes and three nights, and on the fourth night I tooke all my rites of Holy Church and wened not a levyd till day; and after this I langorid
75 forth two dayes and two nights. And on the third night I wened oftentimes to have passyd, and so wened they that were with mee; and, in youngith yet, I thought great sweeme to dye; but for nothing that was in earth that me lekid to levin for, ne for no peyne that I was aferd of, for I trusted in God of His mercy. But it was to have lyved that I might have loved God better and longer tyme,
80 that I might have the more knoweing and lovyng of God in blisse of Hevyn. For methought all the time that I had lived here so little and so short, in reward of that endlesse blisse, I thought, nothing. Wherefore I thought, "Good Lord, may my living no longer be to Thy worshippe?" And I understood by my reason and be my feleing of my peynes that I should dye, and I assented fully with all — with
85 all the will of my herte to be at God will. Thus I durid till day, and be than my body was dede fro the middis downewards as to my feleing. Then was I stered to be sett upright, underlenand with helpe, for to have more fredam of my herte to be at Gods will, and thinkeing on God while my life would lest.
My curate was sent for to be at my endeing, and by than he cam I had sett my
90 eyen and might not speke. He sett the cross before my face and seid, "I have browte thee the image of thy maker and Saviour. Louke thereupon and comfort

68 very, true, genuine. **70 fro**, from. **72 yers**, years. **74 wened not a levyd**, believed I would not live; **langorid**, languished. **75 wened**, thought, supposed. **76 youngith**, youth. **77 sweeme**, a pity, regret. **77–78 me lekid to levin for**, it gave me pleasure to live for. **78 ne**, nor; **aferd**, afraid. **81 methought**, it seemed to me; **in reward of**, in comparison with. **84 feleing**, feeling. **85 God will**, God's will, i.e., at God's disposal; **durid**, endured. **86 dede fro**, dead from; **middis**, middle; **stered**, prompted, took a notion. **87 underlenand**, leaning with support from beneath. **89 by than**, by the time that. **89–90 I had sett my eyen**, my eyes were fixed in the death stare. **90 sett**, placed. **91 browte**, brought; **Louke**, look.

thee therewith." Methought I was wele for my eyen were sett up rightward into Hevyn where I trusted to come be the mercy of God, but nevertheless I assented to sett my eyen in the face of the Crucifix, if I might; and so I dede. For me-
95 thought I might longer duren to loke even forth than right up. After this my sight began to failen and it was all derke about me in the chamber as it had be night, save in the image of the Cross wherein I beheld a comon light, and I wiste not how. All that was beside the Cross was uggely to me as if it had be mekil occupyed with the fends. After this the other party of my body began to dyen so
100 ferforth that onethys I had ony feleing, with shortnesse of onde; and than I went sothly to have passid.

And in this, sodenly all my peyne was taken fro me, and I was as hele, and namely in the other party of my body, as ever I was aforn. I mervalid at this soden change, for methought it was a privy workeing of God and not of kinde,
105 and yet by the feleing of this ease I trusted never the more to levyn. Ne the feleing of this ease was no full ease to me, for methought I had lever a be deliveryd of this world. Than came suddenly to my minde that I should desyre the second wounde of our Lords gracious gift, that my body might be fullfilled with minde and felyng of His blissid passion, for I would that His peynes were
110 my peynes, with compassion, and, afterward, longeing to God. But in this I desired never bodily sight nor sheweing of God, but compassion as a kinde soule might have with our Lord Jesus that for love would beene a dedely man, and therefore I desired to suffer with Him.

IV

Here begynnith the first revelation of the pretious crownyng of Criste etc. in the first chapter, and how God fullfilleth the herrte with most joy, and of His greate meekenesse; and how the syght of the passion of Criste is sufficient strength ageyn all temptations

92 **Methought,** It seemed to me; **eyen,** eyes; **sett,** fixed. 93 **Hevyn,** Heaven. 94 **dede,** did. 95 **duren to loke,** be able to look; **forth than,** straight ahead rather than. 96 **derke,** dark. 97 **wiste,** knew. 98 **mekil,** much. 99 **fends,** fiends; **party,** part. 100 **onethys,** scarcely; **ony feleing,** any feeling; **onde,** breath. 100–01 **went sothly,** truly thought. 101 **passid,** died. 102 **hele,** well. 103 **party,** part; **aforn,** before. 104 **privy,** mysterious; **kinde,** nature. 105 **levyn,** live. 106 **lever a be,** rather have been. 109 **minde,** understanding, realization. 110 **longeing,** longing (possibly belonging). 111 **kinde,** natural, kindly. 112 **would beene a dedely man,** was willing to be a mortal person.

of the fends, and of the gret excellency and mekenesse of the blissid Virgin Mary. The fourth chapter.

115 In this sodenly I saw the rede blode trekelyn downe fro under the garlande hote and freisly and ryth plenteously, as it were in the time of His passion that the garlande of thornys was pressid on His blissid hede. Ryte so, both God and man, the same that sufferd thus for me, I conceived treuly and mightily that it was Himselfe shewed it me without ony mene.

120 And in the same sheweing sodenly the Trinite fullfilled the herte most of joy; and so, I understood, it shall be in Hevyn withoute end to all that shall come there. For the Trinite is God, God is the Trinite. The Trinite is our maker and keeper, the Trinite is our everlasting lover, everlasting joy and blisse, be our Lord Jesus Christ; and this was shewed in the first and in all, for where Jesus appereith the blissid Trinite is understond, as to my sight. And I said, "Bene-
125 dicite, Domine." This I said for reverence in my meneing with a mighty voice, and full gretly was astonyed for wonder and mervel that I had, that He that is so reverend and dredfull will be so homley with a synfull creture liveing in wretched flesh. This I tooke for the time of my temptation, for methowte by the sufferance of God I should be tempted of fends or I dyed. With this sight of the blissid pass-
130 sion, with the Godhede that I saw in myne understonding, I knew wele that it was strength enow to me, ya, and to all creturers leving, ageyn all the fends of Hell and ghostly temptation.

In this He browght our blissid Lady to my understondyng. I saw hir ghostly in bodily likeness, a simple mayde and a meke, young of age and little waxen above
135 a child, in the stature that she was wan she conceived with child. Also God shewid in party the wisedam and the trueth of hir soule, wherein I understood the reverend beholding that she beheld hir God and maker mervelyng with greate reverence that He would be borne of hir that was a simple creature of His makeyng. And this wisdam and trueth, knowyng the greteness of hir maker and
140 the littlehede of hirselfe, that is made, caused hir sey full mekely to Gabriel,

---

114 **rede blode trekelyn**, red blood trickling. 115 **freisly**, afresh; **ryth**, right; **that**, when. 116 **thornys**, thorns. 118 **ony mene**, any intermediary. 119 **herte**, heart. 124 **appereith**, appears. 124–25 **Benedicite, Domine**, Blessed be Thou, Lord. 125 **meneing**, intention. 126 **astonyed**, astonished. 127 **reverend and dredfull**, revered and awe inspiring; **homley**, intimate, familiar (see note); **synfull creture liveing**, sinful creature living. 129 **of fends or I dyed**, by fiends before I died. 131 **enow**, enough; **ya**, yeah, indeed; **leving**, living; **ageyn**, against. 133 **understondyng**, mind. 134 **waxen**, grown. 135 **wan**, when. 136 **party**, part.

"Lo, me, Gods handmayd." In this sight I understoode sothly that she is mare than all that God made beneath hir in worthyness and grace. For aboven hir is nothing that is made but the blissid manhood of Criste, as to my sight.

V

How God is to us everything that is gode, tenderly wrappand us; and all thing that is made, in regard to Almighty God, it is nothing; and how man hath no rest till he nowteth himselfe and all thing for the love of God. The fifth chapter.

145

150

155

160

In this same time our Lord shewed to me a ghostly sight of His homely love- ing. I saw that He is to us everything that is good and comfortable for us. He is oure clotheing, that for love wrappeth us, halsyth us, and all becloseth us for tender love, that He may never leeve us, being to us althing that is gode as to myne understondyng. Also in this He shewed a littil thing the quantitye of an hesil nutt in the palme of my hand, and it was as round as a balle. I lokid there upon with eye of my understondyng and thowte, What may this be? And it was generally answered thus: *It is all that is made.* I mervellid how it might lesten, for methowte it might suddenly have fallen to nowte for littil. And I was answered in my understondyng, *It lesteth and ever shall, for God loveth it; and so all thing hath the being be the love of God.*

In this littil thing I saw three properties: the first is that God made it, the second is that God loveth it, the third, that God kepith it. But what is to me sothly the maker, the keper, and the lover I canot tell, for till I am substantially onyd to Him I may never have full rest ne very blisse; that is to sey, that I be so festined to Him, that there is right nowte that is made betwix my God and me. It needyth us to have knoweing of the littlehede of creatures and to nowtyn allthing that is made for to love and howe God that is unmade. For this is the cause why we be not all in ease of herete and soule, for we sekyn here rest in those things that is so littil, wherin is no rest, and know not our God that is al mighty, al wise, all gode; for He is the very rest. God will be knowen, and Him

141 **sothly,** truly; **mare,** more. 144 **homely,** intimate. 146 **wrappeth . . . becloseth us,** winds about us, embraces us, and entirely encloses us. 149 **hesil nutt,** hazel nut. 151 **lesten,** last. 154 **the being,** existence. 157–58 **substantially onyd,** integrally joined. 158 **ne very,** nor true. 160 **littlehede,** smallness. 160–61 **to nowtyn . . . made,** value as nothing everything created. 161 **howe,** have (see note); **unmade,** without creator. 162 **herete,** heart; **sekyn,** seek. 164–65 **Him liketh,** it pleases Him.

165 liketh that we rest in Him. For all that is beneth Him sufficeth not us. And this is the cause why that no soule is restid till it is nowted of all things that is made. Whan he is willfully nowtid for love, to have Him that is all, then is he abyl to receive ghostly rest.

Also our Lord God shewed that it is full gret plesance to Him that a sily soule 170 come to Him nakidly and pleynly and homely. For this is the kinde yernings of the soule by the touching of the Holy Ghost, as be the understondyng that I have in this sheweing: "God of Thy goodnesse, give me Thyselfe, for Thou art enow to me, and I may nothing aske that is less that may be full worshippe to Thee. And if I aske anything that is lesse, ever me wantith; but only in Thee I have 175 all." And these words arn full lovesome to the soule, and full nere, touchen the will of God and His goodness. For His goodness comprehendith all His creatures and all His blissid works and overpassith without end. For He is the endleshede, and He hath made us only to Himselfe and restorid us be His blissid passion, and kepith us in His blissid love; and all this is of His goodness.

VI

How we shold pray; and of the gret tender love that our Lord hath to mannes soule, willing us to be occupyed in knowing and loveing of Him. The sixth chapter.

180 This sheweing was made to lerne our soule wisely to clevyn to the goodnes of God. And in that time the custome of our prayeing was browte to mende, how we use for lak of understonding and knowing of love to make many menys. Than saw I sothly that is more worshippe to God, and more very delite, that we faithfully pray to Himselfe of His goodness and clevyn thereto be His grace with 185 trew understondyng and stedfast be love, than if we made all the menys that herte can thinke. For if we make all these menys, it is to litil and and not full worshippe to God, but in His goodnes is all the hole, and there failith right nowte.

For thus as I shall say came to my minde: In the same time we pray to God for 190 His holy flesh and for His pretious blode, His holy passion, His deareworthy

166 **nowted**, stripped. 167 **Whan**, When. 169 **sily**, innocent, simple. 170 **kinde yernings**, natural yearning. 172 **enow**, enough. 175 **arn**, are. 180 **lerne**, teach; **clevyn**, cleave. 181 **mende**, mind. 182 **menys**, means, intermediaries. 183 **sothly**, truly. 184 **clevyn**, cleave. 185 **menys**, means, intermediaries. 187 **hole**, whole. 187–88 **failith right nowte**, nothing at all fails. 190 **deareworthy**, precious, excellent.

death and wounds; and all the blissid kindenes, the endles life, that we have of all this, is His goodnes. And we pray Him for His sweete moder love, that Him bare, and all the helpe we have of her is of His godeness. And we pray by His Holy Cross that He dyed on, and all the vertue and the helpe that we have of the Cross, it is of His godeness. And on the same wise, all the helpe that we have of special saints and all the blissed company of Hevyn, the dereworthy love and endles freindshippe that we have of them, it is of His godenes. For God of His godenes hath ordeyned meanys to helpe us, wole faire and fele, of which the chiefe and principal mene is the blissid kinde that He toke of the Mayd, with all the menys that gone aforn and cum after which belongyn to our redemption and to endless salvation.

Wherefore it pleaseth Him that we seke Him and worship be menys, understondyng and knoweing that He is the goodness of all. For the goodness of God is the heyest prayer and it comith downe to the lowest party of our nede. It quickyth our soule and bringith it on life and makyth it for to waxen in grace and vertue. It is nerest in kind and ridiest in grace. For it is the same grace that the soule sekith and evir shall, till we know oure God verily that hath us all in Himselfe beclosyd. For He hath no dispite of that He hath made ne He hath no disdeyne to serve us at the simplest office that to our body longyth in kinde, for love of the soule that He hath made to His owne likness. For as the body is cladde in the cloth, and the flesh in the skyne, and the bonys in the flesh, and the herte in the bouke, so arn we, soule and body, cladde in the goodnes of God and inclosyd; ya, and more homley, for all these may wasten and weren away, and the godenes of God is ever hole, and more nere to us withoute any likenes, for treuly our lover desireth that our soule cleve to Hym with all the might and that we be evermore clevand to His godenes. For of all thing that herete may thinke, it plesyth most God and sonest spedyth, for our soule is so specially lovid of Him that is heiest that it overpassyth the knoweing of all creatures. That is to seyen, there is no creature that is made that may wetyn how mekyl, and how swetely, and how tenderly our Maker loveth us. And therefore we may with His grace and His helpe stond in ghostly beholding with everlestyng merveyling in

192 **moder love,** mother's love. 193 **bare,** bore. 198 **wole,** well (intensive); **fele,** many. 199 **mene,** means; **kinde,** nature; **toke,** took. 200 **menys,** means, helps; **aforn,** before; **cum,** come. 204–05 **quickyth,** gives life to. 206 **nerest . . . grace,** nearest in nature and most ready in grace. 208 **beclosyd,** enclosed; **dispite of,** contempt for. 209 **longyth in kinde,** belongs in nature. 211 **bonys,** bones. 212 **herte,** heart; **bouke,** trunk; **arn,** are. 213 **ya,** indeed; **wasten and weren,** waste and wear. 214 **hole,** whole. 216 **herete,** heart. 217 **spedyth,** prospers. 219 **wetyn,** know; **mekyl,** greatly.

this hey, overpassing, onenestimable love that Almitie God hath to us of His godenes. And therefore we may aske of our lover with reverence all that we willen.

225 For our kindly will is to have God and the gode will of God is to have us, and we may never blyn of willing ne of longyng till we have Him in fullhede of joy; and than may we no more willen. For He will that we be occupyed in knoweing and loveing til the tyme that we shall be fulfilled in Hevyn. And therefore was this lesson of love shewid, with all that followith, as ye shal se. For the strength

230 and the ground of all was shewed in the first sight. For of all thing, the beholding and the lovyng of the Maker makith the soule to seeme lest in his owne sight, and most fillith it with reverend drede and trew mekenes, with plenty of charite to his even Cristen.

VII

How our Lady, beholdyng the gretenes of hir Maker, thowte hirselfe leste; and of the great droppys of blode renning from under the garland; and how the most joy to man is that God most hie and mightie is holyest and curtesiest. Seventh chapter.

And to lerne us this, as to myne understondyng, our Lord God shewed our

235 Lady Saint Mary in the same tyme, that is to mene the hey wisedome and trewth she had in beholding of hir Maker, so grete, so hey, so mightie, and so gode. This gretenes and this noblyth of the beholdyng of God fulfilled her of reverend drede, and with this she saw hirselfe so litil and so low, so simple and so pore, in reward of hir Lord God, that this reverent drede fulfillid hir of mekenes. And

240 thus by this grounde she was fulfillid of grace and of al manner vertues and overpassyth all creatures. In all the tyme that He shewed this that I have seid now, in ghostly sight I saw the bodyly sight lesting of the plentious bledeing of the hede. The grete dropis of blode fel downe from under the garland like pellots semand as it had cum out of the veynis, and in the comeing out it were

245 browne rede, for the blode was full thick, and in the spredeing abrode it were bright rede, and whan it come to the browes, than it vanyshid; notwithstondying

222 **onenestimable**, inestimable. 226 **blyn**, cease. 231 **lest**, least; **his**, its (the soul's). 233 **his even Cristen**, the soul's fellow Christians. 234 **to lerne us**, to teach us. 236 **hey**, high. 239 **in reward of**, in comparison with. 242 **lesting**, lasting. 242–43 **bledeing of the hede**, bleeding of the head. 243 **blode**, blood. 244 **semand . . . veynis**, seeming as if it had come out of the veins. 245 **browne rede**, deep (shining) red.

the bleding continuid till many things were seene and understondyn. The fairehede and the livelyhede is like nothing but the same. The plenteoushede is like
to the dropys of water that fallen of the evys after a greate showre of reyne that
250   fall so thick that no man may numbre them with bodily witte; and for the roundhede, it were like to the scale of heryng in the spreadeing on the forehead. These
three come to my mynde in the tyme: pellotts, for roundhede in the comynge out
of the blode; the scale of heryng, in the spreadeing in the forehede, for roundhede; the dropys of evese, for the plentioushede inumerable. This shewing was
255   quick and lively and hidouse and dredfull, swete and lovely.

   And of all the sight it was most comfort to me, that our God and Lord that is
so reverent and dredefull is so homley and curtes, and this most fullfilled me
with likeing and sekirnes of soule. And to the understondyng of this He shewid
this opyn example. It is the most worshippe that a solemne King or a grete Lord
260   may doe a pore servant if he will be homely with him, and namely if he shewith
it himselfe, of a full trew meneing and with a glad cheere, both prive and partie.
Than thinkyth this pore creature thus: A, what might this nobil Lord doe more
worshipp and joy to me than to shew me that am so simple this mervelous
homlyhede? Sothly it is more joy and likeing to me than he gave me grete gifts
265   and were himselfe strange in maner. This bodily example was shewid so hey that
manys hart might be ravishid and almost forgettyng himselfe for joy of this grete
homlyhede. Thus it fareith be our Lord Jesus and be us, for sothly it is the most
joy that may be, as to my sight, that He that is heyest and mightyest, noblest and
worthyest, is lowest and mekest, homlyest and curteysest. And treuly and sothly
270   this mervelous joy shall be shewne us all whan we se Him. And this will our
Lord, that we willen and trowen, joyen and liken, comfortyn us and solacyn us as
we may with His grace and with His helpe into the tyme that we se it verily. For
the most fulhede of joy that we shal have, as to my sight, is the mervelous
curtesie and homlyhede of our Fader that is our maker in our Lord Jesus Criste
275   that is our brother and our Saviour.

   But this mervelous homlyhede may no man weten in this tyme of life, but he
have it of special shewing of our Lord, or of grete plenty of grace inwardly govyn

---

248 plenteoushede, plenitude. **249 dropys**, drops; **evys**, eaves; **showre of reyne**, shower of
rain. **250 bodily witte**, natural intelligence. **250–51 roundhede**, roundness; **251 heryng**,
herring. **254 dropys of evese**, drops from eaves. **255 hidouse**, hideous. **257 curtes**, courteous. **258 likeing**, happiness, pleasure. **259 opyn**, open. **261 glad cheere, both prive and
partie**, cheerful expression, both in private and in public. **266 manys**, man's. **270-72 And . . .
may**, And our Lord wills this, that we desire and have faith, rejoice and take pleasure,
comfort and console ourselves as we may. **276 weten**, know. **277 govyn**, given.

of the Holy Ghost. But faith and beleve with charite deservith the mede; and so
it is had be grace; for in faith with hope and charete our life is groundyd. The
280 shewyng, made to whome that God will, pleynly techith the same, openyd and
declarid with many privy points longing to our faith which be worshipfull to
knowen. And whan the shewyng, which is goven in a tyme, is passyd and hid,
than the feith kepyth be grace of the Holy Ghost into our life end. And thus be
the shewyng: It is not other than the faith ne less ne more as it may be seene be
285 our Lords meneing in the same matter be than it come to the end.

VIII

**A recapitulation of that is seid; and how it was shewid to hir generally for all. Eighth
chapter.**

And as longe as I saw this sight of the plentious bleding of the hede I might
never stinte of these words, "Benedicite, Domine," in which sheweyng I understode six things. The first is the toknys of the blissid passion and the plentious
sheddyng of His pretious blode. The second is the Maiden that is derworthy
290 moder. The third is the blissfull Godhede that ever was, is, and ever shal bene,
al mighty, al wisdam, al love. The fourth is al thing that He hath made; for wele
I wete that Hevyn and erth and all that is made is mekil and large, faire and
gode, but the cause why it is shewid so litil to my sight was for I saw it in the
presence of Him that is the maker of all thing; for a soule that seith the maker
295 of all, all that is made semith full litil. The fifth is He that made all things for
love; be the same love it is kept and shall be withoute end. The sixth is that God
is al thing that is gode, as to my sight, and the godenes that al thing hath, it is
He. And al these our Lord shewid me in the first sight with time and space to
beholden it.
300 And the bodily sight stinted and the gostly sight dwellid in myne understondyng. And I abode with reverent drede, joyand in that I saw. And I
desired as I durst to se more, if it were His will, or ell lenger time the same.
In al this I was mekil sterid in charite to mine even Cristen, that thei might

277–78 **govyn of**, given by. 278 **mede**, mead, reward. 282 **goven**, given. 285 **be than**,
until. 287 **Benedicite, Domine**, Blessed be Thou, Lord. 288 **toknys**, tokens, signs. 290
bene, be. 292 **wete**, know. 294 **seith**, sees. 295 **semith**, seems. 300 **stinted**, stopped. 302
ell, else. 303 **mekil sterid**, much stirred; **even Cristen**, fellow Christians.

305 seen and knowyn the same that I saw, for I would it were comfort to they. For al this sight was shewid general. Than said I to them that were aboute me, "It is today domys day with me"; and this I said for I went a deid, for that day that a man deith, he is demyd as he shal be without end, as to my understond-yng. This I seid for I would thei lovid God the better for to make hem to have mende that this life is shorte as thei might se in example. For in al this time I 310 went have deid. And that was mervil to me, and sweeme in partie, for methowte this vision was shewid for hem that should leven. And that I say of me, I sey in the person of al myn even Cristen, for I am lernyd in the gostly shewing of our Lord God that He menyth so; and therefore I pray you al for Gods sake, and counsel you for your owne profitt, that ye levyn the beholding of a wretch that 315 it was shewid to, and mightily, wisely, and mekely behold God that of His curtes love and endles godenes wolde shewyn it generally in comfort of us al. For it is God's will that ye take it with gret joy and likyng as Jesus had shewid it on to you all.

IX

Of the mekenes of this woman kepeing hir alway in the feith of Holy Church; and how he that lovyth his evyn Cristen for God lovith all thing. Ninth chapter.

For the shewing I am not goode but if I love God the better. And in as much 320 as ye love God the better, it is more to you than to me. I sey this not to hem that be wise, for thei wote it wele, but I sey it to yow that be simple for ese and comfort, for we arn al one in comfort. For sothly it was not shewid me that God lovid me better than the lest soule that is in grace, for I am sekir that there be many that never had shewing ner sight but of the comon techyng of Holy Church 325 that loven God better than I. For if I loke singularly to myselfe I am right nowte; but in general I am, in hope, in onehede of charite, with al myn evyn Cristen. For in this onehede stond the life of all mankinde that shall be savid.

304 **they,** them. 306 **domys day,** judgment day; **went a deid,** expected to have died. 307 **deith,** dies; **demyd,** judged. 308 **thei lovid,** they loved. 308–09 **make hem to have mende,** make them realize. 310 **went have,** thought to have; **mervil,** strange. 310-11 **sweeme . . . should leven,** partly a pity, for I thought this vision was shown in order to benefit the living. 312 **even Cristen,** fellow Christians; **lernyd,** taught, instructed. 314 **levyn,** believe (see note). 315 **curtes,** courteous. 316 **wolde shewyn,** would show. 317–18 **on to you all,** to you, one and all. 320 **hem,** those. 321 **wote,** know. 323 **sekir,** sure. 326 **onehede,** unity.

For God is all that is good, on to my sight. And God hat made al that is made and God lovith al that He hath made; and he that generaly loveith al his evyn 330 Cristen for God, he lovith al that is. For in mankynd that shall be savid is comprehendid al, that is to sey, all that is made and the Maker of al; for in man is God, and God is in al. And I hope be the grace of God he that beholdith it thus shal be truely taught and mightily comforted if he nedith comforte.

I speake of hem that shal be save, for in this time God shewid me none other. 335 But in al thing I leve as Holy Church levith, preachith, and teachith. For the feith of Holy Church, the which I had afornhand understonden and, as I hope, by the grace of God wilfully kept in use and custome, stode continualy in my sight, willing and meneing never to receive onything that might be contrary therunto. And with this entent I beheld the shewing with al my diligens, for in al this blis- 340 sid shewing, I beheld it as one in Gods meneyng. All this was shewid by thre, that is to sey, be bodily sight, and by word formyd in my understonding, and be gostly sight. But the gostly sight — I cannot ne may not shew it as hopinly ne as fully as I wolde. But I truste in our Lord God Almightie that He shal of His godenes, and for yowr love, make yow to take it more gostly and more swetely 345 than I can or may telle it.

X

The second Revelation is of His discolouryng etc; of our redemption, and the discolour- ing of the vernacle; and how it plesith God we seke Him besily, abiding Him stedfastly and trusting Hym mightily. Tenth chapter.

And after this I saw with bodily sight, in the face of the crucifix that henge before me in the which I behelde continualy, a parte of His passion — despite, spitting and sollowing, and buffetting and many langoryng peynes, mo than I can tel, and often changing of colour. And one time I saw how halfe the face, begyn- 350 ing at the ere, overrede with drie blode til it beclosid to the mid-face. And after that, the tuther halfe beclosyd on the same wise, and therewhiles it vanyssched in this party, even as it came. This saw I bodily — swemely and derkely, and I

328 **on . . . sight**, one (whole) in my sight; **hat**, has. 334 **hem**, those; **save**, saved, i.e., achieve salvation. 335 **leve**, believe; **levith**, believes. 339 **diligens**, diligence. 342 **hopinly**, openly. 343 **wolde**, wish to. 346 **henge**, hung. 348 **sollowing**, soiling (see note); **langoryng**, languishing, lingering; **mo**, more. 350 **ere**, ear; **overrede**, overun. 351 **tuther**, other; **therewhiles**, meanwhile. 352 **swemely**, sorrowfully, fearfully.

desired more bodily sight to have sene more clerely. And I was answered in my reason: If God wil shew thee more, He shal be thy light; thee nedith none but Him. For I saw Him and sowte Hym, for we arn now so blynd and so unwise that we never sekyn God til He of His godenes shewith Him to us. And we ought se of Him graciously, than arn we sterid by the same grace to sekyn with gret desire to se Him more blisfully. And thus I saw Him and sowte Him, and I had Him and I wantid Hym. And this is and should be our comon werkeyng in this, as to my sight.

One tyme mine understondyng was led downe into the see ground, and there I saw hill and dalis grene, semand, as it were, mosse begrowne, with wrekke and with gravel. Than I understode thus, that if a man or a woman were under the broade watyr, if he might have sight of God, so as God is with a man continually, he should be save in body and soule and take no harme; and, overpassing, he should have mor solace and comfort than al this world can telle. For He will that we levyn that we se Him continually thowe that us thinketih that it be but litl, and in this beleve He makith us evermore to getyn grace. For He will be sene and He wil be sowte, He wil be abedyn and He wil be trosted.

This second sheweing was so low and so litil and so simple that my sprets were in grete travel in the beholding, mornand, dredfull, and longand. For I was sum time in doute whither it was a shewing. And than divers times our gode Lord gave me more sight whereby I understode treuly that it was a shewing. It was a figure and likenes of our foule dede hame, that our faire, bright, blissid Lord bare for our sins. It made me to thinke of the holy vernacle of Rome which He hath portrayed with His owne blissid face whan He was in His herd passion wilfully going to His deth and often chongyng of colour. Of the brownehede and blakehede, reulihede and lenehede of this image, many mervel how it might be, stondyng He portraied it with His blissid face, which is the faire hede of Heavyn, flowre of erth, and the fruite of the mayden wombe. Than how might this image be so discolouring and so fer fro faire?

I desire to sey like as I have understond be the grace of God. We know in our faith and beleve be the teaching and preching of Holy Church, that the blissid

---

355 sowte, sought. **356 sekyn**, seek. **356–57 And . . . Him**, If we see anything of Him. **357 sterid**, stirred, prompted; **sekyn**, seek. **358 sowte**, sought. **361 see ground**, bottom of the sea. **362 dalis . . . wrekke**, green dales, seeming as if it were grown over with moss, with wrak. **367 levyn**, believe; **thowe that us thinkeith**, although we think. **369 abedyn**, abided, waited for; **trosted**, trusted. **370 low**, humble; **sprets**, spirits. **371 travel**, travail; **mornand, dredfull**, mourning, fearful. **374 dede hame**, skin, slough; mortal covering (fig., flesh). **378 reulihede and lenehede**, piteousness and thinness. **379 stondyng**, understanding that.

385 Trinite made mankinde to His image and to His likenes. In the same maner wise
we knowen that whan man felle so deepe and so wretchidly be synne, there was
none other helpe to restore man but throw Him that made man. And that made
man for love, be the same love He would restore man to the same blisse and
overpassing. And like as we were like made to the Trinite in our first makyng,
390 our Maker would that we should be like Jesus Criste, our Saviour in Hevyn without ende, be the vertue of our geynmakyng. Than atwix these two He would, for
love and worshippe of man, make Himselfe as like to man in this dedely life, in
our foulehede and our wratchidnes, as man myght be without gilte. Whereof it
meneith as it was aforseyd — it was the image and likenes of our foule blak dede
395 hame wherein our faire bryte blissid Lord God is hid. But ful sekirly I dar sey,
and we owen to trowen, that so faire a man was never none but He, till what
tyme His faire colour was chongyd with travel and sorrow and passion, deyeng.
Of this it is spoken in the eighth Revelation where it tretith more of the same
likenes. And there it seith of the vernacle of Rome, it mevyth be dyvers
400 chongyng of colour and chere, sometyme more comfortably and lively and sometime more rewfull and dedely, as it may be seene in the eighth Revelation.

And this vision was a lernyng to myn understondyng that the continual sekyng
of the soule plesith God ful mekyl, for it may do no more than sekyn, suffrin,
and trusten. And this wrought in the soule that hath it be the Holy Ghost. And
the clernes of fyndyng is of His special grace whan it is His will. The sekyng with
405 feith, hope, and charite plesyth our Lord, and the finding plesyth the soule and
fulfillith it with joy. And thus was I lernyd to myn understondyng, that sekyng is
as good as beholdyng for the tyme that He will suffer the soule to be in travel.
It is God wille that we seke Him to the beholdyng of Him, for be that He shall
shew us Himselfe of His special grace whan He wil. And how a soule shall have
410 him in His beholdyng, He shal teche Himselfe; and that is most worshipp to Him
and profitt to thyselfe, and most receivith of mekenes and vertues with the grace
and ledyng of the Holy Goste. For a soule that only festenith him on to God
with very troste, either be sekyng or in beholdyng, it is the most worshipp that
he may don to Him, as to my sight.
415 These arn two werkyng that mown be seene in this vision. That on is sekyng;

385 **be synne**, through sin. **386 And that made**, And He who made. **388 overpassing**, transcendence. **390 geynmakyng**, remaking. **391 dedely**, mortal. **393-94 dede hame**, skin, slough, mortal covering (fig., flesh). **395 owen to trowen**, ought to believe. **396 travel**, travail. **399 chere**, expression. **400 rewfull and dedely**, rueful and like death. **401 lernyng**, teaching. **402 ful mekyl**, very much; **sekyn**, seek. **404 sekyng**, seeking. **407 travel**, travail. **408 God wille**, God's will. **409-10 have him**, conduct itself. **415 mown**, may; **on**, one.

the other is beholdyng. The sekyng is common; that, every soule may have with His grace, and owith to have, that discretion and techyng of the Holy Church. It is God wil that we have thre things in our sekyng. The first is that we sekyn wilfully and bisily withouten slauth as it may be throw His grace, gladly and merili

420 withoute onskilful hevynes and veyne sorow. The second is that we abide Him stedfastly for His love withoute gruching and strieving ageyns Him in our lives end, for it shall lesten but a while; the thred, that we trosten in Him mightily of ful sekird feith, for it is His wil. We knowen He shall appere sodenly and blisfully to al His lovers, for His werkyng is privy, and He wil be perceivid; and His

425 appering shal be swith sodeyn, and He wil be trowid, for He is full hend and homley. Blissid mot He ben.

XI

The third Revelation etc.; how God doth al thing except synne, never chongyng His purpose without end, for He hath made al thing in fulhede of goodnes. The eleventh chapter.

And after this I saw God in a poynte, that is to sey in myn understonding, be which sight I saw that He is in al things. I beheld with avisement, seing and knowing in sight with a soft drede, and thought, What is synne? For I saw treuly

430 that God doth al thing be it never so litil. And I saw truly that nothing is done be happe, ne be aventure, but al thing be the foreseing wisedome of God. If it be happe or adventure in the sight of man, our blindhede and our onforesight is the cause, for the things that arn in the foreseing wisdam of God fro withoute beginning (which rightfully and worshippfully and continualy He ledyth to the

435 best end as they comen aboute) fallyn to us sodenly, ourselfe unwetyng; and thus be our blindhede and our onforsighte, we seyen these ben happis and aventures. But to our Lord God thei be not so.

Wherefore me behovith nedes to grant that al thing that is done, it is wel

---

416–17 The sekyng . . . Church, The seeking is common; that is available in the discretion and teaching of Holy Church which every soul may have, and ought to have, by God's grace. **419 slauth,** sloth; **throw,** through. **420 onskilful,** senseless, unreasonable; **veyne,** vain. **421 gruching,** grudging; **ageyns,** against. **422 thred,** third. **425 swith sodeyn,** very sudden; **trowid,** believed; **hend,** courteous. **426 mot,** may. **427 poynte,** point. **428 with avisement,** thoughtfully, with full clarity. **431 be happe, ne be aventure,** by chance nor by accident. **435 unwetyng,** unknowing. **436 ben happis and aventures,** are chances and accidents. **438 me behovith nedes to grant,** I must concede.

done, for our Lord God doth alle. For in this time the werkyng of cretures was
440 not shewid, but of our Lord God in the creature. For He is in the mydde poynt
of all thyng, and all He doith; and I was sekir He doith no synne. And here I
saw sothly that synne is no dede, for in al this was not synne shewid. And I
wold no lenger mervel in this, but beheld our Lord, what He wold shewen. And
thus as it might be for the time, the rightfulhede of Gods werkyng was shewid to
445 the soule.

Rightfulhede hath two faire properties: it is right and it is full, and so arn al
the werks of our Lord God. And thereto nedith neither the werkyng of mercy
ner grace, for it ben al rightfull, wherin feilith nougte. And in another time He
shewid for the beholdyng of synne nakidly, as I shal sey, where He usith werkyng
450 of mercy and grace. And this vision was shewid to myne understondeng. For our
Lord will have the soule turnid truly into the beholdyng of Him, and generally
of all His werks, for they arn full gode, and al His doings be easye and swete,
and to gret ease bringing the soule that is turnyd fro the beholdyng of the blind
demyng of man on to the faire, swete demyng of our Lord God.

455 For a man beholdith some dedes wele done and some dedes evil. But our Lord
beholdyth hem not so. For as al that hath being in kinde is of Godds makyng, so
is al thing that is done in propertie of Gods doing. For it is easye to understonde
that the best dede is wele done. And so wele as the best dede is done and the
heiest, so wele is the lest dede done, and al in propertie and in the ordir that our
460 Lord hath it ordeynit to from withoute begynning, for ther is no doer but He. I
saw ful sekirly that He chongyth never His purpos in no manner thyng, nor never
shall, withoute end. For ther was nothyng onknowen to Him in His rightfull
ordenance from without begynnyng. And therefore al thyng was sett in ordir, or
anything was made, as it should stonde withoute end, and no maner thyng shall
465 failen of that poynt. For He made al thinge in fulhede of godenes, and therefore
the blissid Trinite is ever ful plesid in al His werks. And al this shewid He ful
blisfully meneing thus: Se I am God; se I am in al thing; se I doe al thyng; se I
left never myne hands of myn werks, ne never shall withoute ende; se I lede al
thing to the end I ordeynd it to fro withoute beginnyng be the same might, wis-
470 dam, and love that I made it. How should anything be amysse? Thus migtily,
wisely, and lovinly was the soule examynyd in this vision. Than saw I sothly that
me behovyd nedis to assenten with gret reverens, enjoyand in God.

---

441 sekir, certain. **442 dede**, deed. **443 wold**, would; **wold shewen**, would show. **448 ben
al**, is all; **feilith nougte**, nothing fails. **454 demyng**, judgment. **459 heiest**, highest. **463 or**,
before. **472 me behovyd nedis to assenten**, I must necessarily assent.

XII

The fourth Revelation etc.; how it likith God rather and better to wash us in His blode from synne than in water, fore His blode is most pretius. Twelfth chapter.

And after this I saw, beholding the body plentiously bleding in seming of the scorgyng, as thus: The faire skynne was brokyn ful depe into the tender flesh with
475 sharpe smyting al about the sweete body. So plenteously the hote blode ran oute that there was neither sene skynne ne wound, but as it were al blode. And whan it come wher it should a fallen downe, than it vanyshid. Notwitstondyng the bleding continued a while til it migt be sene with avisement, and this was so plenteous to my sigt that methowte if it had be so in kind and in substance for
480 that tyme, it should have made the bed al on blode and a passid over aboute.

And than cam to my minde that God hath made waters plentiuous in erthe to our service and to our bodily ease for tender love that He hath to us, but yet lekyth Him better that we take full homely hys blissid blode to wassch us of synne, for there is no licur that is made that He lekyth so wele to give us. For it
485 is most plentiuous as it is most pretious, and that be the vertue of His blissid godhede. And it is our kinde and al blisfully beflowyth us be the vertue of His pretious love. The dereworthy blode of our Lord Jesus Criste, as verily as it is most pretious, as verily it is most plentiuous. Beholde and se: The pretious plenty of His dereworthy blode desendith downe into Helle and braste her bands
490 and deliveryd al that were there which longyd to the curte of Hevyn. The pretious plenty of His dereworthy blode overflowith al erth and is redye to wash al creaturs of synne which be of gode will, have ben, and shal ben. The pretious plenty of His dereworthy blode ascendid up into Hevyn to the blissid body of our Lord Jesus Christe, and there is in Him, bleding and praying for us to the Father,
495 and is and shall be as long as it nedith. And evermore it flowith in all Hevyns enjoying the salvation of al mankynde that arn there and shal ben, fulfilling the noumber that failith.

473–74 **seming of the scorgyng**, seaming, furrowing, of the scourging (see note). **477 should a**, should have. **478 migt**, might; **avisement**, clarity. **479 sigt**, sight. **480 al on blode and a passid over aboute**, bloody all over and have passed entirely over it. **484 licur**, liquor. **486 it is our kinde**, it is of the same nature as our own. **489 braste her bands**, burst their bonds. **490 longyd**, belonged; **curte**, courte. **495 it nedith**, it is needed.

XIII

The fifth Revelation is that the temptation of the fend is overcome be the passion of Criste, to the encres of joy of us, and to His peyne everlestingly. Thirteenth chapter.

And after, er God shewid ony words, He sufferd me to beholden in Him a conable tyme, and all that I had sene, and all intellecte that was therein, as the simplicite of the soule migte take it. Than He, without voice and openyng of lippis, formys in my soule these words: *Herewith is the fend overcome.* These words seyd our Lord menening His blissid passion as He shewid aforn. In this shewid our Lord that the passion of Him is the overcomming of the fend. God shewid that the fend hath now the same malice that he had aforn the incarnation. And as sore he travilith and as continually he seeth that all sent of salvation ascappyn him worshipply be the vertue of Cristes pretious passion. And that is his sorow and ful evyl he is attemyd, for all that God sufferith him to doe turnith us to joye and him to shame and wo. And he hath as mech sorow when God givith him leave to werkyn as when he werkyth not. And that is for he may never doe as yvel as he would, for his migte is al tokyn in Godds hand. But in God may be no wreth, as to my syte. For our gode Lord endlesly hath regarde to His owne worshippe and to the profite of al that shall be savid. With might and ryht He withstondith the reprovid, the which of mallice and shrewidnes bysyen hem to contriven and to done agens Gods wille. Also I saw our Lord scorne his malice and nowten his onmigte, and He wil that we doe so.

For this sigte I lauhyd migtily, and that made hem to lauhyn that were about me, and ther lauhyng was a likeing to me. I thowte that I wold that al myn evyn Christen had seen as I saw and than should thei al lauhyn with me. But I saw not Criste lawhyn; for I understode that we may lauhyn in comforting of ourselfe and joying in God, for the devil is overcome. And then I saw Him scorne his malice; it was be ledyng of myn understondyng into our Lord, that is to sey, an inward sheweing of sothfastnes, withoute chongyng of chere. For as to my sight, it is a worshipfull property that is in God which is durabil.

And after this I fel into a sadhede, and seid, "I se three things, game, scorne,

498 **er**, before. 499 **conable**, suitable. 500 **migte**, might. 501 **formys**, forms. 502 **menening**, referring to. 506 **ascappyn**, escape; **worshipply be**, honorably by. 507 **attemyd**, esteemed. 508 **mech**, much. 510 **migte**, might; **tokyn**, taken. 511 **wreth**, wrath. 515 **onmigte**, powerlessness. 516 **sigte**, sight; **I lauhyd migtily**, I laughed mightily; **lauhyn**, laugh. 517 **likeing**, pleasure. 518–19 **lauhyn, lawhyn**, laugh. 522 **sothfastnes**, truth. 524 **sadhede**, sober mood; **game**, joy.

525 and arneste; I se game that the fend is overcome. I se scorne that God scornith
him and he shal be scornyd. And I se arneste that he is overcome be the blissfull
passion and deth of our Lord Jesus Criste; that was done in ful arnest and with
sad travelle." And I seid, "He is scornid." I mene that God scornith him; that is
to sey, for He seeth him now as He shall done withoute end. For in this God
530 shewid that the fend is dampnid. And this ment I when I seid he shall be scornyd
at domys day generally of all that shal be savyd to hose consolation he hath gret
invye. For than he shall seen that all the wo and tribulation that he hath done
to them shal be turnid to encres of their joy without ende. And al the peyne and
tribulation that he would a brougte hem to shal endlesly goe with him to Helle.

XIV

**The sixth Revelation is of the worshippfull thanke with which He rewardith His ser-
vants, and it hath three joyes. Fourteenth chapter.**

535 After this our good Lord seid, *I thanke thee of thy travel and namely of thy
youthe.* And in this myn understondyng was lifted up into Hevyn, where I saw our
Lord as a lord in his owne house, which hath clepid al his derworthy servants
and freinds to a solemne feste. Than I saw the Lord take no place in His owne
house, but I saw Him rialy regne in His hous, and fulfillid it with joy and mirth,
540 Hymselfe endlesly to gladen and to solacyn His derworthy frends ful homeley and
ful curtesly, with mervelous melody of endles love in His owen faire blissid
chere, which glorious chere of the godhede fulfillith Hevyns of joy and bliss.

God shewid three degrees of blis that every soule shal have in Hevyn that
wilfully hath servid God in any degre in erthe. The first is the worshipful thanke
545 of our Lord God that he shal receyvn whan he is deliverid of peyne. This thanke
is so high and so worshipful that him thinkith it fillith him, thow there were no
more. For methowte that all the peyne and travel that might be suffryd of all
liveing men might not deserve the worshipfull thanke that one man shall have
that wilfully hath servid God. The second, that all the blissid creatures that arn
550 in Hevyn shall se that worshipfull thankyng, and He makyth his service knowen
to al that arn in Hevyn. And in this time this example was shewid. A king, if he
thanke his servants, it is a gret worship to hem; and if he makyth it knowen to

525 **arneste**, earnest, seriousness. 526 **arneste**, earnestly. 529 **done**, do. 530 **dampnid**,
damned. 531 **hose**, whose. 532 **invye**, envy. 537 **clepid**, called. 540 **to solacyn**, to make
comfortable. 544 **thanke**, thanks.

all the reme, than is his worshippe mekil incresid. The third is that as new and as leking as it is underfongyn that tyme, rigte so shall it lesten withoute ende. And I saw that homely and swetely was this shewid, that the age of every man shal be knowen in Hevyn, and shal be rewardid for his wilful service and for his time. And namely the age of hem that wilfully and frely offir her yongith to God, passingly is rewardid and wonderly is thankyd. For I saw that whan or what tyme a man or woman be truly turnid to God, for on day service and for his endles wille he shall have al these three degres of blisse. And the more that the lovand soule seeth this curtesy of God, the lever he is to serve Him al the dayes of his life.

XV

The seventh Revelation is of oftentymes felyng of wele and wo etc.; and how it is expedient that man sumtymes be left withoute comfort, synne it not causeing. Fifteenth chapter.

And after this He shewid a soveren gostly lekyng in my soule. I was fulfillid of the everlesting sekirnes migtily susteinid withoute any peynful drede. This felyng was so gladd and so gostly that I was in al peace and in reste, that there was nothing in erth that should a grevid me. This lestenid but a while, and I was turnyd and left to myselfe in hevynes and werines of my life and irkenes of myselfe that onethis I coude have patience to leve. There was no comfort nor none ease to me, but feith, hope, and charite. And these I had in truthe, but litil in feling. And anone after this our blissid Lord gave me ageyne the comfort and the rest in soule in likyng and sekirnes so blisful and so mycti, that no drede, no sorow, ne peyne bodily that might be suffrid, should have desesid me. And than the peyne shewid ageyn to my feling, and than the joy and the lekyng, and now that one, and now that other, dyvers tymes, I suppose aboute twenty tymes. And in the same tyme of joy I migte have seid with Seynt Paul, nothing shal depart me from the charite of Criste. And in the peyne I migte have seid with Peter, Lord save me, I perish.

This vision was shewid me after myn understondyng that it is spedeful to some soulis to fele on this wise, somtime to be in comfort, and somtyme to faile and

553 **reme**, realm. 554 **leking**, pleasing; **underfongyn**, received; **rigte**, right. 557 **hem**, those; **her yongith**, their youth. 559 **on day**, one day's. 561 **lever**, readier, more inclined. 562 **soveren gostly lekyng**, sovereign spiritual delight. 565 **lestenid**, lasted. 566 **irkenes of**, irriation with. 567 **onethis**, scarcely; **leve**, live. 570 **mycti**, mighty. 571 **desesid me**, made me uneasy. 573 **dyvers**, different. 577 **spedeful**, efficacious.

580 to be left to hemselfe. God wille we knowen that He kepyth us even alike sekir in wo and in wele. And for profitt of manys soule, a man is sumtyme left to himselfe, althowe synne is not ever the cause. For in this tyme I synned not wherfore I shulde be left to myselfe, for it was so soden. Also I deservyd not to have this blissid felyng. But frely our Lord gevyth whan He wille, and suffrith us in wo sumtyme, and both is one love. For it is Godds wil we hold us in comfort

585 with al our migte for blisse is lestinge without ende, and peyne is passand and shal be browte to nougte to hem that shall be savyd. And therefore it is not Godds will that we folow the felynge of peyne in sorow and mornyng for hem, but sodenly passing over and holden us in endless likyng.

XVI

The eighth Revelation is of the last petiuous peynes of Christe deyeng, and discoloryng of His face and dreyeng of His flesh. Sixteenth chapter.

After this Criste shewid a partie of His passion nere His deyeng. I saw His

590 swete face as it was drye and blodeles with pale deyeng, and sithen more pale, dede, langoring, and than turnid more dede into blew, and sithen more browne blew, as the flesh turnyd more depe dede. For His passion shewid to me most propirly in His blissid face, and namly in His lippis. There I saw these four colowres, tho that were aforn freshe, redy, and likyng to my sigte. This was a swem-

595 ful chonge to sene, this depe deyeng, and also the nose clange and dryed, to my sigte, and the swete body was brown and blak, al turnyd oute of faire lifely colowr of Hymselfe on to drye deyeng. For that same tyme that our Lord and blissid Savior deyid upon the Rode, it was a dry, harre wynde and wonder colde, as to my sigte. And what tyme the pretious blode was bled oute of the swete body

600 that migte passe therfro, yet there dwellid a moysture in the swete flesh of Criste, as it was shewyd.

Blodeleshede and peyne dryden within and blowyng of wynde and cold com-myng fro withouten metten togeder in the swete body of Criste. And these four,

580 **manys,** man's. 582 **soden,** sudden. 585 **passand,** passing. 590 **sithen,** after. 591 **langoring,** languishing. 591-92 **dede . . . browne blew,** deathly to blue, and after a duller blue. 594-95 **tho . . . clange,** those that before were fresh, red, and pleasant in my eyes. This was a grievous change to see, this deep dying, and also the nose shriveled. 596 **lifely,** life-like. 598 **Rode,** Cross; **harre,** keen, fierce. 600 **migte,** might. 602 **Blodeleshede,** Bloodlessness.

tweyn withouten and tweyn within, dryden the fleshe of Criste be process of tyme.
605 And thow this peyne was bitter and sharpe, it was full longe lestyng as to my
sighte and peynfully dreyden up all the lively spirits of Crists fleshe. Thus I saw
the swete fleshe dey, in semyng be party after party, dryande with mervelous
peynys. And as longe as any spirit had life in Crists fleshe, so longe sufferid He
peyne. This longe pynyng semyd to me as if He had bene seven night ded deyand
610 at the poynt of outpassing awey, sufferand the last peyne. And than I said, it
semyd to me as if He had bene seven night dede, it menyth that the swete body
was so discoloryd, so drye, so clongen, so dedely, and so peteuous as He had be
seven night dede, continuly deyand. And methowte the deyeng of Crists flesh was
the most peyne, and the last, of His passion.

XVII

**Of the grevous bodyly threst of Criste causyd four wysys and of His petouous coronyng;
and of the most payne to a kinde lover. Seventeenth chapter.**

615 And in this deyng was browte to my mynde the words of Criste, "I threst." For
I saw in Criste a doble threst, one bodely, another gostly, the which I shal speke
of in the thirty-first chapter. For this word was shewid for the bodyly threst
the which I understode was causid of failyng of moysture, for the blissid flesh
and bonys was left al alone without blode and moysture. The blissid bodye dreid
620 alone long tyme with wryngyng of the naylys, and weyte of the bodye. For I
understode that for tenderness of the swete hands and of the swete fete, be the
gretnes, hardhede, and grevoushed of the naylis, the wounds wexid wide and the
body saggid for weyte be long tyme hanging, and peircing and wrangyng of the
hede and byndyng of the crowne, al bakyn with drye blode, with the swete heire
625 clyngand, and the drye flesh, to the thornys, and the thornys to the flesh, deyand.
And in the begynnyng, while the flesh was fresh and bledand, the continuant
sytyng of the thornys made the wounds wyde. And ferthermore I saw that the
swete skyn and the tender flesh, with the heere and the blode, was al rasyd and

---

607 party after party, step by step; **dryande**, drying. **609 pynyng**, torture, suffering. **610
than I seid**, when I said. **612 clongen**, withered; **peteuous**, pitiable. **613 deyand**, dying.
616 threst, thirst. **619 bonys**, bones. **620 wryngyng of the naylys**, twisting, drilling in, of the
nails; **weyte**, weight. **623 wrangyng**, twisting. **624 bakyn**, baked. **625 clyngand**, clinging;
deyand, dying. **626–31 And . . . moysture**, And in the beginning, while the flesh was still

630 losyd abov from the bone with the thornys where thorow it were daggyd on many
pecys as a cloth that were saggand as it wold hastely have fallen of for hevy and
lose while it had kynde moysture. And that was grete sorow and drede to me.
For methowte I wold not for my life a sen it fallen. How it was don I saw not,
but understode it was with the sharpe thornys and the boystrous and grevous
setting on of the garland onsparably and without pety. This continuid a while,
635 and sone it began to chongyn, and I beheld and merveled how it migt ben; and
than I saw it was for it began to dreyen and stynte a party of the weyte and sette
abute the garland. And thus it envyronyd al aboute, as it were garland upon
garland; the garland of the thornys was dyed with the blode, and the tother
garland and the hede al was on colour, as cloderyd blode whan it is drey. The
640 skynne of the flesh that semyd of the face and of the body was smal, ronkyllid,
with a tannyd colour lyke a dry borde whan it is akynned, and the face more
browne than the body.

I saw four maner of dryengs. The first was blodeless; the secund was payne
folowyng after; the thred, hangyng up in the eyr as men hang a cloth to drye; the
645 forth, that the bodily kynd askyd licour, and ther was no manner of comfort
mynystid to Hym in al His wo and disese. A, hard and grevous was His peyne,
but mech more hard and grevous it was whan the moysture faylid and al beganne
to drye thus clyngand. These were the paynys that shewdyn in the blissful hede.
The first wrought to the deyng whyl it was moyst; and that other, slow, with
650 clyngyng dryand, with blowing of the wynde from withowten that dryed Him
more, and peynd with cold, than myn herte can thingke; and other paynys, for
which paynys I saw that all is to litil that I can sey, for it may not be told. The
which shewing of Cristes peynys fillid me ful of payne. For I wiste wele He
suffryd but onys, but as He wold shewn it me and fillen me with mynde as I had
655 aforn desyryd.

fresh and bleeding, the constant piercing of the thorns made the wounds wide. And furthermore, I saw that the sweet skin and the tender flesh, with the hair and the blood, were
raised and loosened out from the bone with the thorns, where it [the skin] was pierced
through in many pieces; [it was] like a cloth that is sagging, as if it would very soon have
fallen off because of its heaviness and looseness, while it had natural moisture. **634 pety,**
pity. **635 ben,** be. **636 dreyen,** dry; **stynte,** diminish, stop; **weyte,** weight. **637 abute,** about.
638 tother, other. **639 cloderyd,** clotted. **640 smal,** thin; **ronkyllid,** wrinkled. **641 a tannyd . . .
akynned,** a tanned color like a dry board when it is scorched. **643 dryengs,** dryings. **644
eyr,** air. **645 askyd licour,** needed moisture. **646 mynystid,** ministered. **648 clyngand,**
withering up. **650 clyngyng dryand,** withering drying. **651 peynd,** made to suffer, tortured;
thingke, think. **653 wiste,** knew. **654 onys,** once; **mynde,** realization.

And in al this tyme of Cristes paynys I felte no payn, but for Cristes paynys. Than thowte me, I knew but litil what payne it was that I askyd, and as a wretch repentid me, thynkand if I had wiste what it had be, lothe me had be to have praydd it; for methowte it passid bodely dethe, my paynes. I thowte, Is any payne

660   like this? And I was answered in my reason: Helle is another payne, for there is despeyr. But of al paynes that leden to salvation, this is the most payne: to se thy love suffir. How might any payne be more to me than to se Him that is al my life, al my blisse, and al my joy suffren? Here felt I sothfastly that I lovyd Criste so mech above myselfe that there was no payne that might be suffrid leke to that

665   sorow that I had to se Him in payne.

XVIII

Of the spiritual martyrdam of our Lady and other lovers of Criste, and how al things suffryd with Hym goode and ylle. Eighteenth chapter.

Here I saw a part of the compassion of our Lady Seynt Mary, for Christe and she were so onyd in love that the gretnes of His lovyng was cause of the mekyl-hede of hyr payne. For in thys I saw a substance of kynd love continyyd be grace that creatures have to Hym, which kynde love was most fulsomely shewyd in His

670   swete moder, and overpassyng. For so mech as she lovid Him more than al others, hir panys passyd al others. For ever the heyer, the myghtyer, the sweter that the love be, the mor sorow it is to the lover to se that body in payne that is lovid. And al His disciples and al His trew lovers suffrid panys more than ther owne bodyly deyng. For I am sekir by my myn owne felyng that the lest of hem

675   lovid Hym so far above hemself that it passyth al that I can sey. Here saw I a gret onyng betwyx Christe and us, to myn understondyng. For whan He was in payne, we were in peyne. And al cretures that might suffre payne suffrid with Hym, that is to sey, al cretures that God hathe made to our service. The firma-ment, the erth, faledyn for sorow in hyr kynde in the tyme of Crists deyng. For

680   longith it kyndely to thir properte to know Hym for ther God in whome al ther

657–59 **Than . . . praydd it,** Then I thought, I knew very little what payne it was that I was asking for, and like a wretch I repented, thinking if I had known what it would be, I would have been loath to have prayed for it. 661 **despeyr,** despair. 667 **onyd,** joined. 667–68 **mekylhede,** greatness. 668 **continyyd,** continued. 669 **fulsomely,** abundantly; fully. 671 **panys,** pains. 676 **onyng,** empathy, union. 679 **faledyn,** failed; **hyr,** their. 680 **thir,** their; **ther,** their.

vertue stondyth. Whan He faylid, than behovyd it nedis to them for kyndnes to faylon with Hym as mech as thei myght for sorow of His penys. And thus thei that were His frends suffryd peyne for love.

685 And generaly al, that is to sey, thei that knew Hym not, suffrid for feylyng of al manner of comfort save the myghty, privy kepyng of God. I mene of two manner of folke, as it may be understode by two personys: that on was Pilate, that other was Sain Dionyse of France, which was that tyme a paynym. For whan he saw wonderous and mervelous sorowes and dreds that befallen in that tyme,

690 he seyd, "Either the world is now at an end or ell He that is maker of kynde suf-fryth." Wherfor he did write on an auter, "This is the auter of onknown God." God of His godenes that maketh the planets and the elements to werkyn of kynd to the blissid man and the cursid, in that tyme it was withdrawen from bothe. Wherfore it was that thei that knew Him not were in sorow that tyme. Thus was our Lord Jesus nawted for us, and we stond al in this manner nowtid with Hym;

695 and shal done til we come to His blisse, as I shal sey after.

XIX

Of the comfortable beholdyng of the crucifyx; and how the desyre of the flesh without consent of the soule is no synne. And the flesh must be in peyne, suffring til bothe be onyd to Criste. Nineteenth chapter.

In this I wold a lokyd up of the Crosse, and I durst not, for I weste wele whyl I beheld in the Cross I was seker and save; therefore I wold not assenten to put my soule in perel, for beside the Crosse was no sekernes for uggyng of fends. Than had I a profir in my reason as it had be frendly seyd to me, *Loke up to*

700 *Hevyn, to His Fader;* and than saw I wele with the feyth that I felte that ther was nothyn betwix the Crosse and Hevyn that myght have desesyd me. Either me behovyd to loke up or else to answeren. I answered inwardly with al the myghts of my soule, and said, "Nay, I may not, for Thou art my Hevyn." This I seyd for I wold not, for I had lever a ben in that peyne til domys day than to come to Hevyn

681–82 **than . . . faylon with Hym**, then because of their nature they necessarily failed with Him; **penys**, pains. 684 **feyling**, failing. 685 **privy kepyng**, mysterious care. 686 **on**, one. 687 **paynym**, pagan. 689 **ell**, else. 690 **auter**, altar. 694 **nawted**, made nothing, a cipher. 696 **wold a lokyd**, would have looked; **weste**, knew. 698 **uggyng**, horror. 699 **profir**, proposition. 700 **feyth**, faith. 701 **desesyd me**, made me uneasy. 704 **lever a ben**, rather have been; **domys day**, judgment day.

705 otherwyse than by Hym. For I wiste wele that He that bonde me so sore, He
sholde onbynde me whan that He wolde.

Thus was I lerid to chose Jesus to my Hevyn, whome I saw only in payne at
that tyme. Me lekyd no other Hevyn than Jesus, which shal be my blisse whan I
come there, and this hath ever be a comfort to me, that I chase Jesus to my Hevyn

710 be His grace in al this tyme of passion and sorow. And that hat be a lernyng to
me that I should evermor done so — chesyn only Jesus to my Hevyn in wele and
wo. And thow I as a wretch had repentid me — I sayd aforn if I had wiste what
peyne it had be, me had be loth to have prayed — here saw I sothly that it was
grutching and daming of the flesh without assent of the soule, in whych God

715 assignyth no blame. Repenting and wilful choys be two contrarys which I felte
both in one at that tyme, and tho be two parties, that one outward, that other
inward. The outeward party is our dedely fleshede which is now in peyne and wo,
and shal be in this life, whereof I felt mech in this tyme, and that party was that
repentid. The inward party is an high blisfull life, which is al in pece and in love,

720 and this was more privily felte, and this party is in which, mightyly, wysly, and
wilfully, I chase Jesus to my Hevyn. And in this I saw sothly that the inward
party is master and soverayn to the outeward, and not charging ne takyng hede
to the will of that, but al the entent and will is sett endlesly to be onyd into our
Lord Jesus. That the outeward part should draw the inward to assent was not

725 shewid to me, but that the inward drawith the outeward by grace and bothe shal
be onyd in blisse without end be the vertue of Criste — this was shewid.

XX

**Of the onspekabyl passion of Criste, and of three things of the passion alway to be
remembrid. Twentieth chapter.**

And thus saw I our Lord Jesus langring long tyme, for the onyng of the Godhede gave strength to the manhode for love to suffre more than al man myght
suffryn. I mene not allonly more peyne than al men myght suffre, but also that

730 He suffrid more peyne than al men of salvation that ever was from the first

707 **lerid**, taught. 709 **chase**, chose. 710 **hat be**, has been. 711 **done so**, do so; **chesyn**,
choose. 712 **repentid me**, repentid, changed my mind; **wiste**, known. 713 **me had be loth**,
I should have been loath. 714 **grutching and daming**, grudging and curse. 715 **wilful choys**,
deliberate choice. 716 **tho be**, those are. 721 **chase**, chose. 722 **soverayn**, sovereign; **hede**,
heed. 723 **onyd into**, made one with. 727 **langring**, languishing. 729 **allonly**, only.

begynnyng into the last day myght tellyn or ful thynkyn, havyng regard to the worthynes of the heyest, worshipful kyng, and the shamly, dispitous, peynful dethe. For He that is heyest and worthyest was fullyest nowtyd and utterlyest dispisid. For the heyest poynte that may be sean in the passion is to thynkyn and
735   knowen what He is that suffryd.

And in this He browte a part in mende the heyte and noblyth of the glorius Godhede and, therwith, the pretioushed and the tendernes of the blisfull body which be together onyd, and also the lothhede that is in oure kynd to suffre peyne. For as mech as He was most tender and clene, ryght so He was most strong
740   and myghty to suffir. And for every mannys synne that shall be savid He suffrid, and every manys sorow and desolation He saw, and sorowid for kyndenes and love. For in as mekyl as our Lady sorowid for His peynes, as mekyl He suffrid sorrow for her sorow, and more, in as mekyl as the swete manhode of Hym was worthier in kynd. For as long as He was passible, He suffryd for us and sorowyd
745   for us. And now He is uprysyn and no more passibyl, yet He suffryt with us. And I, beholdyng al this be His grace, saw that the love of Hym was so strong whych He hath to our soule, that wilfully He ches it with gret desyr and myldly He suffrid it with wel payeyng. For the soule that beholdyth it thus, whan it is touchid be grace, he shal veryly se that the peynys of Crists passion passen al
750   peynys; that is to sey, which peynys shal be turnyd into everlestyng passyng joyes by the vertue of Crists passion.

XXI

Of three Beholdyngs in the passion of Criste, and how we be now deyng in the Crosse with Criste, but His chere puttyt away al peyne. Twenty-first chapter.

Tis Goddys wille, as to myn understondyng, that we have three manner of beholdyngs in His blissid passion. The first is the herd peyn that He suffrid with contrition and compassion. And that shewid our Lord in this tyme, and gave me
755   myght and grace to se it. And I loked after the departing with al my myght and wet have seen the body al ded, but I saw Hym not so. And ryth in the same tyme that methowte, be semyng, the life myght ne lenger lesten and the shewyng of

---

732 **shamly, dispitous**, shameful, pitiless. 734 **sean**, seen. 736 **heyte and noblyth**, height and nobility. 738 **lothhede**, loathing. 740 **mannys**, man's. 741 **manys**, man's. 747 **ches**, chose; **desyr**, desire. 748 **wel payeyng**, much satisfaction. 750 **passyng**, transcendent. 756 **wet**, expected to; **ryth**, right. 757 **be semyng**, by appearances.

the end behovyd nedis to be, sodenly, I beholdyng in the same Crosse, He chongyd His blissfull chere. The chongyng of His blisful chere chongyd myn, and
760 I was as glad and mery as it was possible. Than browte our Lord merily to my mynde, *Where is now ony poynte of the peyne or of thin agreefe?* And I was full mery. I understode that we be now, in our Lords menyng, in His Crosse with Hym in our peynys and our passion, deyng. And we wilfully abydyng in the same Cross with His helpe and His grace into the last poynte, sodenly He shall chonge
765 His chere to us, and we shal be with Hym in Hevyn.

Betwix that one and that other shal be no tyme, and than shal al be browte to joy, and so mente He in this shewyng, *Where is now ony poynt of thy peyne or thyn agreefe?* And we shal be full blissid. And here saw I sothfastly that if He shewid now us His blissful chere, ther is no peyne in erth nor in other place that should
770 us agrevyn, but al things should be to us joy and blisse. But for He shewith to us time of passion as He bare in this life and His Crosse, therefore we arn in desese and travel with Hym as our frelete askyth. And the cause why He suffrith is for He wil of His godeness make us the heyer with Hym in His bliss. And for this litil peyne that we suffre here, we shal have an hey endles knowyng in God whych
775 we myght never have without that; and the harder our peynys have ben with Him in His Cross, the more shall our worshippe be with Hym in His kyngdom.

XXII

The ninth Revelation is of the lekyng etc., of three Hevyns, and the infinite love of Criste, desiring every day to suffre for us, if He myght, althow it is not nedeful. Twenty-second chapter.

Than seyd our good Lord Jesus Christe, askyng, *Art thou wele payd that I suffrid for thee?* I sayd, "Ya, good Lord, gramercy; ya, good Lord, blissid mot thou be." Than seyd Jesus, our kinde Lord, *If thou art payde, I am payde; it is a*
780 *joy, a blis, an endles lekyng to me that ever suffrid I passion for the, and if I myht suffre more, I wold suffre more.* In this felyng my understondyng was lifte up into Hevyn, and there I saw thre Hevyns, of which syght I was gretly mervelyd. And

759 **chere**, countenance, expression. 761 **agreefe**, sorrow. 762 **menyng**, intention, disposition, understanding. 769–70 **should us agrevyn**, would make us sad. 771–72 **desese and travel**, distress and labor. 772 **frelete askyth**, frailty requires. 777 **payd**, pleased, satisfied. 778 **gramercy**, thank you. 779 **payde**, pleased. 780–81 **I myht suffre**, I might suffer. 781 **lifte**, lifted. 782 **gretly mervelyd**, made to marvel greatly.

thow I se thre Hevyns, and all in the blissid manhode of Criste, non is more, non is less, non is heyer, non is lower, but evyn lyke in blis.

785 For the first Hevyn Christe shewyd me His Fader, in no bodyly lyknes, but in His properte and in His werkyng; that is to sey, I saw in Criste that the Fader is. The werkyng of the Fader is this, that He gevyth mede to His son Jesus Criste. This geft and this mede is so blisful to Jesus, that His Fader myht have goven Hym no mede that myght have lykyd Hym better. The first Hevyn — that is the

790 plesyng of the Fader — shewid to me as an Hevyn, and it was ful blisfule, for He is ful plesed with al the dedes that Jesus hath done aboute our salvation. Where-fore we be not only His be His beyeng but also by the curtes geft of His Fader. We be His blis, we be His mede, we be His worshippe, we be His corone; and this was a singular mervel and a full delectable beholdying, that we be His corone.

795 This that I sey is so grete blis to Jesus that He settith at nowte al His travel, and His herd passion, and His cruel and shamful deth.

And in these words, *If that I might suffre more, I would suffer more,* I saw sothly that as often as He myght deyen, so often He wold, and love should never let Him have rest til He had don it. And I beheld with gret diligens for to wetyn

800 how often He would deyn if He myght, and sotly the noumbre passid myn under-stondyng and my wittis so fer that my reson myghte not ne coude comprehend it; and whan He had thus oft deyid, or should, yet He would sett it at nowte for love, for al thynkyth Him but litil in reward of His love. For thowe the swete manhood of Criste might suffre but onys, the godenes in Him may never sesin of

805 profir. Every day He is redy to the same if it myght be. For if He seyd He wold for my love make new Hevyns and new erth, it were but litil in reward, for this might be done every day if He wold, withoute any travel. But for to dey for my love so often that the noumbre passith creature reson — it is the heyest profir that our Lord God myght make to manys soule, as to my syte.

810 Than menyth He thiss: How shold it than be that I shold not do for thi love al that I myght, which dede grevyth me not, sith I wold for thi love dey so often having no reward to my herd peynys? And here saw I for the second beholdyng in this blissid passion, the love that made Him to suffre passith as far al His peynes as Hevyn is above erth, for the peynes was a nobele, worshipfull dede don

815 in a tyme be the werkyng of love. And love was without begynnyng, is, and shall

---

788 mede, reward. **788–89 Fader . . . mede**, Father might have given Him no reward. **792 beyeng**, buying (fig., redemption). **793 corone**, crown. **799 diligens**, diligence. **800 sotly**, truly. **801 coude**, could. **803 al thynkyth Him**, He considers all; **in reward of**, considering. **804 sesin**, cease. **808 creature**, human.

be without endyng; for which love He seyd ful swetely these words, *If I myght suffre more, I wold suffre more.* He sayd not, "If it were nedeful to suffre more"; for thow it were not nedeful, if He myght suffre more, He wold. This dede and this werke about our salvation was ordeynyd as wele as God myght ordeyn it.
820   And here I saw a full blisse in Criste, for His blisse shold not a be full if it myte any better have be done.

XXIII

How Criste wil we joyen with Hym gretly in our redemption and to desire grace of Hym that we may so doe. Twenty-third chapter.

And in these three words, *It is a joy, a blis, an endles lykyng to me,* were shewid three Hevyns, as thus: For the joy I understode the plesance of the Fader, and for the blis, the worshippe of the Son, and for the endles lykyng the
825   Holy Gost. The Fader is plesid, the Son is worshippid, the Holy Gost lykith. And here saw I for the thred beholdyng in His blisful passion, that is to sey, the joy and the blis that make Hym to lekyn it. For our curtes Lord shewid His passion to me in five manners, of which the first is the bledyng of the hede, the second is discoloryng of His face, the third is the plentiuous bledyng of the body
830   in semys of the scorgyng, the fourth is the depe deyng. These four are aforseyd for the peynys of the passion. And the fifth is that was shewid for the joy and the bliss of the passion.
For it is Goddys wille that we have trew lekyng with Hym in our salvation, and therin He wil we be myghtyly comfortid and strengthnid, and thus wil He
835   merily with His grace that our soule be occupyed. For we arn His blisse; for in us He lekyth without end, and so shal we in Hym, with His grace. And al that He hath done for us, and doth, and ever shal, was never coste ne charge to Hym, ne myte be, but only that He dede in our manhood begynnyng at the sweete incarnation and lesting to the blissid upriste on Esterne morow. So long
840   durid the cost and the charge aboute our redemption in dede, of which dede He enjoyeth endlesly, as it is afornseyd. Jesus wil we takyn hede to the blis that

823 plesance, pleasure. **824 lykyng,** enjoyment. **826 thred,** third. **827 curtes,** courteous. **830 semys of the scorgyng,** weals from the scourging (see note 473–74). **831 that,** that which. **833 Goddys,** God's. **839 upriste on Esterne morow,** resurrection on Easter morning. **841 wil,** desires.

is in the blisful Trinite of our salvation, and that we desiren to have as mech
gostly lykyng with His grace, as it is afornseyd. That is to sey, that the likyng of
our salvation be like to the joy that Criste hath of our salvation, as it may be
845   whil we arn here. Al the Trinite wroute in the passion of Criste, minystryng
abundance of vertues and plenty of grace to us be Hym; but only the Mayden
Son suffrid, whereof all the blissid Trinite endlesly enjoyeth. And this was
shewid in these words, *Art thou wel payd?* and be that other word that Criste
sayd, *If thou art payed, than am I paide*; as if He seyd, "It is joy and likyng enow
850   to me and I aske nowte ell of the for my travel, but that I myght wel payen the."

And in this He browte to mend the property of a glad gevere. A glad gever
takyth but litil hede of the thyng that he gevith, but al his desire and al his
intent is to plesyn hym and solacyn hym to whome he gevyth it. And if the
receiver take the geft heyly and thankfully, than the curtes gever settith at nowte
855   all his coste and al his travel for joy and delite that he hath, for he hath plesid
and solacid hym that he lovyth. Plenteously and fully was this shewid. Thynke
also wisely of the gretnes of this word *evere,* for in that was shewid an high
knowing of love that He hath in our salvation with manyfold joyes that folow of
the passion of Criste. One is that He joyeth that He hath don it in dede, and
860   He shal no more suffre; another, that He browte us up into Hevyn and made us
for to be His corone and endles blisse. Another is that He hath therwith bawte
us from endless peynys of Helle.

XXIV

**The tenth Revelation is that our Lord Jesus shewith in love His blissid herte cloven in
two enjoyand. Twenty-fourth chapter.**

Than with a glad chere our Lord loked into His syde and beheld, enjoyand;
and with His swete lokyng He led forth the understondyng of His creture be the
865   same wound into Hys syde withinne. And than He shewid a faire, delectabil
place and large enow for al mankynd that shal be save to resten in pece and in
love. And therwith He browte to mende His dereworthy blode and pretious
water which He lete poure al oute for love. And with the swete beholdyng He
shewid His blisful herte even cloven on two. And with this swete enjoyyng He
870   shewid onto myn understondyng, in party, the blissid Godhede, steryng than the

845 **wroute,** wrought. 849 **enow,** enough. 850 **ell,** else. 851 **mend,** mind; **gevere,** giver.
853 **solacyn,** give solace to, please. 856 **solacid,** satisfied. 861 **bawte,** bought (fig., redeemed).

pure soule for to understonde, as it may be said; that is to mene, the endles love that was without begynnyng, and is, and shal be ever.

And with this our gode Lord seyd full blisfully, *Lo, how that I lovid the;* as if He had seid, "My derling, behold and se thy Lord, thy God that is thy maker and

875 thyn endles joy; se what likyng and bliss I have in thy salvation, and for my love enjoy now with me." And also, for more understondyng, this blissid word was seyd: *Lo, how I lovid the. Behold and se that I lovid the so mekyl ere I deyd for the that I wold dey for the, and now I have deyd for the, and suffrid wilfuly that I may. And now is al my bitter peyne and al my hard travel turnyd to endles joy and bliss*

880 *to me and to the. How should it now be that thou should onythyng pray me that lekyth me, but if I shuld ful gladly grant it the? For my lekyng is thy holynes and thyn endles joy and bliss with me.*

This is the understondyng simply as I can sey of this blissid word, *Lo, how I lovid the.* This shewid our gode Lord for to make us glad and mery.

XXV

The eleventh Revelation is an hey gostly shewing of His Moder. Twenty-fifth chapter.

885 And with this same chere of myrth and joy, our gode Lord lokyd downe on the ryte syde and browte to my mynde where our Lady stode in the tyme of His passion, and seid, *Wilt the se here?* And in this swete word, as if He had seyd, "I wote wele thou wold se my blissid moder, for after myselfe she is the heyest joy that I myte shew the and most lykyng and worshippe to me, and most she is desyrid

890 to be seene of my blissid cretures." And for the hey, mervelous, singular love that He hath to this swete mayden, His blissid moder our Lady Seyt Mary, He shewid hir heyly enjoyng as be the menyng of these swete words, as if He seyd, "Wil thou se how I love hir that thou myte joy with me in the love that I have in her and she in me?" And also to more understondyng this swete word our Lord

895 God spekyth to al mankynde that shal be save, as it were al to one person, as if He seyd, "Wilt tho seen in hir how thou art lovid? For thy love I made her so hey, so noble, and so worthy, and this likyth me, and so wil I that it doith the." For after Hymselfe, she is the most blisful syte.

But herof am I not lerid to longen to seen hirr bodyly presense while I am here,

900 but the vertues of hir blissid soule, her truth, her wisdam, hir charite, wherby I

---

886 ryte, right. **888 wold se**, would wish to see. **899 lerid . . . hirr**, taught to long to see her.

may leryn to know myselfe and reverently drede my God. And whan our gode Lord had shewid this, and seid this word, *Wilt thou seen hir?* I answerid and seyd, "Ya, good Lord, gramercy; ya, good Lord, if it be thy wille." Oftentymes I prayd this and I wend a seen hir in bodily presens, but I saw hir not so. And

905 Jesus in that word shewid me a gostly syte of hir. Ryte as I had seen hir aforn litil and simple, so He shewid hir than hey and noble and glorious and plesyng to Hym above al creatures; and He wil that it be knowen that al those that lyke in Hym should lyken in hir and in the lykyng that He hath in hir and she in Him.

And to more understondyng He shewid this example: as, if a man love a creature

910 syngularly above al creatures, he wil make al creature to loven and to lyken that creature that he lovith so mekyl. And in this word that Jesus seid, *Wilt thou se hir?* methowte it was the most likyng word that He might have gove me of hir with the gostly shewyng that He gave me of hir. For our Lord shewid me nothyng in special but our Lady Seynt Mary, and hir He shewid three tymys. The

915 first was as she conceyvyd, the second was as she was in hir sorows under the Cross, the third is as she is now in likyng, worshippe, and joye.

XXVI

The twelfth Revelation is that the Lord our God is al sovereyn beyng. Twenty-sixth chapter.

And after this our Lorde shewid Hym more gloryfyed, as to my syte, than I saw Him beforne, wherin I was lernyd that our soule shal never have rest til it comith to Hym knowing that He is fulhede of joy, homley and curtesly blisful and

920 very life. Our Lord Jesus oftentymes seyd, *I it am, I it am, I it am that is heyest, I it am that thou lovist, I it am that thou lykyst, I it am that thou servist, I it am that thou longyst, I it am that thou desyrist, I it am that thou menyst, I it am that is al, I it am that Holy Church prechyth and teachyth the, I am that shewed me here to thee.* The nombre of the words passyth my witte and al my understondyng

925 and al my mights, and it arn the heyest, as to my syte. For therin is compre-hendid, I cannot tellyn — but the joy that I saw in the shewyng of them passyth al that herte may willen and soule may desire; and therefore the words be not declaryd here. But every man, after the grace that God gevyth him in under-stondyng and lovyng, receive hem in our Lords menyng.

903 gramercy, thank you. **904 wend a seen hir**, expected to have seen her. **912 gove**, given. **914 tymys**, times.

XXVII

The thirteenth Revelation is that our Lord God wil that we have grete regard to all His deds that He hav don in the gret noblyth of al things makyng and of etc; how synne is not knowin but by the peyn. Twenty-seventh chapter.

930   After this the Lord browte to my mynd the longyng that I had to Hym aforn. And I saw that nothyng letted me but synne, and so I beheld generally in us al. And methowte, if synne had not a ben, we should al a ben clene and like to our Lord as He made us. And thus, in my foly, aforn this tyme, often I wondrid whi by the gret forseyng wysdam of God the begynyng of synne was not lettid. For
935   than, thowte me, al shuld a be wele. This steryng was mikel to forsakyn, and nevertheless mornyng and sorow I made therefor without reason and discretion.
        But Jesus, that in this vision enformid me of all that me nedyth, answerid by this word, and seyd: *Synne is behovabil, but al shal be wel, and al shal be wel, and al manner of thyng shal be wele.* In this nakid word *synne,* our Lord browte to my
940   mynd generally al that is not good, and the shamfull dispite and the utter nowt-yng that He bare for us in this life, and His dyeng, and al the peynys and pas-sions of al His creatures, gostly and bodyly — for we be all in party nowtid, and we shall be nowtid followyng our Master Jesus till we be full purgyd, that is to sey, till we be fully nowtid of our dedly flesh and of al our inward affections
945   which arn not very good — and the beholdyng of this with al peynys that ever wern or ever shal be; and with al these I understond the passion of Criste for most peyne and overpassyng. And al this was shewid in a touch, and redily passid over into comforte. For our good Lord wold not that the soule were afferd of this uggly syte.
950   But I saw not synne, for I beleve it hath no manner of substance ne no party of being, ne it myght not be knowin, but by the peyne that it is cause of; and thus peyne — it is somethyng, as to my syte, for a tyme, for it purgith and makyth us to knowen our selfe and askyn mercy. For the passion of our Lord is comforte to us agens al this, and so is His blissid wille. And for the tender love
955   that our good Lord hath to all that shal be save, He comfortith redyly and swetely, menyng thus: *It is sothe that synne is cause of all this peyne, but al shal be wele, and al shall be wele, and all manner thing shal be wele.* These words were seyd full tenderly, shewyng no manner of blame to me ne to non that shall

931 **letted,** hindered. 934 **forseyng,** foreseeing; **lettid,** prevented. 935 **a be,** have been; **steryng,** agitation. 938 **behovabil,** necessary; fits in (see note 936). 942 **in party nowtid,** partly despised. 946 **wern,** were. 949 **afferd,** afraid.

960 be safe. Than were it a gret unkindness to blame or wonder on God for my synne, sythen He blamyth not me for synne. And in these same words I saw a mervelous, hey privitye hid in God, which privity He shall openly make knowen to us in Hevyn, in which knowyng we shal verily see the cause why He suffrid synne to come, in which syte we shall endlesly joyen in our Lord God.

XXVIII

How the children of salvation shal be shakyn in sorowis, but Criste enjoyth wyth compassion; and a remedye agayn tribulation. Twenty-eighth chapter.

965 Thus I saw how Criste hath compassion on us for the cause of synne. And ryte as I was aforn in the passion of Criste fulfillid with peyne and compassion, like in this I was fulfild a party with compassion of al myn even Cristen, for that wel, wel belovid people that shal be savid. That is to sey, Gods servants, Holy Church, shal be shakyn in sorows and anguis and tribulation in this world, as men shakyn a cloth in the wynde. And as to this our Lord answerid in this manner:
970 *A gret thing shall I makyn hereof in Hevyn, of endles worshipps and everlestyng joyes.* Ya, so ferforth I saw that our Lord joyth of the tribulations of His servants. With reuth and compassion to ech person that He lovyth to His bliss for to bringen, He levyth upon them something that is no lak in Hys syte, wherby thei are lakid and dispisyd in thys world, scornyd, rapyd, and outcasten. And this He
975 doith for to lettyn the harme that thei shuld take of the pompe and the veyn glory of this wrechid lif, and mak ther way redy to come to Hevyn, and heynen them in His bliss without end lestyng. For He seith, *I shall al tobreke you for your veyn affections and your vicious pryde, and after that I shal togeder gader you, and make you mylde and meke, clene and holy, by onyng to me.* And than I saw
980 that ech kynde compassion that man hath on his even Cristen with charite, it is Criste in him.

That same nowting that was shewid in His passion, it was shewid ageyn here in this compassion, wherein were two maner of understondyngs in our Lords menyng. The one was the bliss that we arn bowte to, wherin He will be enjoyen.
985 That other is for comforte in our peyne, for He will that we wettyn that it shal al be turnyd to worshippe and profite be vertue of His passion, and that we

960 **sythen**, since. 972 **reuth**, ruth, pity; **ech**, each. 974 **lakid**, blamed; **rapyd**, abused. 975 **lettyn**, prevent, lessen. 976 **heynen**, raise. 977 **tobreke**, utterly shatter. 982 **nowting**, humiliation.

wetyn that we suffir not alone, but with Him, and seen Hym our grounde, and that we seen His penys and His nowting passith so fer al that we may suffre that it may not be ful thowte; and the beholdyng of this will save us from gruching and 990 dispeir in the felyng of our peynys. And if we se sothly that our synne deservyth it, yet His love excusith us, and of His gret curtesye He doith awey al our blame, and He holdyth us with ruth and pite as childer, inocents and unlothfull.

XXIX

Adam synne was gretest, but the satisfaction for it is more plesyng to God than ever was the synne harmfull. Twenty-ninth chapter.

But in this I stode beholdyng generally, swemly and mournyng, seyng thus to our Lord in my menyng with ful gret drede: "A, good Lord, how myte al ben wele 995 for the grete hurte that is come by synne to the creatures?" And here I desirid as I durst to have sum more open declaryng wherwith I myte be esyd in this. And to this our blisfull Lord answerd full mekely and with ful lovely chere and shewid that Adams synne was the most harme that ever was don or ever shal to the world ende. And also He shewid that this is openly knowen in al Holy Chirch 1000 in erth. Furthermore He leryd that I should behold the glorious asyeth, for this asyeth makyng is more plesyng to God and more worshipfull for manys salvation without comparison than ever was the synne of Adam harmfull. Than menyth our blissid Lord thus in this techyng, that we should take hede to this: *For sythe I have made wele the most harme, than it is My wil that thou knowe thereby that I* 1005 *shal make wel al that less.*

XXX

How we shuld joye and trusten in our Savior Jesus not presumyng to know His privy counsell. Thirtieth chapter.

He gave me understondyng of two parties. That one party is our Savior and our salvation. This blissid parte is hopyn and clere and faire and lite and plentiuous,

989–90 **gruching and dispeir,** grudging and despair. **992 childer,** children. **993 swemly,** sadly. **996 esyd,** eased. **1000 asyeth,** reparation. **1001 manys,** man's. **1003 sythe,** since. **1007 hopyn,** open; **lite,** luminous, without burden.

for al mankynde that is of good wille, and shal be, is comprehendid in this parte. Herto arn we bounden of God and drawen and councellid and lerid inwardly be 1010 the Holy Gost and outwardly be Holy Church in the same grace. In this will our Lord we be occupyed, joyeng in Him, for He onjoyeth in us, and the more plentiuously that we take of this with reverens and mekenes the more thanke we deserven of Hym and the more spede to ourselfe, and thus, may we sey, enjoying our part is our Lord. That other is hid and sperid from us, that is to sey, al 1015 that is besiden our salvation. For it is our Lords privy councell, and it longyth to the ryal lordship of God to have His privy councell in pece, and it longyth to His servant for obedience and reverens not to wel wetyn His conselye.

Our Lord hath pety and compassion on us, for that sum creatures make them so besy therin. And I am sekir if we wisten how mekil we shuld plese Hym and 1020 ese our selfe to leven it, we wolden. The seynts that be in Hevyn, thei wil nothyng wetyn but that our Lord will shewen hem, and also their charite and their desire is rulid after the wil of our Lord, and thus owen we to willen like to hem. Than shal we nothyng willen ne desiren but the wille of our Lord, like as thei do. For we arn al on in Goddis menyng. And here was I lerynyd that we shal 1025 trosten and enjoyen only in our Savior, blisful Jesus, for althynge.

XXXI

Off the longyng and the spiritual threst of Criste which lestyth and shall lesten til domys day. And be the reason of His body, He is not yet full gloryfyed ne al unpassible. Thirty-first chapter.

And thus our good Lord answerid to al the question and doubts that I myte makyn, sayeing ful comfortably, *I may makyn al thing wele, I can make al thing wele, and I wil make al thyng wele, and I shall make al thyng wele, and thou shal se thiself that al manner of thyng shal be wele.* That He seyth, *I may,* I understond for 1030 the Fader, and He seith, *I can,* I understond for the Son, and where He seith, *I will,* I understond for the Holy Gost, and wher He seith, *I shall,* I understond for the unite of the blissid Trinite, three persons and one trouthe; and where He seith, *Thu shal se thi selfe,* I understond the onyng of al mankynd that shalle be save into the blisful Trinite. And in thes five words God wil be onclosid in 1035 rest and in pees, and thus shal the gostly threst of Criste have an end.

1009 **councellid,** counseled. 1011 **onjoyeth,** takes pleasure. 1014 **sperid,** barred, closed. 1022 **owen,** ought. 1035 **threst,** thirst.

For this is the gostly thrist of Criste, the luf longyng that lestith and ever shal til we se that syte on Domys Day. For we that shal be save and shal be Crists joye and His blis, some be yet here, and some be to cum, and so shal sum be into that day. Therefore this is His thrist: a love longyng to have us al togeder
1040 hole in Him to His blis, as to my syte. For we be not now as fully as hole in Him as we shal be then. For we knowen in our feith, and also it was shewid in alle, that Criste Jesus is both God and man. And amenst the Godhede, He is Hymselfe heyest blis, and was from without begynnyng, and shall be from with-oute end, which endles blis may never be heyned ne lownyd in the selfe. For this
1045 was plentiuously sen in every shewyng, and namely in the twelfth, wher He seith, *I am that is heyest.*

And anemst Crists manhood, it is knowen in our feith, and also shewyd, that He with the vertue of Godhede, for love, to bring us to His blis, suffrid peynys and passions and deid. And these be the werks of Crists manhode wherin He enjoyeth,
1050 and that shewid He in the ninth Revelation, wher He seith, *It is a joye, a blis, a endles lykyng to me that ever I suffrid passion for the.* And this is the blis of Crists werks, and thus He menyth where He seith in the selfe shewing, we be His blis, we be His mede, we be His worship, we be His corone. For anemst that Criste is our hede, He is glorifyed and onpassible, and anemst His body, in which
1055 al His members be knitt, He is not yet ful glorifyed ne al onpassible. For the same desire and threst that He had upon the Cross, which desire, longyng, and thrist, and, as to my syte, was in Him fro withoute begynnyng, the same hath He yet and shal, into the tyme that the last soule that shal be savid is cum up to His bliss.
1060 For as verily as there is a properte in God of ruth and pity, as veryly there is a property in God of threst and longyng. And of the vertue of this longyng in Criste, we have to longen ageyn to Him, withoute which no soule comyth to Hevyn. And this propertye of longyng and threst comyth of the endles goodnes of God, ryte as the property of pite comith of His endles goodnes, and thow long-
1065 yng and pite arn two sundry properties, as to my syte. And in this stondyth the poynt of the gostly thrist which is lestyng in Hym as long as we be in nede, us drawing up to His blis. And al this was sen in the shewyng of compassion, for that shal secyn on Domys Day. Thus He hath ruth and compassion on us, and He hath longyng to have us, but His wisdam and His love suffrith not the end to
1070 cum til the best tyme.

1040 **hole**, whole. 1042 **amenst**, as concerns (see note). 1044 **heyned ne lownyd**, raised nor lowered. 1047 **anemst**, concerning. 1055 **onpassible**, impassible. 1056 **threst**, thirst. 1058 **cum**, come. 1064–65 **thow ... properties**, And [this is true] even though longing and pity are two separate qualities. 1068 **secyn**, cease.

XXXII

How al thyng shal be wele and Scripture fulfillid, and we must stedfastly holdyn us in the faith of Holy Chirch as is Crists wille. Thirty-second chapter.

On tyme our good Lord seid, *Al thyng shal be wele,* and another tyme He seid, *Thu shalt sen thiself that al manner thyng shal be wele.* And in these two, the soule toke sundry understondyng. On was this: that He wil we wetyn that not only He takith hede to noble thyngs and to grete, but also to litil and to smale, to low and to simple, to on and to other. And so menyth He in that He seith, *Al manner thyngs shal be wele.* For He will we wetyn the leste thyng shal not be forgottyn. Another understondyng is this: that there be dedes evyl done in our syte and so grete harmes takyn, that it semyth to us that it were impossibil that ever it shuld cum to gode end, and upon this we loke sorowyng and morning therefore, so that we cannot restyn us in the blisful beholdyng of God as we shuld doe. And the cause is this, that the use of our reason is now so blynd, so low, and so symple, that we cannot know that hey, mervelous wisdam, the myte, and the goodness, of the blisful Trinite; and thus menyth He wher He seith, *Thou shalt se thiself that al maner thyng shal be wele.* As if He seid, "Take now hede faithfuly and trostily, and at the last end thou shalt verily sen it in fulhede of joye." And thus in these same five words afornseid, *I may make al thyngs wele* etc., I understond a myty comforte of al the works of our Lord God that arn for to comen.

Ther is a dede the which the blisful Trinite shal don in the last day, as to my syte. And whan the dede shall be and how it shal be done, it is onknown of all creatures that are beneath Criste, and shal be, till whan it is don. And the cause He wil we know is for He wil we be the more esyd in our soule and pesid in love, levyng the beholdyng of al tempests that myte lettyn us of trewth, enjoyeng in Hym. This is the grete dede ordeynyd of our Lord God from without begynnyng, treasured and hid in His blissid breast, only knowen to Hymself, be which dede He shal make al thyngs wele. For like as the blisful Trinite made al thyngs of nowte, ryte so the same blissid Trinite shal make wele al that is not wele.

And in this syte I mervelid gretely and beheld our feith, merveland thus: Our feith is growndid in Goddys word, and it longyth to our feith that we levyn that Goddys word shal be savid in al things. And one peynt of our feith is that many creatures shal be dampnyd — as Angells that fellyn out of Hevyn for pride which

1071 **On,** one. 1073 **On,** one; **wetyn,** understand. 1079 **loke,** look; **morning,** mourning. 1085 **trostily,** trustfully. 1092 **pesid,** made peaceful. 1100 **peynt,** point.

be now fends, and man in herth that deyth oute of the feith of Holy Church, that is to say, thei that be ethen men, and also man that hath receyvid Christendam and livith uncristen life, and so deyth out of charite — all these shall be 1105 dampnyd to Helle without end, as Holy Church techyth me to belevyn.

And stondyng al this, methowte it was impossibil that al manner thyng should be wele as our Lord shewid in this tyme. And as to this I had no other answere in shewyng of our Lord God but this: *That is impossible to the is not impossible to Me. I shal save My worde in al things, and I shal make al thing wele.* Thus I was 1110 tawte by the grace of God that I should stedfasty hold me in the faith as I had afornehand understonden, and therewith that I should sadly levyn that al thyng shal be wele, as our Lord shewid in the same tyme. For this is the great dede that our Lord shal done, in which dede He shal save His word in al thing, and He shal make wele al that is not wele. And how it shal be don there is no creature 1115 benethe Criste that wot it, ne shal wetyn it, till it is don, as to the understondyng that I toke of our Lords menyng in this tyme.

XXXIII

Al dampnyd soule be dispisid in the syte of God, as the devil; and these Revelations withdraw not the feith of Holy Church, but comfortith; and the more we besy to know Gods privites, the less we knowen. Thirty-third chapter.

And yet in this I desired as I durst that I myte have had ful syte of Helle and Purgatory. But it was not my mening to maken prefe of anythyng that longyth to the feith. For I levyd sothfastly that Hel and Purgatory is for the same end that 1120 Holy Church techith. But my menyng was that I myte háve seen for leryng in al thyng that longyth to my feith, wherby I myte liven the more to Gods worship, and to my profit. And for my desire I coude of this ryte nowte, but as it is aforseid in the fifth shewing, wher that I saw that the devil is reprovid of God and endlesly dampned. In which syte I understode that al creatures that arn of the 1125 devils condition in this life, and therin enden, there is no more mention made of hem aforn God and al His holy than of the devil, notwithstondying that thei be of mankynd, whether they have be cristenyd or not.

For thow the Revelation was made of goodnes, in which was made litil mention of evil, yet I was not drawne therby from any poynt of the feith that Holy

1102 **herth**, earth. 1103 **ethen**, heathen. 1106 **And stondyng**, And this being so. 1108 **That**, What. 1110 **stedfasty**, steadfastly. 1111 **sadly levyn**, firmly believe. 1118 **to maken prefe**, to try to prove out, to test; **longyth**, belongs. 1122 **coude**, knew, could learn.

1130 Church techyth me to levyn. For I had syte of the passion of Criste in dyvers shewyngs, in the first, in the second, in the fifth, and in the eighth, as it is seid aforn, wheras I had in party a felyng of the sorow of our Lady and of His trew freinds that sen Hym in peyne. But I saw not so propirly specyfyed the Jewes that deden Hym to ded, notwithstondyn I knew in my feith that thei wer accursid

1135 and dampnyd without end, savyng those that converten be grace. And I was strengthyd and lered generaly to kepe me in the feith in every pointe, and in al as I had afore understoden, hopyng that I was therin with the mercy and the grace of God, desyring and prayng in my menyng that I myte continue therin on to my lifs end. And it is Gods will that we have gret regard to al His dedes that

1140 He hath don, but evermore it us nedyth levyn the beholdyng what the dede shal be; and desir we to be leke our brethren which be seynts in Hevyn that wille ryth nowte but God wille. Than shal we only enjoyen in God, and ben wel payd both with hyding and with shewyng. For I saw sothly in our Lordis menyng, the more we besyn us to knowen His privities in this or any other thyng, the ferther

1145 shal we be from the knowing thereof.

XXXIV

God shewyth the privityes necessarye to His lovers; and how they plese God mekyl that receive diligently the prechyng of Holy Church. Thirty-fourth chapter.

Our Lord God shewid to manner of privityes. On is this gret privyte with al the prive peynts that longen therto, and these privites He wil we knowen hid into the tyme that He wil clerly shewen hem to us. That other arn the privytes that He wil maken opyn and knowen to us; for He wil we wetyn that it is His

1150 wil we knowen hem. It arn privytes to us, not only that He wil it ben privytes to us, but it arn privytes to us for our blyndnes and our onknowyng. And therof hath He gret ruthe; and therfore He wil Hymself maken hem more opyn to us wherby we may knowen Hym, and loven Hym, and clevyn to Him. For al that is spedeful to us to wetyn and to knowen, ful curtesly wil our Lord will shewen us,

1155 and that is this, with al the prechyng and techyng of Holy Church.

1134 deden Hym to ded, put Him to death. **1136 lered**, taught. **1137 hopyng**, hoping. **1144 besyn us**, busy ourselves. **1146 to**, two; **privityes**, secrets, mysteries. **1153–55 For al . . . Holy Church**, For all that is helpful to us to know and understand, our Lord will [make it His] will most courteously to show us what it is [what these things are] by and through all the preaching and teaching of Holy Church.

God shewid ful gret plesance that He hath in al men and women that mytyly and mekely and wilfully taken the prechyng and techyng of Holy Church, for it is His Holy Church. He is the ground, He is the substance, He is the techyng, He is the techer, He is the leryd, He is the mede wherfor every kynd soule travellith.

1160 And this is knowen and shall be knowen to every soule to which the Holy Gost declarith it. And hope sothly that al those that seke this, He shal spedyn; for they seke God. Al this that I have now seid, and more that I shal sey after, is comfortyng ageyn synne. For in the thred shewyng when I saw that God doith al that is don, I saw no synne, and than saw I that al is wele. But whan God

1165 shewid me for synne, than seid he, *Al shal be wele.*

XXXV

How God doith al that is good and suffrith worshipfully al by His mercy, the which shal secyn whan synne is no longer suffrid. Thirty-fifth chapter.

And whan God almyty had shewid so plenteuously and so fully of Hys godenes, I desired to wetyn a certeyn creature that I lovid, if it shuld continu in good lyvyng, which I hopid be the grace of God was begonne. And in this syngular desire it semyd that I lettyd myselfe, for I was not taught in this tyme. And than was I

1170 answerid in my reson, as it were be a freindful mene: "Take it generally and behold the curtesy of thi Lord God as He shewith to the, for it is mor worship to God to behold Hym in al than in any special thyng." I assentid, and therewith I leryd that it is more worship to God to knowen al things in general than to lyken in onythyng in special. And if I shuld do wysely after this techyng, I

1175 shuld not only be glad for nothyng in special, ne gretly disesid for no manner of thyng, for al shal be wele. For the fulhede of joy is to beholden God in al. For be the same blissid myte, wisdam, and love that He made al thyng, to the same end our good Lord ledyth it continually, and therto Hymselfe shal bryng it. And whan it is tyme we shal sen it. And the grounde of this was shewid in the first

1180 and more openly in the third, wher it seyth I saw God in a peynte.

Al that our Lord doeth is rythful, and that He suffrith is worshipful, and in these two is comprehendid good and ille. For al that is good our Lord doith; and that is evil, our Lord suffrith. I sey not that ony evil is worshipful, but I sey the sufferance of our Lord God is worshipfull, wherby His goodnes shal be know

---

1163 **ageyn**, against; **thred**, third.　　1170 **freindful mene**, friendly intermediary.　　1180 **peynte**, point.　　1181 **rythful**, righteous.

1185 withoute end in His mervelous mekeness and myldhede by the werkyng of mercy
and grace. Rythfulhede is that thyng that is so goode that may not be better
than it is. For God Hymselfe is very rythfulhede, and al His werkes arn don
rythfully as they arn ordeynid from wythout begynnyng by His hey myte, His hey
wisdom, His hey goodnes. And ryth as He ordeynid onto the best, ryth so He
1190 werkyth continualy and ledyth it to the same end. And He is ever ful plesid with
Hymselfe and with al His werks. And the beholdyng of this blisful accord is ful
swete to the soule that seith by grace. Al the sowlys that shal be savid in Hevyn
without ende be mad rythful in the syte of God, and be His owen goodnes, in
which rythfulhede we arn endlesly kept and mervelously, aboven al creatures.

1195   And mercy is a werkyng that comith of the goodnes of God, and it shal lestyn
in werkyng al along, as synne is suffrid to pursue rythful souls. And whan synne
hath no lenger leve to pursue, than shal the werkyng of mercy secyn, and than
shal al be browte to rythfulhede and therein stondin withoute ende. And by His
sufferaunce we fallyn, and in His blisful love, with His myte and His wisdom, we
1200 are kept. And be mercy and grace we arn reysid to manyfold more joyes. And
thus in rythfulhede and in mercy He wil be knowen and lovid now without ende.
And the soul that wisely beholdyth it in grace, it is wel plesyd with bothen and
endlesly enjoyeth.

XXXVI

Of another excellent dede that our Lord shal don, which be grace may be known a party here, and how we shul enjoyen in the same, and how God yet doith myracles. Thirty-sixth chapter.

     Our Lord God shewid that a dede shall be done, and Hymselfe shal don it. And
1205 I shal do nothyng but synne, and my synne shal not lettyn His goodnes werkyng.
And I saw that the beholdyng of this is an heyly joy in a dredful soule, which
evermore kyndly be grace desirith Godds wille. This dede shal be begonne here,
and it shal be worshipful to God and plentously profitable to His lovers in erth.
And ever as we come to Hevyn we shalle sen it in mervelous joye. And it shal
1210 lestyn thus in werkyng on to the last day; and the worship and the bliss of it
shal lestyn in Hevyn aforn God and al His holy without end. Thus was this dede
sene and understond in our Lords menyng, and the cause why He shewid it, is

1192 seith, sees; sowlys, souls. 1197 secyn, cease. 1206 dredful, reverent. 1211 His holy,
His saints.

81

to maken us enjoyen in Hym and in al His werks. Whan I saw His shewing continuid, I understod that it was shewid for a grete thyng that was for to come, 1215 which thyng God shewid that Hymselfe should don it, which dede hath these properties afornseid. And this shewid He wel blisfully, menand that I should take it wysely, feithfully, and trostily.

But what this dede shuld be, it was kepid privy to me. And in this I saw that He wil not we dredyn to know the thyngs that He shewith. He shewith hem for 1220 He will we know hem, be which knowing He will we love Hym and lekyn and end-lesly enjoyen in Hym. And for the grete love that He hat to us, He shewith us al that is worshipfull and profitable for the tyme. And the thyngs that He will now hav privy, yet of His grete goodness He shewith hem close, in which shewyng He will we leven and understonden that we shal sen it verily in His endles bliss.

1225 Than owe we to enjoyen in Hym for al that He shewith and al that He hidyth. And if we wilfully and mekely doe thus, we shal fynd therin gret ese, and endles thanks we shall have of Hym therfore. And thus is the understondyng of this word, that it shal be don by me, that is the general man, that is to sey, al that shal be save. It shalle be worshipful and mervelous and plenteuous; and God 1230 Hymself shal don it. And this shal be the heyest joye that may ben, to beholden the dede that God Hymselfe shal don. And man shal do ryte nowte but synne. Than menyth our Lord God thus, as if He seid, "Behold and se: here hast thou matter of mekenes, here hast thou matter of love, here hast thou matter to nowten thyself, her hast thou matter to enjoyen in me, and for my love enjoye 1235 in me, for of al thyngs, therwith myte thou most plese me."

And as long as we arn in this lif, what tyme that we be our folly turne us to the beholdyng of the reprovyd, tenderly our Lord God toucht us, and blisfully clepyth us seyand in our soule: *Lete be al thi love, my dereworthy child. Entend to me. I am enow to the, and enjoye in thi Savior and in thi salvation.* And that this 1240 is our Lordys werkyng in us, I am sekir. The soule that is aperceyvid therein be grace shal sen it and felen it. And thow it be so that this dede be truly taken for the general man, yet it excludith not the special; for what our good Lord will do be His pore creatures, it is now onknowen to me.

But this dede and the tother afornseid, they arn not both on, but two sundry. 1245 But this dede shal be don sooner, and that shal be as we come to Hevyn. And to whom our Lord gevyth it, it may be knowen her in party. But the gret dede afornseid shal nether be knowen in Hevyn ner erth till it is don.

And moreover, He gave special understondyng and techyng of werkyng of

1217 **trostily**, with trust, confidence. 1221 **hat to**, has for. 1224 **leven**, believe. 1225 **owe we**, we ought. 1234 **her**, here. 1238 **clepyth us**, calls out to us; **Entend**, Attend, Listen.

miracles. As thus: *It is knowen that I have done miracles her aforn, many and fele,*
1250 *heygh and mervelous, worshipful and grete, and so as I have don, I do now con-*
tinualy, and shal don in coming of tyme. It is know that afor miracles comen
sorow and anguish and tribulation. And that is that we showld know our owne
febilnes and our myschevis that we arn fallen in by synne to meken us and
maken us to dreden God, cryen for helpe and grace. Myracles commen after that,
1255 and that of the hey myte, wisdam, and goodnes of God shewand His vertue and
the joyes of Hevyn so as it may be in this passand life; and that for to strength
our feith, and to encresyn our hope in charite; wherfor it plesyth Hym to be
knowen and worshippid in miracles. Than menyth He thus: He wil that we be
not born overlow for sorrow and tempests that fallen to us, for it hath ever so
1260 ben aforn myracle comyng.

XXXVII

**God kepyth His chosen ful sekirly althowe thei synne, for in these is a godly will that
never assayed to synne. Thirty-seventh chapter.**

God browte to my mynd that I shuld synne, and for lykyng that I had in
beholdyng of Hym, I entended not redily to that shewyng. And our Lord full
mercifully abode and gave me grace to entendyn, and thys shewyng I toke singularly to myselfe. But be al the gracious comforte that folowyth, as ye shal seen,
1265 I was leryd to take it to al my even Cristen, al in general and nothing in special.
Thowe our Lord shewid me I should synne, by *me* alone is understode *al.* And
in this I concyvid a soft drede; and to this our Lord answerid: *I kepe the ful*
sekirly. This word was seid with more love and sekirness and gostly kepyng than
I can or may telle. For as it was shewid that I should synne, ryth so was the com-
1270 forte shewid, sekirnes and kepyng for al myn even Cristen. What may make me
more to love myn evyn Cristen than to seen in God that He lovyth all that shal
be savid as it wer al on soule?
For in every soule that shal be savid is a godly wil that never assentid to
synne ne never shal. Ryth as there is a bestly will in the lower party that may
1275 willen no good, ryth so ther is a godly will in the heyer party which will is so
good that it may never willen yll, but ever good. And therfore we arn that He

1249 **fele**, many, several. 1250 **heygh**, high. 1253 **myschevis**, troubles, evils; **to meken us**,
to make us meek. 1263 **entendyn**, attend, pay attention. 1267 **concyvid a softe drede**,
conceived a quiet fear. 1274 **Ryth**, Just; **bestly**, bestial. 1276 **yll**, evil.

lovith, and endlesly we do that that Hym lykyt, and this shewid our Lord in the holehede of love that we stonden in in His syght. Ya, that He lovith us now as wele whil we arn here, as He shal don whan we arn there afore His blissid face.

1280 But for faylyng of love on our party, therefore is al our travel.

XXXVIII

Synne of the chosen shall be turnyd to joye and worship. Exemple of David, Peter, and John of Beverley. Thirty-eighth chapter.

Also God shewid that synne shal be no shame but worship to man. For ryth as to every synne is answeryng a peyne be trewth, ryth so for every synne to the same soule is goven a bliss by love. Ryth as dyvers synnes arn punyshid with dyvers peynes after that thei be grevous, ryth so shal thei be rewardid with dyvers

1285 joyes in Hevyn after thei have be peynful and sorowful to the soule in erthe. For the soule that shal come to Hevyn is pretious to God, and the place so worshipful that the goodnes of God suffrith never that soul to synne that shal come there but which synne shal be rewardid. And it is made knowen without end, and blisfully restorid be overpassyng worshipps.

1290 For in thys syte myn understondyng was lift up into Hevyn, and than God browte merily to my minde David and other in the Old Law without numbre. And in the New Law He browte to my mynd first Mary Magdalen, Peter and Paul, and Thomas of Inde, and Saynt John of Beverly, and other also without noumbre, how thei are knowen in the church in erth with ther synnes, and it is

1295 to hem no shame, but al is turnyd hem to worship. And therfore our curtes Lord shewith for them here in party like as it is there in fulhede. For ther the token of synne is turnyd to worshippe.

And Seynt John of Beverley, our Lord shewid hym ful heyly in comfort to us for homlyhed, and browte to my mynde how he is an hende neybor and of our

1300 knowyng. And God called hym Seynt John of Beverley pleynly as we doe, and that with a full glad, swete chere, shewyng that he is a ful hey seynt in Hevyn in His syght, and a blisfull. And with this he made mention that in his youngth and in his tendyr age he was a derworthy servant to God, mekyl God lovand and dredand; and nevertheless God suffrid him to fall, hym mercyfully kepand that

1305 he perishid not ne lost no tyme. And afterward God reysyd hym to manyfold

---

1277 that that Hym lykyt, that which pleases Him. **1283 goven,** given. **1290 lift,** lifted. **1299 hende neybor,** courteous, affable neighbor.

84

more grace; and be the contrition and mekenes that he had in his living, God hat goven hym in Hevyn manyfold joyes overpassing that he shuld hav had if he had not fallen. And that thys is soth, God shewith in erth with plentiuous miracles doyng aboute his body continuly. And al was this to make us glad and mery in love.

XXXIX

Of the sharpnes of synne and the godenes of contrition, and how our kynd Lord will not we dispair for often fallyng. Thirty-ninth chapter.

1310   Synne is the sharpest scorge that any chousyn soule may be smyten with, which scorge al forbetyth man and woman and noyith him in his owne syte, so ferforth that otherwhile he thynkyth hymself he is not worthy but as to synken in Helle, til whan contrition takyth hym be touchyng of the Holy Gost and turn- yth the bitternes in hopes of Gods mercy; and than he begynnyth his woundis
1315   to helyn, and the soule to quickyn tunyd into the life of Holy Chirch. The Holy Gost ledyth hym to confession wilfully to shewyn his synnes nakidly and truely, with grete sorow and grete shame that he hath defoulyd the fair ymage of God. Than undertakyth he penance for every synne, enjoynid by his domysman; that is groundid in Holy Church be the teaching of the Holy Ghost. And this is on
1320   mekenes that mekyl plesyt God; and also bodely sekenes of Gods sendyng, and also sorow and shame from withoute, and reprove and dispyte of this world, with al manner grevance and temptations that wil be cast in, bodily and gostly. Ful pretiously our Lord kepyth us whan it semyth to us that we arn nere for- sakyn and cast away for our synne and because we have deservyd it. And because
1325   of mekenes that we gettyn hereby we arn reysyd wol hey in Godds syte be His grace, with so grete contrition, also with compassion and trew longyng to God. Than thei be sodenly delyveryd of synne and of peyne and taken up to bliss, and made even hey seynts. Be contrition we arn made clene; be compassion we arn made redy; and be trew longyng to God we arn made worthy. Thes arn three
1330   menys, as I understond, wherby that al soulis come to Hevyn, that is to seyn, that have ben synners in erth and shal be save.

1310 **chousyn**, chosen. 1311–13 **al forbetyth . . . Helle**, beats down man and woman and makes them irritated with themselves, so much that sometimes, in their own view, they think themselves worthy of nothing but to sink into Hell. 1317 **ymage**, image. 1318 **domysman**, judge. 1330 **menys**, means, ways.

For be these medycines behovyth that every soule be helyd. Thow he be helyd, his wounds arn seen aforn God, not as wounds, but as worships. And so on the contraryewise, as we ben ponishid here with sorow and with penance, we shal be
1335 rewardid in Hevyn be the curtes love of our Lord God Almyty that wil that non that come there lose his travel in no degre. For He holdyth synne as sorow and peyne to His lovers, in whome He assigneth no blame for love.

The mede that we shal underfongyn shal not be litil, but it shal be hey, glorious, and worshipfull; and so shal shame be turnyd to worship and more joye.
1340 For our curtes Lord wil not that His servants dispeir for often ne for grevous fallyng. For our fallyng lettyth not Hym to love us. Peas and love arn ever in us beand and werkand. But we be not alway in pese and in love. But He wil that we takin hede thus: that He is ground of al our hole life in love, and furthermore that He is our everlestyng keper and mytyly defendith us ageyn our enemys that
1345 ben ful fel and fers upon us; and so mech our nede is, the more — for we gyven Hym occasion be our fallyng.

XL

Us nedyth to longyn in love with Jesus, eschewyng synne for love; the vyleness of synne passith al peynes; and God lovith wol tenderly us while we be in synne, and so us nedyth to doe our neybor. Fortieth chapter.

This is a severayn frendshyp of our curtes Lord, that He kepyth us so tenderly whil we be in synne. And furthermore He touchyth us ful privily and shewyth us our synne be the swete lyte of mercy and grace. But whan we seen ourselfe so
1350 foule, than wene we that God were wroth with us for our synne, and than aren we steryd of the Holy Gost be contrition into prayers and desire to amendyng of our life with al our mytes, to slakyn the wreth of God, on to the tyme we fynd a rest in soule and softnes in consciens, and than hope we that God hath forgoven us our synnes. And it is soth. And than shewith our curtes Lord Hymselfe to the
1355 soul wol merily and with glad cher with frendful welcummyng as if He had ben in peyn and in prison, sayand swetely thus: "My derlyng, I am glad thou art

1332 helyd, healed.   **1338 mede**, reward; **underfongyn**, receive.   **1340 dispeir**, despair.
1342 beand and werkand, existing and working.   **1345 fel and fers**, evil and fierce; **and so mech . . . the more**, and in as much as our need is [great] the more [He defends us].   **1347 severayn**, sovereign.   **1348 privily**, inwardly.   **1353 consciens**, conscience.   **1355 frendful**, friendly.

comen to me; in al thi wo I have ever be with the, and now seist thou my lovyng, and we be onyd in bliss." Thus arn synnes forgoven be mercy and grace,
and our soule worshipfully receivid in joye, like as it shal be when it comyth to
1360   Hevyn, as oftentymes as it comys be the gracious werkyng of the Holy Gost and
the vertue of Crists passion.

Here understond I sothly that al manner thyng is made redy to us be the grete
goodnes of God so ferforth that what tyme we ben our selfe in peas and charite
we be verily save. But for we may not have this in fulhede whil we arn here,
1365   therefore it befallyth us evermore to leven in swete prayor and in lovely longyng
with our Lord Jesus. For He longyth ever to bryng us to the fulhede of joy, as it
is aforseid where He shewith the gostly threst. But now because of al this
gostly comfort that is afornseyd, if ony man or woman be sterid be foly to seyn
or to thinken, "If this be soth, than were it good to synne to have the more
1370   mede," or ell to chargyn the less to synne — beware of this steryng. For sothly if
it come it is ontrew, and of the enemy of the same trew love that techith us all
this comforte. The same blissid love techith us that we should haten synne only
for love. And I am sekir, by myn owen felyng, the more that every kinde soul
seith this in the curtes love of our Lord God, the lother is hym to synne, and the
1375   more he is ashamid.

For if afor us were layd al the peynes in Helle and in Purgatory and in erth —
deth and other — and synne, we should rather chose al that peyne than synne.
For synne is so vile and so mekyl to haten, that it may be liken to no payne,
which peyne is not synne. And to me was shewid no herder helle than synne. For
1380   a kynde soule hath non helle but synne. And we gevyn our intent to love and
mekenes, be the werkyng of mercy and grace we arn mad al fair and clene. And
as mygty and as wyse as God is to save man, as wyllyng He is, for Criste Hymselfe is ground of all the lawis of Cristen men; and He tawth us to doe good
ageyn ille. Here may we se that He is Hymselfe this charite, and doith to us as
1385   He techith us to don. For He will we be like Hym in holehede of endless love
to ourselfe and to our even Cristen. No more than His love is broken to us for
our synne, no more will He that our love be broken to ourselfe and to our evyn
Cristen. But nakidly hate synne and endlesly loven the soule as God lovith it;
than shal we haten synne lyke as God hatith it, and love the soule as God lovyth
1390   it. For this word that God seid is an endless comfort: *I kepe the sekirly.*

1365 **leven**, live. 1370 **chargyn**, charge, set down. 1374 **the lother . . . synne**, the more
loath he is to sin. 1378 **to haten**, to be hated. 1380 **And we gevyn**, If we give. 1383 **lawis**,
laws; **tawth**, taught. 1384 **ageyn**, in opposition to.

XLI

The fourteenth Revelation is as afornseyd etc. It is impossible we shuld pray for mercy and want it; and how God will we alway pray thow we be drey and barryn, for that prayer is to Him acceptabil and plesante. Forty-first chapter.

After this, our Lord shewid for prayers, in which shewing I se two conditions in our Lordis menyng. On is rytfulnes; another is sekir troste. But yet often-tymes our troste is not full, for we arn not sekir that God herith us, as us thynkith, for our onworthynes and for we felyn ryth nowte, for we arn as barren
1395 and dry oftentimes after our prayors as we wer aforn. And this, in our felyng, our foly, is cause of our wekenis. For thus have I felt in myselfe. And al this browte our Lord sodenly to my mend and shewed these words and said: *I am ground of thi besekyng. First it is my wille that thou have it, and sythen I make the to willen it, and sithen I make the to besekyn it, and thou besekyst it. How shuld it*
1400 *than be that thou shuld not have thyn besekyng?* And thus in the first reason with the three that followen, our good Lord shewith a mytye comforte as it may be seen in the same words. And in the first reason, thus He seith: *And thou besekyst it.* There He shewith ful grete plesance and endles mede that He will gevyn us for our besekyng. And in the sixth reason, there He seith: *How shuld it*
1405 *than be?* etc., this was seid for an impossible. For it is most impossible that we shuld besekyn mercy and grace and not have it. For of all thyng that our good Lord makyth us to besekyn, Hymselfe hath ordeynid it to us from withoute begynnyng.

Here may we seen that our besekyng is not cause of Godis goodness, and that
1410 shewid He sothfastly in al these swete words when He seith: *I am grounde.* And our good Lord wille that this be knowen of His lovers in erth, and the more that we knowen, the more shuld we besekyn, if it be wisely taken; and so is our Lords menyng. Besekyng is a new, gracious, lestyng will of the soule onyd and festenyd into the will of our Lord be the swete privy werke of the Holy Gost. Our
1415 Lord Hymselfe, He is the first receyvor of our prayors, as to my syte, and takyth it ful thankfully and heyly enjoyand; and He sendyth it up aboven, and settith it in tresour wher it shal never perishen. It is ther aforn God with al His holy, continuly receyvyd, ever spedand our nedys. And whan we shal underfongyn our bliss it shal be gevyn us for a degre of joye with endles worshipful thankyng of Hym.
1420 Full glad and mery is our Lord of our prayors, and He lokyth therafter, and

---

1392 Lordis, Lord's. **1398 besekyng,** prayer, beseeching; **sythen,** after. **1405 for an impossible,** as an impossibility, a logical absurdity. **1417 tresour,** treasury; **His holy,** His saints.

He wil have it. For with His grace He makyth us lyke to Hymself in condition as we arn in kynd, and so is His blisful will, for He seith thus: *Pray inderly thow the thynkyth it savowr the nott. For it is profitable thow thou fele not, thow thou se nowte, ya, thow thou thynke thou myghte nowte. For in dryhede and in barrenhede,*
1425 *in sekenes and in febelnes, than is thyn prayers wel plesant to me, thow thou thynk-yth it savowr the nowte but litil; and so is al thy levyng prayers in my syte.* For the mede and the endles thanke that He wil gevyn us, therfore He is covetous to have us pray continuly in His syhte. God acceptith the good will and the travel of His servant, howsoever we felen. Wherfore it plesyth Hym that we werkyn
1430 and in our prayors and in good levyng be Hys helpe and His grace resonably with discrecion, kepand our myght to Hym, til whan that we have Hym that we sekyn in fulhede of joy — that is, Jesus. And that shewid He in the fifteenth Revelation aforn this word: *Thou shalt have Me to thy mede.*

And also to prayors longyth thankyng. Thankyng is a new, inward knowing
1435 with gret reverens and lovely drede turnyng ourselfe with all our myghts into the werkyng that our good Lord steryth us to, enjoyng and thankyng inwardly. And sometyme, for plenteoushede, it brekyth out with voyce, and seith, "Good Lord, grante mercy. Blissid mot Thou be." And sumtyme whan the herte is drey and felyth not, or ell be temptation of our enemy, than it is dreven by reason
1440 and be grece to cryen upon our Lord with voyce, rehersyng His blissid passion and His gret goodnes. And the vertue of our Lords word turnyth into the soule, and quicknith the herte, and entrith it be His grace into trew werkyng, and makyth it prayen wel blisfully and trewly to enjoyen our Lord; it is a ful blisfull thankyng in His syte.

XLII

Off three thyngs that longyn to prayor, and how we shuld pray; and of the goodnes of God that supplyeth alway our imperfection and febilnes whan we do that longyth to us to do. Forty-second chapter.

1445 Our Lord God wille we have trew understondyng, and namely in three thyngs that longyn to our prayors. The first is be whom and how that our prayors springyth. Be whome, He shewith when He seith, *I am ground*; and how, be His goodnes, for He seith, first, *It is my wille.* For the secund, in what manner and how we should usen our prayors, and that is that our wil be turnyd into the will of

1422 inderly, earnestly. **1439 felyth,** feels. **1440 grece,** grace.

1450   our Lord, enjoyand; and so menith He whan He seith, *I mak the to willen it.* For the thred, that we knowen the frute and the end of our prayors: that is, to be onyd and lyk to our Lord in al thyng. And to this menyng and for this end was al this lovely lesson shewid; and He wil helpyn us, and we shall make it so — as He seith Hymselfe. Blissid mot He ben.

1455   For this is our Lords wille, that our prayors and our troste ben both alyk large. For if we trost not as mekyl as we preyen, we doe not ful worship to our Lord in our prayors, and also we taryen and peyn ourselfe. And the cause is, as I leve, for we know not truly that our Lord is ground on whom our prayors springith. And also that we know not that it is goven us be the grace of His 1460   love. For if we knew this, it would maken us to trosten to have, of our Lords gyfte, al that we desire. For I am sekir that no man askyth mercy and grace with trew menyng, but mercy and grace be first geyvin to hym. But sumtyme it cumyth to our mynd that we have prayd long tyme, and yet, thynkyth us, that we have not our askyng. But herfor should we not be hevy, for I am sekir be our 1465   Lords menyng, that eyther we abyden a better tyme, or more grace, or a better gyfte. He will we have trow knowyng in Hymself that He is beyng; and in this knowyng He will that our understondyng be growndid with al our mytys, and al our entent, and al our menyng. And in this grownd He will that we taken our stede and our wonynge. And be the gracious lyte of Hymself, He will we have 1470   understondyng of the thyngs that folow.

    The first is our noble and excellent makyng; the second, our pretious and derworthy agen byeing; the thred, althyng that He hath made benethen us to serven us, and, for our love, kepith it. Than menyth He thus, as if He seyd: Behold and se that I have don al this, beforn thi prayors, and now thou art, and 1475   prayest me. And thus He menyth that it longyth to us to wetyn that the gretest deds be don as Holy Church techyth. And in the beholdyng of thys with thankyng, we owte to pray for the dede that is now in doyng, and that is that He reule us and gyde us to His worshippe in thys lif and bryng us to His bliss. And therfore He hath don all. Than menyth He thus, that we sen that He doth it, 1480   and we prayen therfor. For that on is not enow. For if we prayen and sen not that He doth it, it makyth us hevy and doutful; and that is not His worshippe. And if we sen that He doth and we pray not, we do not our dette — and so may it not ben, that is to seyen, so is it not in His beholdyng. But to sen that He doth it and to pray forthwith, so is He worshippid and we sped.

1457 **taryen and peyn,** delay and trouble. 1458 **leve,** believe. 1460 **trosten,** trust. 1467 **mytys,** powers. 1468 **will,** desires. 1468–69 **our stede . . . wonynge,** our standing place and our dwelling. 1472 **agen byeing,** redemption. 1476 **deds,** deeds. 1477 **dede,** deed. 1482 **dette,** debt.

1485   Althyng that our Lord hath ordeynyd to don, it is His will that we prayen therfor, other in speciyal or in generall; and the joy and the bliss that it is to Hym, and the thanke and the worshippe that we shall have therfore, it passyth the understondyng of cretures, as to my syte. For prayor is a rythwis understondyng of that fulhede of joye that is for to cume with wel longyng and sekir

1490   troste. Faylyng of our bliss that we ben kyndly ordeynid to makyth us for to longen. Trew understondyng and love, with swete mynd in our Savior, graciously makyth us for to trosten. And in these two werkyngs our Lord beholdyth us continuly. For it is our dett, and His goodnes may no less assignen in us. Than longyth it to us to don our diligens, and whan we have don it, than shal us yet

1495   thinken that is nowte; and soth, it is. But do we as we may, and sothly aske mercy and grace. Al that us faylyth, we shal fynd in Hym; and thus menyth He wher He seith: *I am grounde of thy besekyng.* And thus in this blisful word, with the shewing, I saw a full overcomyng agens al our wekenes and al our douteful dredis.

XLIII

What prayor doth, ordeynyd to God will; and how the goodnes of God hath gret lekyng in the deds that He doth be us, as He wer beholden to us, werkyng althyng ful swetely. Forty-third chapter.

    Prayor onyth the soule to God; for thow the soule be ever lyke to God in kynde

1500   and substance restorid be grace, it is often onlyke in condition be synne on manys partye. Than is prayor a wittnes that the soule will as God will, and comfortith the conscience and ablith man to grace. And thus He techith us to prayen, and mytyly to trosten that we shal have it. For He beholdith us in love, and wil makyn us partyner of His gode dede. And therfore He steryth us to prayen

1505   that that likyth Hym to don; for which prayors and gode will that He wil have of His gyft, He wil reward us and gevyn us endless mede. And this was shewid in this word, *And thou besekyst it.* In this word God shewid so gret plesance and so gret lykyng as He were mekyl beholden to us for every god dede that we don, and yet it is He that doth it. And for that we besekyn Hym mytyly to don althyng

1486 **other,** either. 1494 **diligens,** diligence. 1499 **onyth,** binds, unites; **thow,** though. 1501 **will,** desires. 1502 **ablith,** makes able, fits the individual for. 1504 **steryth,** prompts, stirs. 1507 **And thou besekyst,** And you beseech.

1510   that Him lekyt, as if He seid, "What myte then plese Me more, than to besekyn
mytyly, wisely, and wilfully to do that thyng that I shal don?" And thus the
soule be prayor accordyth to God.

But whan our curtes Lord of His grace shewith Hymselfe to eur soule, we
have that we desire, and than we se not for the tyme what we shuld more pray,
1515   but al our entent with al our myte is sett holy to the beholdyng of Hym, and
this is an hey, unperceyvable prayor as to my syte. For al the cause wherfor we
prayen, it is onyd into the syte and beholdyng of Hym to whome we prayen,
mervelously enjoyand with reverent drede and so grete sweteness and delite in
Hym, that we can pray ryth nowte but as He steryth us for the tyme.

1520   And wel I wote the mor the soule seeth of God, the more it desyrith Hym be
His grace. But whan we sen Hym not so, than fele we nede and cause to pray —
for faylyng — for ablyng of ourselfe to Jesus. For whan the soule is tempested,
troublid, and left to hymself be onreste, than it is tyme to prayen to maken
hymselfe supple and buxum to God. But he be no manner of prayor makyth God
1525   supple to hym.   For He is ever alyke in love. And thus I saw that what tyme we
se nedys wherfore we prayen, than our good Lord folowyth us, helpand our
desire. And whan we of His special grace planely beholden Hym seying non
other nedys, than we folowen Hym, and He drawith us into Hym be love. For I
saw and felt that His mervelous and fulsome goodnes fulfillith al our mytys, and
1530   then I saw that His continuate werkyng in al manner thing is don so godely, so
wysely, and so mytyly that it overpassyt al our imagynyng and all that we can
wenyn and thynken; and than we can do no more but behold Hym, enjoyeng
with an hey, myty desire to be al onyd into Hym, and entred to His wonyng, and
enjoy in Hys lovyng, and deliten in His godeness.

1535   And then shal we, with His swete grace, in our owen meke continuat prayors,
come into Hym now in thys life be many privy tuchyngs of swete gostly syghts
and felyng, mesurid to us as our simplehede may bere it, and this wrowte, and
shal be, be the grace of the Holy Gost, so long til we shal dey in longyng for
love. And than shal we all come into our Lord, ourselfe clerely knowand and
1540   God fulsomely havyng; and we endlessly ben al had in God, Hym verily seand,
and fulsomly feland, Hym gostly heryng, and Hym delectably smellyng, and Hym

1513 **eur**, your (see note). 1519 **steryth**, inspires. 1522 **ablyng**, fitting. 1524 **buxum**, obedient. 1526 **nedys wherfore we prayen**, that we need to pray. 1527 **seying**, seeing. 1529
fulsome, abundant; **mytys**, powers. 1530 **continuate**, continual. 1533 **hey**, high, great;
wonyng, dwelling place. 1535 **continuat**, continual. 1540 **fulsomely**, completely, to the
full; **seand**, seeing. 1541 **feland**, feeling; **heryng**, hearing.

swetely swelowyng; and than shal we sen God face to face, homly and fulsumly.
The creature that is made shal sen and endlesly beholden God which is the maker.
For thus may no man sen God and leven after, that is to sey, in this dedly life.
1545 But whan He of His special grace wil shewn Him here, He strengthyth the
creature above the selfe, and He mesurith the shewing after His own wille as it
is profitable for the tyme.

XLIV

**Of the properties of the Trinite; and how mannys soule, a creature, hath the same
properties, doyng that that it was made for: seyng, beholdyng, and mervelyng his God,
so, by that, it semyth as nowte to the selfe. Forty-fourth chapter.**

God shewid in al the Revelations oftentymes that man werkyth evermore His
will and His wership lestyngly withoute ony styntyng. And what this worke is was
1550 shewid in the first, and that in a mervelous grounde. For it was shewid in the
werkyng of the soule of our blisfull Lady Seynt Mary, treuth and wisdam; and
how, I hope, be the grace of the Holy Gost, I shal say as I saw.
Treuth seith God, and wisedam beholdyth God; and of these two comyth the
thred, that is, an holy, mervelous delyte in God, which is love. Wher treuth and
1555 wisdam is, verily there is love, verily commend of hem bothyn, and al of God
makyng. For He is endles soverain trueth, endles severeyn wisdam, endles sovereyn love onmade. And man soule is a creature in God, which hath the same
propertyes made, and evermore it doith that it was made for: It seith God, it
beholdyth God, and it lovyth God, wherof God enjoyith in the creature, and the
1560 creature in God, endlesly mervelyng, in which mervelyng he seith his God, his
Lord, his Maker, so hey, so gret, and so good in reward of hym that is made,
that onethys the creature semyth owte to the selfe. But the clertye and the
clenes of treuth and wisdam makyth hym to sen and to beknowen that he is
made for love, in which God endlesly kepyth him.

1542 **swelowyng**, swallowing. 1544 **leven**, live; **dedly**, mortal. 1555 **commend**, coming.
1556–57 **soverain, severeyn, sovereyn**, sovereign. 1558 **made**, created, i.e., not self-
generated. 1561 **in reward of**, in comparison with. 1562 **onethys**, scarcely; **owte**, anything; **clertye**, clarity.

XLV

Of the ferme and depe jugement of God and the variant jugement of man. Forty-fifth chapter.

1565   God demyth us upon our kynde substance which is ever kept on in Hym hoole and save without end, and this dome is of His rythfulhede. And man jugith upon our changeabil sensualyte, which semyth now on, now other, after that it takyth of the parties and shewyth outward. And this wisdam is medyllid, for sumtyme it is good and esye and sumtyme it is herd and grevous. And in as mekil

1570   as it is good and esy it longyth to the rythfulhede. And in as mekyl as it is herd and grevous, our good Lord Jesus reformyth it be mercy and grace throw the vertue of His blissid passion and so bryngith into the rythfulhede. And thow these two be thus accordid and onyd, yet it shal be knowen, both, in Hevyn without end. The first dome, which is of God rythfulhed, and that is of His hey, endless life;

1575   endless life; and this is that faire swete dome that was shewid in al the fair revelation in which I saw Him assigne to us no manner of blame.

And thow this was swete and delectabil, yet only in the beholdyng of this, I cowd nowte be full esyd. And that was for the dome of Holy Church, which I had aforn understond and was continuly in my syte. And therfore be this dome

1580   methowte me behovyd neds to know me a synner, and be the same dome I understode that synners arn worthy sumtime blame and wreth. And these two cowth I not se in God. And there my desir was more than I can or may tell. For the heyer dome God shewid Hymselfe in the same tyme, and therfore me behovyd neds to taken it, and the lower dome was lern me aforn in Holy Church,

1585   and therfore I myte in no way levyn the lower dome. Than was this my desire — that I myte sen in God in what manner that the dome of Holy Church herin techyth is trew in His syte, and how it longyth to me sothly to knoyn it, wherby thei myte both be savid so as it wer worshipfull to God and ryte way to me. And to al this I had non other answere but a mervelous example of a lord and of a

1590   servant, as I shal seyn after, and that ful mytyly shewid.

And yet I stond in desire, and will into my end, that I myte be grace knowen these two domys as it longyth to me. For al hevenly and al erthly things that longyn to Hevyn arn comprehendid in thes two domys. And the more understondyng be the gracious ledyng of the Holy Gost that we have of these two domys

---

1565–66 hoole and save, whole and safe. **1568 medyllid,** mixed. **1578 cowd nowte,** could not; **dome,** judgment. **1582 cowth,** could. **1585 levyn,** leave (see note). **1587 longyth . . . knoyn it,** pertains to me to know it truly.

1595 the more we shal sen and known our faylyngs. And ever the more that we sen hem, the more kyndly be grace we shal longen to be fulfillid of endles joye and bliss. For we arn made therto, and our kindly substance is now blisful in God, and hath ben sithen it was made, and shall, without end.

XLVI

We cannot knowen ourself in this life but be feith and grace, but we must know ourself synners; and how God is never wreth, being most nere the soule, it kepyng. Forty-sixth chapter.

But our passand lif that we have here in our sensualite knowith not what our-
1600 self is. Than shal we verily and clerly sen and knowen our Lord God in fulhede of joy. And therfore it behovyth neds to be that the nerer we be our bliss, the more we shall longen; and that both be kynd and be grace. We may have knowing of ourselfe in this life be continuant helpe and vertue of our hey kynd, in which knowing we may encrecin and wexen be forthing and speding of mercy and
1605 grace. But we may never full know ourselfe in to the laste poynte, in which poynte this passend life and manner of peyne and wo shall have an end. And therfore it longyth properly to us, both be kynd and be grace, to longen and desiren with al our myghts to knowen ourselfe in fulhede of endles joye.

And yet in al this tyme from the begynnyng to the end I had two manner of
1610 beholdyng. That one was endless continuant love with sekirnes of kepyng and blisfull salvation. For of this was al the shewyng. That other was the common techyng of Holy Church in which I was aforn enformyd and growndid and wilfully haveing in use and understondyng. And the beholdyng of this come not from me. For be the shewing I was not sterid ne led therfrom in no manner poynte,
1615 but I had therin teching to loven it and liken it, wherby I myte, be the helpe of our Lord and His grace, encrese and resyn to more hevynly knowyng and heyer lovyng. And thus in al this beholdyng methowte it behovyd nedys to sen and to knowen that we arn synners, and don many evill that we owten to leven, and levyn many good dedes ondon that we owten to don, wherfore we deserve peyne
1620 and wreth.

And notwithstondyng al this, I saw sothfastly that our Lord was never wreth

1604 **encrecin and wexen be forthing,** increase and grow with the helping. 1613–14 **And . . . me,** And this way of looking at things stayed with me. 1616 **encrese and resyn,** increase and rise.

ne never shall. For He is God — good, life, trueth, love, peas. His charite and His unite suffrith Hym not to be wroth. For I saw trewly that it is agens the properte of myte to be wroth, and agens the properte of His wisdam, and agens 1625 the properte of His goodnes. God is the goodnes that may not be wroth, for He is not but goodnes. Our soule is unyd to Hym, onchangable goodnes, and betwix God and our soule is neyther wroth nor forgifenes in Hys syte. For our soule is fulsomly onyd to God of His owen goodnes, that atwix God and soule may ben ryth nowte. And to this understondyng was the soul led by love, and drawne be 1630 mygte in every shewing. That it is thus, our good Lord shewid, and how it is thus sothly, of His gret goodnes; and He will we desire to wetyn, that is to seyen, as it longyth to His creature to wetyn it. For althyng that the simple soule understode, God will that it be shewid and knowen. For the thyngs that He will have privy, mytyly and wisely Hymselfe He hydeth hem for love. For I saw in the 1635 same shewing that mech privity is hid, which may never be knowen into the tyme that God of His goodnes hath made us worthy to sen it. And therwith I am wele paid, abyding our Lords will in this hey mervel. And now I yeele me to my moder Holy Church as a simple child owyth.

XLVII

We must reverently mervelyn and mekly suffren, ever enjoyand in God; and how our blyndhede, in that we se not God, is cause of synne. Forty-seventh chapter.

Tweyn poynts longen to our soule be dett. On is that we reverently mervelyn. 1640 That other is that we mekely suffryn, ever enjoyand in God; for He will we wetyn that we shal in short tyme se clerly in Hymself al that we desire. And notwithstondyng al this, I beheld and mervelyd gretly: What is the mercy and forgivenes of God? For be the techyng that I had aforn, I understode that the mercy of God shuld be the forgevenes of His wreth after the tyme that we have 1645 synned. For methowte to a soule whose menyng and desire is to loven, that the wreth of God wer herder than any other peyne. And therfor I toke that the forgevness of His wreth shuld be one of the principal poynts of His mercy. But for nowte that I myte beholden and desyrin I could no se this poynte in al the shewyng. But how I understode and saw of the werks of mercy I shal sey sumdel, 1650 as God wil geve me grace.

1637 yeele me, yield myself. **1638 owyth**, ought to do. **1639 longen**, pertain; **On**, One. **1648 no**, not. **1649 sumdel**, something.

I understode this: Man is chongeable in this lif and be frelte and overcummyng fallith into synne. He is onmytye and onwise of hymself, and also his
wil is overleyd, and in this tyme he is in tempest and in sorow and wo. And the
cause is blindhede, for he seith not God. For if he sey God continuly, he shuld
1655 have no mischevous felyng, ne no manner steryng the yernyng that servyth to
synne. Thus saw I and felt in the same tyme; and methowte that the syte and the
felyng was hey and plentiuous, and gracious in reward that our commen felyng
is in this lif, but yet I thowte it was but smal and low in reward of the great
desire that the soule hath to sen God.

1660 For I felt in me five manner of werkyngs, which be these: enjoying, morning,
desir, drede, and sekir hope. Enjoyeng, for God gave me understondyng and
knowing that it was Hymself that I saw. Morning, and that was for faylyng.
Desir, and that was that I myte sen Hym ever more and more, understondyng
and knowyng that we shal never have ful rest til we sen Hym verily and clerly in
1665 Hevyn. Drede was for it semyd to me in al that tyme that that syte shuld fayle
and I ben left to myselfe. Sekir hope was in the endles love, that I saw I shuld
be kept be His mercy and browte to His bliss. And the joyeing in His syte with
this sekir hope of His mercyful kepyng made me to have felyng and comforte so
that morneing and drede were not gretly peynfull. And yet in al this I beheld in
1670 the shewing of God that this manner syte of Him may not be continuant in this
lif, and that for His owen worship and for encreas of our endles joy. And therefore
we failen oftentymes of the syte of Hym, and anon we fallen into ourself and
than fynde we no felyng of ryth — nowte but contrarioust that is in ourselfe, and
that of the elder rote of our first synne with all that followyn of our contrivans;
1675 and in this we arn traveylid and tempestid with felyng of synnys and of peynes
in many dyvers manner, gostly and bodyly, as it is knowen to us in this lif.

XLVIII

**Off mercy and grace and their propertyes; and how we shall enjoy that ever we suffrid
wo patiently. Forty-eighth chapter.**

But our good Lord the Holy Gost, which is endles lif wonnyng in our soule,
ful sekirly kepyth us, and werkyth therin a peas, and bryngith it to ese be grace,

1651–52 **frelte and overcummyng**, frailty and defeats. 1652 **onmytye and onwise**, powerless
and foolish. 1654 **sey**, saw. 1655 **mischevous**, ill. 1660 **morning**, mourning. 1673 **contrarioust**,
contrariness, perversity. 1674 **rote**, root. 1675 **traveylid**, belabored. 1677 **wonnyng**, dwelling.

and accordith it to God, and makyth it buxum. And this is the mercy and the wey
1680 that our Lord continuly ledyth us in as longe as we ben here in this lif which is
chongeabile. For I sow no wrath but in mannys partie, and that forgevyth He in us.
For wreth is not ell but a frowardness and a contrarioste to peace and to love.
And eyther it commyth of faylyng of myte, or of faylyng of wisdam, or of faylyng
of goodnes, which faylyng is not in God, but it is on our partie, for we be synne
1685 and wretchidnes have in us a wretchid and continuant contrariuste to peace and
to love, and that shewid He full often in His lovely chere of ruth and pety. For
the ground of mercy is love, and the werkyng of mercy is our kepyng in love,
and this was shewid in swich manner that I cowth not aperceyven of the partye
of mercy otherwise but as it were alone in love, that is to sey, as to my syte.

1690   Mercy is a swete, gracious werkyng in love medilyd with plenteuous pitte. For
mercy werkith, us kepand; and mercy workyth, turnyng to us althyng to good.
Mercy be love suffrith us to faylen be mesur, and in as mech as we faylen, in so
mekyl we fallen, and in as mekyl as we fallen, so mekyl we dyen. For us behovyth
nedes to deyen, in as mech as we failen syght and felyng of God that is our lif.
1695 Our faylyng is dredful, our falling is shamefull, and our deyng is sorowfull. But
in al this the swete eye of pite and love cummyth never of us, ne the werkyng of
mercy cessyth not. For I beheld the properte of mercy and I beheld the properte
of grace, which have two manner werkyng in one love. Mercy is a pitifull
propirte which longyth to the moderhode in tendyr love. And grace is a wor-
1700 shipful propirte which longyth to the ryal Lordshipp in the same love. Mercy
werkyth, kepyng, suffring, quecknyng, and helyng; and al is of tendernes of love.

    And grace werkyth, reysing, rewardyng, and endlessly overpassyng that our
lovyng and our travel deservyth, spreding abrode, and shewyng the hey, plentiuous largess of Godds ryal Lordship in His mervelous curtesye; and this is of
1705 the abondance of love. For grace werkyth our dredfull faylyng into plentiuous
endles solace, and grace werkyth our shamefull fallyng into hey worship reysyng,
and grace werkyth our sorowfull deying into holy blisfull lif. For I saw full sekirly that ever as our contrarioust werkyth to us here in erth peyne, shame, and
sorow, ryth so on the contrariewise, grace werkyth to us in Hevyn solace, worship,
1710 and bliss; and overpassyng — so fer forth that whan we cum up and receivyn the
swete reward which grace hath wrowte to us, than we shal thankyn and blissyn our
Lord, endlesly enjoyand that ever we suffrid wo. And that shal be for a properte

1679 **buxum**, obedient. 1681 **sow**, saw. 1682 **all**, else; **frowardness and a contrarioste**,
perversity and an opposition. 1685 **contrariuste**, contrariness. 1688 **cowth**, could. 1691
turnyng . . . good, turning everything to good for us. 1696 **of us**, away from us. 1697
cessyth, ceases. 1699 **propirte**, quality.

of blissid love that we shall know in God, which we myte never a knowen withoute wo goeing afore. And whan I saw all this, me behovid nedis to granten that
1715   the mercy of God and the forgiveness is to slaken and wasten our wreth.

XLIX

**Our lif is growndid in love withoute the which we perish; but yet God is never wroth,
but in our wreth and synne He mercifully kepith us, and tretith us to peace, rewarding
our tribulations. Forty-ninth chapter.**

For this was an hey mervel to the soule which was continely shewid in al, and
with gret diligens beholden: that our Lord God anempts Hymself may not for-
gevyn, for He may not be wroth. It were impossible. For this was shewid, that
our lif is all groundid and rotid in love, and without love we may not levyn. And
1720   therfore to the soul that of His special grace seyth so forforth of the hey, mervelous godenes of God, and that we arn endlesly onyd to Hym in love, it is the
most impossible that may ben that God shuld be wreth. For wreth and frendship
be two contraries. For He that westith and destroyith our wreth, and makyth us
meke and mylde, it behovyth neds to ben that He be ever on in love, meke and
1725   myld, which is contrarious to wreth. For I saw ful sekirly that wher our Lord
apperith, peas is taken and wreth hath no place. For I saw no manner of wreth
in God, neyther for short tyme ne for longe, for sothly, as to my syte, if God
myte be wroth a touch we shuld never have lif, ne stede, ne beyng.
For verily as we have our beyng of the endles myte of God and of the endless
1730   wisdam and of the endless godeness, as verily we have our kepyng in the endles
myte of God, in the endles wisdom, and in the endless goodnes. For thow we
felyn in us wretches, debates, and strives, yet arn we al mannerfull beclosyd in
the mildhede of God and in His mekehede, in His benignite, and in His buxumhede. For I saw full sekirly that al our endles frendship, our stede, our lif, and
1735   our beyng is in God. For that same endles goodnes that kepith us whan we
synne that we perish not, the same endles goodnes continuly tretyth in us a
peace agaynst our wreth and our contrarious fallyng, and makyth us to sen our
nede with a trew drede, mytyly to sekyn into God to have forgivenes with a
gracious desire of our salvation. For we may not be blisfully save til we be verily
1740   in peace and in love, for that is our salvation. And thow we, be the wreth and

1720 **seyth**, sees. 1728 **a touch**, a bit; **stede**, standing place. 1732 **wretches**, times of
wretchedness. 1733–34 **buxumhede**, obedience. 1734 **stede**, place.

the contrariouste that is in us, be now in tribulation, desese, and wo, as fallyth to our blindnes and frelte, yet arn we sekirly safe be the mercifull kepyng of God that we perish not. But we arn not blisfully saf in havyng of our endles joy till we ben al in peace and in love, that is to sey, ful plesid with God and with al

1745 His werks, and with al His domys, and lovand and pessible with ourselfe and with our even Cristen, and with al that God lovith, as love likyth. And this doeth Gods goodnes in us.

Thus saw I that God is our very peace, and He is our sekir keper whan we arn oureselfe at onpeace, and He continuly werkith to bring us into endles peas. And

1750 thus whan we, be the werkyng of mercy and grace, be made meke and mylde, we arn ful safe. Sodenly is the soule onyd to God whan it is trewly pesid in the selfe, for in Him is fonden no wreth. And thus I saw whan we arn all in peace and in love, we fynde no contrariouste, ne no manner of lettyng; of that contrariouste which is now in us, our Lord of His goodnes makyth it to us ful profitable. For

1755 that contrarioust is cause of our tribulations and al our wo, and our Lord Jesus takyth hem and send hem up to Hevyn, and there arn thei made more swete and delectable than herte may thynken or tongue may tellen. And whan we cum thither we shal fynd hem redy al turnyd into very faire and endless worships. Thus is God our stedfast ground, and He shal be our full bliss and make us

1760 onchongeable as He is whan we arn there.

L

How the chosen soule was nevere ded in the syte of God, and of a mervel upon the same; and three things boldid hir to aske of God the understondyng of it. Fiftieth chapter.

And in this dedly lif, mercy and forgivenes is our wey and evermore ledyth us to grace. And be the tempest and the sorow that we fallen in on our parte, we be often dede as to manys dome in erth, but in the syte of God, the soule that shal be save was never dede ne never shall. But yet here I wondrid and mervelid

1765 with al the diligens of my soul menand thus: Good Lord, I se the that art very truth and I know sothly that we synne grevously al day and ben mekyl blame-worthy, and I ne may neyther levyn the knowyng of this sothe, ner I ne se the shewyn to us no manner of blame. How may this be? For I knew be the common techyng of Holy Church, and be myn owne felyng, that the blame of our synne

1770 continuly hangith upon us from the first man into the tyme that we come up

1745 **domys**, judgments; **pessible**, at peace.

100

into Hevyn. Than was this my mervel, that I saw our Lord God shewand to us no more blame than if we were as clene and as holy as angelys be in Hevyn.

And atwix these two contraries my reason was gretly traveylid by my blyndhede and cowde have no rest for drede that His blyssid presens shuld passyn
1775   from my syte, and I to be left in onknowyng how He beholdyth us in our synne. For either behovid me to sen in God that synne were al don awey, or ell me behovid to sen in God how He seith it, wherby I myte trewly knowen how it longyth to me to se synne and the manner of our blame. My longyn indurid, Hym continuly beholding, and yet I cowde have no patience for great awer and
1780   perplexitie, thynkand: If I take it thus that we be not synners ne no blameworthy, it semyth as I shuld eryn and faile of knoweing of this soth. And if it be so that we be synners and blameworthy, Good Lord, how may it than ben that I can not sen this sothnes in The, which art my God, my maker, in whom I desire to sen al trueths?

1785   For three poynts makyn me herdy to ask it. The first is for it is so low a thyng, for if it wer an hey, I should ben adred. The second is that it is so common, for if it were special and privye, also I shuld ben adred. The third is that it nedyth me to wetyn it, as me thynkyth, if I shall levyn here, for knowyng of good and evill wherby I may be reason and grace the more depart hem on sundre,
1790   and loven goodnes and haten evill as Holy Church techyth. I cryed inwardly with al my myte sekyng into God for helpe, menand thus, "A, Lord Jesus, King of bliss, how shall I ben esyd? Ho that shal techyn me and tellyn me that me nedyth to wetyn if I may not at this tyme sen it in The?"

LI

The answere to the doute afor by a mervelous example of a lord and a servant; and God will be abidyn, for it was nere twenty yeres after ere she fully understode this example; and how it is understod that Crist syttith on the ryth hand of the Fader. Fifty-first chapter.

And than our curtes Lord answerd in shewing full mystily a wondirful example
1795   of a lord that hath a servant, and gave me syte to my understondyng of botyrn, which syght was shewid double in the lord, and the syte was shewid dowble in the servant. Than on partie was shewid gostly in bodily lyknes, and the other

---

1779 awer, trouble (see note). **1781 eryn,** err. **1785 makyn . . . it,** make me courageous enough to ask this. **1792 Ho,** Who. **1793 sen,** see. **1794 mystily,** obscurely, as if through a mist; symbolically (see note). **1795 botryn,** both.

partie was shewid more gostly without bodyly lyknes. For the first, thus: I saw two persons in bodyly likenes, that is to sey, a lord and a servant, and therewith God gave me gostly understondyng. The lord sittith solemnly in rest and in peace; the servant standyth by, aforn his lord reverently, redy to don his lords will. The lord lookyth upon his servant ful lovely, and swetely and mekely he sendyth hym to a certain place to don his will. The servant, not only he goeth, but suddenly he stirtith and rynnith in grete haste for love to don his lords will, and anon he fallith in a slade and takith ful grete sore. And than he gronith and monith and waylith and writhith, but he ne may rysen ne helpyn hymself be no manner wey.

And of all this the most myscheif that I saw him in was faylyng of comforte. For he cowde not turne his face to loke upon his lovyng lord which was to hym ful nere, in whom is ful comfort; but as a man that was febil and onwise for the tyme, he entended to his felyng, and induryd in wo, in which wo he suffrid seven grete peynes.

The first was the sore brosyng that he toke in hys fallyng, which was to hym felable peyne. The second was the hevynes of his body. The third was febilnes folowyng of these two. The fourth, that he was blinded in his reason and stonyed in his mend so forforth that almost he had forgotten his owne luf. The fifth was that he myte not rysen. The sixth was most mervelous to me, and that was that he lay alone. I lokid al aboute and beheld, and fer ne nere, hey ne low, I saw to him no helpe. The seventh was that the place which he lay on was a lang, herd, and grevous. I merveled how this servant myte mekely suffren there al this wo.

And I beheld with avisement to wetyn if I cowth perceyve in hym any defaute, or if the lord shuld assigne in hym any blame. And sothly ther was none seen. For only his good will and his grete desire was cause of his fallyng. And he was as unlothful and as good inwardly as whan he stode afor his lord redy to don his wille. And ryth thus continualy his lovand lord ful tenderly beholdyth him, and now with a double cher — on outward, ful mekely and myldely with grete ruth and pety, and this was of the first; another inward, more gostly, and this was shewid with a ledyng of my understondyng into the lord which I saw hym heyly enjoyen for the worshipful resting and nobleth that he will and shall bryng his servant to be his plenteuous grace; and this was of that other shewyng. And now my understondyng led agen into the first, both kepand in mynd. Than seith this curtes lord in his menyng: *Lo, lo my lovid servant, what harme and disese he hath*

1804 **rynnith**, runs. 1805 **slade**, valley. 1813 **brosyng**, bruising. 1816 **stonyed**, stunned, astonished; **mend**, mind; **luf**, love. 1820 **lang**, long. 1830 **nobleth**, nobility, honor.

takeyn in my service for my love, ya, and for his good will; is it not skyl that I
1835   *reward hym his afray and his drede, his hurt and his mayme, and al his wo? And*
not only this, but fallith it not to me to gevyn a geft that be better to hym and more
worshipfull than his own hole shuld have ben? And ell me thynkyth I dede hym no
grace. And in this an inward gostly shewing of the lords menyng descendid into
my soule, in which I saw that it behovith neds to ben, stondyng his grete and his
1840   own worship, that his dereworthy servant which he lovid so mech shuld ben
verily and blisfully rewardid without end aboven that he shuld a ben if he had
not fallen; ya, and so ferforth that his fallyng and his wo that he hath taken
therby shall be turnyd into hey and overpassing worship and endles bliss.

And at this poynte the shewing of the example vanishid, and our good Lord
1845   led forth myn understondyng in syte and in shewing of the Revelation to the
end. But notwithstondyng al this forthledyng, the mervelyng of the example cam
never from me for methowth it was goven me for an answere to my desir. And
yet cowth I not taken therin ful understondyng to myn ese at that tyme. For in
the servant that was shewid for Adam, as I shal seyn, I saw many dyvers properties
1850   that myten be no manner way ben aret to single Adam. And thus in that tyme I
stode mekyl in onknowyng. For the full understondyng of this mervelous example
was not goven me in that tyme, in which mystye example three propertes of the
revelation be yet mekyl hidde. And notwithstondyng this, I saw and understode
that every shewing is full of privities. And therfore me behovith now to tellen
1855   three propertes in which I am sumdele esyd. The frest is the begynnyng of techyng that I understod therein in the same tyme. The second is the inward lernyng
that I have understodyn therein sithen. The third, al the hole revelation from
the begynnyng to the end, that is to sey, of this boke, which our Lord God of
His goodnes bryngyth oftentymes frely to the syte of myn understondyng. And
1860   these three arn so onyd as to my understondyng that I cannot, ner may, depart
them. And be these three as on, I have techyng wherby I owe to leyvyn and
trostyn in our Lord God, that of the same godenes that He shewid it, and for
the same end, ryth so, of the same goodnes and for the same end, He shal
declaryn it to us when it is His wille.
1865   For twenty yeres after the tyme of the shewing, save three monethis, I had
techyng inwardly, as I shal seyen. *It longyth to the to taken hede to all the pro-*
pertes and condition that weryn shewd in the example thow thou thynke that they

---

1834 skyl, reasonable. **1835 reward . . . drede**, compensate him for this attack and for his
fear. **1837 hole**, wholeness, health; **And ell**, Or else. **1850 aret**, attributed. **1852 mystye**,
symbolic, obscure (see note to line 1794). **1855 sumdele**, somewhat. **1860 depart**, separate. **1861 owe**, ought. **1862 trostyn**, trust. **1865 monethis**, months. **1866 hede**, heed.

ben mysty and indifferent to thy syte. I assend wilfully with grete desire, and seeing inwardly with avisement al the poynts and propertes that wer shewid in the
same tyme as ferforth as my witt and understondyng wold servyn, begynning
myn beholding at the lord and at the servant, and the manner of sytting of the
lord and the place that he sate on and tho color of his clothyng, and the manner
of shapp and his cher withouten and his nobleth and his godeness within; at the
manner of stondyng of the servant, and the place wher and how, at his manner
of clothyng, the color and the shappe, at his outward havyng, and at his inward
goodnes and his onlothfulhede.

The lord that sate solemnly in rest and in peace, I understond that he is God.
The servant that stode aforn the lord, I understode that it was shewid for Adam,
that is to seyen, on man was shewid that tyme, and his fallyng, to maken therby
understonden how God beholdith a man and his fallyng. For in the syte of God,
al man is on man, and on man is all man. This man was hurte in hys myte and
made ful febil, and he was stonyed in his understondyng, for he turnyd from the
beholdyng of his lord. But his will was kept hole in God sygte, for his will I saw
our lord commenden and approven. But hymselfe was lettid and blyndyd of the
knowing of this will, and this is to him grete sorow and grevous disese. For
neither he seith clerly his lovyng lord, which is to him ful meke and mylde, ne
he seith trewly what himself is in the sygte of his lovyng lord. And wel I wote
whan these two are wysely and treuly seyn, we shall gettyn rest and peas her in
parte, and the fulhede of the bliss of Hevyn be His plentiuous grace. And this was a
begynnyng of techyng which I saw in the same tyme wherby I myte com to knowyng
in what manner He beholdyth us in our synne. And than I saw that only paynys
blamith and punishith, and our curtis Lord comfortith and sorowith, and ever
He is to the soule in glad cher, lovand and longand to bryngen us to bliss.

The place that our Lord sat on was symple, on the erth, barren and desert,
alone in wildernes. His clothyng was wide and syde, and ful semely as fallyth to
a lord. The color of His cloth was blew as asure, most sad and fair. His cher was
merciful. The color of His face was faire browne with fulsomely featours; His
eyen were blak, most faire and semely, shewand ful of lovely pety; and within Him,
an hey ward, longe and brode, all full of endles hevyns. And the lovely lokeing
that He loked upon His servant continuly, and namely in his fallyng, methowte
it myte molten our herts for love and bresten hem on to for joy. The fair lokyng

1868 **mysty and indifferent**, unclear and irrelevant; **assend**, assented. 1872 **sate**, sat; **tho**,
the. 1875 **havyng**, behavior. 1876 **onlothfulhede**, alacrity, good will. 1882 **stonyed**, stunned,
stricken. 1884 **lettid**, hindered. 1895 **syde**, long, ample. 1896 **sad**, dignified. 1897 **fulsomely featours**, full, regular features. 1899 **hey ward**, high refuge. 1901 **on to**, in two.

shewid of a semely medlur which was mervelous to beholden. That on was ruth and pety, that other was joye and bliss. The joy and bliss passith as fer reuth and pite as Hevyn is aboven erth. The pite was erthly, and the blis was hevenly.

1905 The ruth in the pite of the Fadir was of the falling of Adam, which is His most lovid creatur. The joy and the bliss was of His dereworthy Son, which is evyn with the Fadir. The merciful beholdyng of His lofly cher fulfilled al erth and descendid downe with Adam into Helle, with which continuant pite Adam was kept from endles deth. And this mercy and pite dwellyth with mankind into the

1910 tyme we com up into Hevyn.

But man is blindid in this life, and therfore we may not sen our Fader, God, as He is. And what tyme that He of His goodnes will shewin Hym to man, He shewith Him homley as man. Notwithstonding I saw sothly we owen to knowen and levyn that the Fader is not man. But His sitting on the erth barreyn and

1915 desert is this to menyn: He made mans soule to ben His owen cyte, and His dwellyng place, which is most plesyng to Hym of al His werks. And what tyme that man was fallen into sorow and peyne, he was not al semly to servyn of that noble office. And therfore our kind Fader wold adyten him no other place, but sitten upon the erth abeydand mankynd which is medlid with erth till what time

1920 be His grace His derworthy Son had bowte ageyn His cyte into the noble fayrhede with His herd travel. The blewhede of the clothing betokinith His stedfastnes; the brownhede of His fair face with the semely blakhede of the eyen was most accordyng to shew His holy sobirnes. The larghede of His clothyng which were fair, flamand abowten, betokenith that He hath beclesid in hym all hevyns and

1925 al joy and blis. And this was shewid in a touch, wher I sey, myn understondyng was led into the Lord, in which I saw Him heyly enjoyen for the worshipful restoring that He wil and shal bring His servant to be His plenteous grace.

And yet I mervellyd, beholdyng the lord and the servant afornseid. I saw the lord sitten solemnly and the servant stondand reverently aforn his lord, in which

1930 servant is double understondyng, on withouten, another within. Outward, he was clad simply as a labourer which wer disposid to travel, and he stode ful nere the lord, not even fornempts hym, but in partie asyd, that on the lift. His clothyng was a white kirtle, sengil, old and al defacid, died with swete of his body, streyte fittyng to hym and short, as it were an handful benethe the knee,

1902 **medlur**, mixture. **1907 lofly**, lovely. **1915 is this to menyn**, means this; **cyte**, city, site. **1918 adyten him**, prepare for him, assign to him. **1919 abeydand**, waiting for; **medlid**, mingled. **1922 eyen**, eyes. **1932 fornempts**, right before; **asyd**, aside; **lift**, left. **1933 kirtle**, coat, tunic; **sengil**, single; **died with swete**, stained with sweat. **1934 streyte fit-tyng**, skimpy, close.

1935　bar, semand as it shuld sone be weryd up redy to be raggid and rent. And in this I mervelid gretly, thynkand: This is now an onsemely clothyng for the servant that is so heyly lovid, to stondyn afor so worship lord.

And inward, in him was shewid a ground of love, which love he had to the lord was even like to the love that the lord had to hym. The wisdam of the ser-
1940　vant saw inwardly that ther was on thing to don which shuld be to the worshipp of the lord. And the servant, for love, haveing no reward to hymselfe ne to nothing that might fallen on him, hastely he stirt and ran at the sendyng of his lord to don that thing which was his will and his worship. For it semyd be his outward clothyng as he had ben a continuant labourer of leng tyme. And be the
1945　inward syte that I had both in the lord and in the servant, it semyd that he was anew, that is to sey, new begynnyng to travellyn, which servant was never sent out aforn.

Ther was a tresor in the erth which the lord lovid. I mervelid and thowte what it myte ben. And I was answered in myn understondyng: It is a mete which is
1950　lovesome and plesant to the lord. For I saw the lord sitten as a man, and I saw neither mete ner drynke wherwith to servyn hym. This was on mervel. Another mervel was that this solemn lord had no servant but on, and hym he sent owte. I beheld, thynkyng what manner labour it myte ben that the servant shud don, and than I understode that he shuld don the gretest labor and herdest travel that
1955　is. He shuld ben a gardiner, delvyn and dykyn, swinkin and swetyn, and turne the earth upsodowne, and sekyn the depnes, and wattir the plants in tyme, and in this he shuld continu his travel and make swete flods to rennen, and noble and plenteous fruits to springen which he shuld bryng aforn the lord and servyn hym therwith to his lykyng. And he shuld never turne agen till he had dygte this
1960　mete al redye as he knew that it lekyd the lord, and than he shuld take this mete with the drinke in the mete, and beryn it ful worshipfully aforn the lord.

And al this tyme the lord shuld sytten on the same place abydand his servant whome he sent out. And yet I merveylid from whens the servant came. For I saw in the lord that he hath wythyn hymselfe endles lif and al manner of goodnes,
1965　save that tresor that was in the erth, and that was groundyd in the lord in mervelous depenes of endles love. But it was not all to the worship till this servant had dygte thus nobly it, and browte it aforn him, in hymself present. And without the lord was nothing but wildernes. And I understod not all what this example ment, and therfore I merveylid whens the servant cam.

1935 **weryd up**, worn out. 1949 **mete**, food. 1953 **myte . . . don**, might be that the servant should do. 1955 **delvyn and dykyn**, digging and ditching; **swinkin**, working; **swetyn**, sweating. 1959–60 **dygte this mete**, prepared this food. 1967 **dygte**, prepared.

1970 In the servant is comprehendid the Second Person in the Trinite, and in the
servant is comprehendid Adam, that is to sey, al man. And therfore whan I sey
the Son, it menyth the Godhede which is even with the Fadir; and whan I sey
the *servant*, it menyth Christs manhood which is rythful Adam. Be the nerehede
of the servant is understode the Son, and be the stondyng on the left syde is under-
1975 stod Adam. The lord is the Fadir, God; the servant is the Son, Christ Jesus; the
Holy Gost is even love which is in them both. Whan Adam fell, God Son fell.
For the rythfull onyng which was made in Hevyn, God Son myte not fro Adam,
for by Adam I understond all man. Adam fell fro lif to deth into the slade of
this wretchid world, and after that into Hell. Gods Son fell with Adam into the
1980 slade of the Mayden wombe which was the fairest dawter of Adam, and therfor
to excuse Adam from blame in Hevyn and in erth, and mytyly He fetchid him
out of Hell.

Be the wisdam and goodnes that was in the servant is understode Godds Son.
Be the por clothyng as a laborer standand nere the left syde is understode the
1985 manhood and Adam, with al the mischef and febilnes that folowith. For in al
this, our good Lord shewid His owne Son and Adam but one man. The vertue
and the goodnes that we have is of Jesus Criste, the febilnes and the blindnes
that we have is of Adam; which two wer shewid in the servant. And thus hath
our good Lord Jesus taken upon Him al our blame, and therfore our Fadir may,
1990 ne will, no more blame assigne to us than to His owen Son, derworthy Criste.
Thus was He the servant aforne His comeing into erth, stondand redy aforne
the Fader in purpos till what tyme He would send hym to don that worshipfull
dede be which mankynde was browte ageyn into Hevyn, that is to seyn, notwithstondyng that He is God, evyn with the Fadir as anempts the Godhede. But in
1995 His forseeing purpose that He wold be man to saven man in fulfilling of His
Faders will, so He stode afore His Fader as a servant wilfully takyng upon Hym
al our charge. And than He stirt full redily at the Faders will, and anon He fell
full low in the Maydens womb, haveing no reward to Himselfe ne to His herd
peyns. The which kirtle is the flesh; the syngulhede is that there was ryte now
2000 atwix the godhod and manhede. The steytehede is povertye. The eld is of Adams
waring; the defaceing of swete, of Adams travel. The shorthede shewith the
servant labour. And thus I saw the Son stonding, sayeing in His menyng: *Lo,
my der Fader, I stond befor The in Adams kirtle alredy to sterten and to rennen. I*

1973 rythful, fittingly; **nerehede,** closeness. **1980 slade,** valley. **1994 anempts,** pertains to.
1996 Hym, Himself. **2000 steytehede,** skimpiness. **2001 waring,** wearing; **defaceing of
swete,** disfigurement of the sweat; **travel,** labor.

wold ben in the erth to don Thy worship whan it is Thy will to send me. How long shal I desiren?

2005   Ful sothfastly wist the Son whan it was the Fader will, and how long He shal desiren. That is to sey, anempt the Godhede, for He is the wisdam of the Fader. Wherfor this mening was shewid in understondyng of the manhode of Criste. For all mankynd that shal be savid be the swete incarnation and blisful passion

2010   of Criste, al is the manhood of Criste. For He is the hede, and we be His members, to which members the day and the tyme is onknown whan every passand wo and sorow shal have an end and the everlestyng joy and bliss shall be fulfylid, which day and time for to se al the company of Hevyn longyth. And al that shall ben under Hevyn that shal come thider, ther wey is be longyng and desire,

2015   which desir and longing was shewid in the servant stondyng aforen the Lord, or ell thus, in the Sons stondyng aforn the Fadir in Adams kirtle. For the langor and desire of al mankynd that shal be savid aperid in Jesus, for Jesus is al that shal be savid, and al that shal be savid is Jesus — and al of the charite of God, with obediens, mekeness, and patience, and vertues that longyn to us.

2020   Also in this mervelous example I have techyng with me as it were the begynnyng of an ABC, wherby I may have sum understondyng of our Lordis menyng. For the privities of the Revelation ben hidd therin, notwithstondyng that al the shewing arn ful of privityes. The syttyng of the Fadir betokynyth His Godhede, that is to sey, for shewyng of rest and peas, for in the Godhede may be no travel.

2025   And that He shewid Hymselfe as Lord, betokynith to our manhode. The stondyng of the servant betokynyth travel; on syde and on the left betokynyth that he was not al worthy to stonden ever ryth aforn the Lord. His stertyng was the Godhede, and the rennyng was the manhede. For the Godhede sterte from the Fadir into the Maydens wombe, falling into the taking of our kynde. And in this falling

2030   He toke gret sore. The sore that He toke was our flesh in which He had also swithe felyng of dedly peynis. Be that He stod dredfully aforn the Lord, and not even ryth, betokynith that His clothyng was not honest to stond in even ryth aforn the Lord. Ne that myte not, ne shuld not, ben His office whil He was a laborer. Ne also He myte not sitten in rest and peace with the Lord till He had

2035   woon His peace rythfully with His herd travel. And be the left syde, that the Fadir left His owne Son wilfully in the manhode to suffre all mannys paynys without sparing of Him.

     Be that His kirtle was in poynte to be raggid and rent is understonden the sweppys and the scorgis, the thornys and the naylys, the drawyng and the draggyng,

2022 privities, secrets. **2030 sore,** physical pain. **2030–31 also swithe,** at once. **2031 stod dredfully,** stood in awe. **2032 even ryth,** on the righthand of God. **2035 woon,** achieved, won. **2039 sweppys,** blows; **scorgis,** whippings.

2040 His tendir flesh rendyng — as I saw in sum partie the flesh was rent from the
hedepanne, falland in pecys into the tyme the bledyng failyd, and than it began
to dryand, agen clyngand to the bone. And be the wallowyng and wrythyng,
gronyng and monyng, is understonden that He myte never rysen al mytyly from
the tyme that He was fallen into the Maydens wombe till His body was slaine
2045 and ded, He yeldyng the soule in the Fadirs hands with al mankynd for whom
He was sent.

And at this poynte He began first to shewen His myte, for He went into Helle,
and whan He was there He reysid up the gret rote out of the depe depenes, which
rythfully was knit to Hym in hey Hevyn. The body was in the grave till Estern
2050 morow, and from that tyme He lay never more. For then was rythfully endid the
walowyng and the wrythyng, the groning and the monyng. And our foule dedly
flesh that Gods Son toke on Hym, which was Adams old kirtle, streyte, bare and
short, than be our Savior was made fair, now white and bryte, and of endles
cleness, wyde and syde, fairer and richer than was than the clothyng which I saw
2055 on the Fadir. For that clothyng was blew, and Christs clothyng is now of a fair
semely medlur which is so mervelous that I can it not discrien, for it is al of
very worshipps.

Now sittith not the Lord on erth in wilderness, but He sittith in His noblest
sete which He made in Hevyn most to His lekyng. Now stondith not the Son aforn
2060 the Fadir as a servant aforn the Lord, dredfully, unornely clad, in party nakid,
but He stondith aforn the Fadir ever rythe rechely clad in blissfull largess with
a corone upon His hede of pretious richess. For it was shewid that we be His
corone, which corone is the Fadirs joye, tho Sonys worshippe, the Holy Gost
lekyng, and endless mervelous bliss to all that be in Hevyn. Now stondith not the
2065 Son aforn the Fadir on the left syde as a laborer, but He sittith on His Fadirs
ryte hond in endles rest and peace. But it is not ment that the Son syttith on
the ryte hond, syde be syde, as on man sittith be another in this lif, for ther is
no such syttyng, as to my syte, in the Trinite. But He sittith on His Fadirs ryte
hand, that is to sey, in the heyest noblyth of the Fadirs joyes. Now is the spouse,
2070 Gods Son, in peace with His lowvid wife which is the fair mayden of endles
joye. Now sittith the Son, very God and man, in His cety in rest and peace
which His Fadir hath adyte to Him of His endles purpose, and the Fadir in the
Son, and tho Holy Gost in the Fadir and in the Son.

2041 hedepanne, skull. **2048 rote,** rout, i.e., throng, company of souls. **2052 streyte,**
scanty. **2054 wyde and syde,** ample and long; **than was than,** than was then. **2056 medlur,**
mixture. **2059 sete,** seat, site. **2060 unornely,** without ornament, plainly. **2063 tho,** the.
2071 cety, city. **2072 adyte,** assigned.

LII

God enjoyeth that He is our fadir, mother, and spouse, and how the chosen have here a medlur of wele and wo, but God is with us in three manner; and how we may eschew synne but never it perfectly as in heaven. Fifty-second chapter.

    And thus I saw that God enjoyeth that He is our fader, God enjoyeth that He
2075   is our moder, and God enjoyeth that He is our very spouse, and our soule is His
lovid wife. And Criste enjoyeth that He is our broder and Jesus enjoyeth that
He is our Savior. Ther arn five hey joyes, as I understond, in which He wil that
we enjoyen, Hym praysyng, Him thankyng, Him loveing, Him endlesly blissand.
Al that shall be savid, for the tyme of this life, we have in us a mervelous medlur
2080   bothen of wele and wo. We have in us our Lord Jesus uprysen; we have in us
the wretchidnes and the mischefe of Adams fallyng, deyand. Be Criste we are
stedfastly kept, and be His grace touchyng, we are reysid into sekir troste of
salvation. And be Adams fallyng we arn so broken in our felyng on divers
manner, be synes and be sondry peynes, in which we arn made derke and so blinde
2085   that onethys we can taken ony comfort.
    But in our menyng we abiden God, and faithfully trosten to have mercy and
grace. And this is His owen werkyng in us, and of His godeness He opynyth the
eye of our understondyng be which we have syte, sumtyme more and sumtyme
less, after that God gevyth abilite to takyn. And now we arn reysid into that on,
2090   and now we are suffrid to fallen into that other. And thus is this medle so mervelous in us that onethys we knowen of ourselfe or of our evyn Cristen in what
wey we stonden, for the merveloushede of this sundry felyng, but that ilke holy
assent that we assenten to God whan we felyn Hym, truly willand to be with
Him with al our herte, with al our soule, and with all our myte. And than we
2095   haten and dispisen our evil sterings and all that myte be occasion of synne,
gostly and bodily. And yet nevertheles whan this sweteness is hidde, we falyn
ageyn into blindhede, and so into wo and tribulation on divers manner. But
than is this our comfort, that we knowen in our feith, that be the vertue of
Criste which is our keper we assenten never therto, but we grutchin ther agen
2100   and duryin in peyne and wo, prayand into that tyme that He shewith Him agen
to us. And thus we stonden in this medlur all the dayes of our life.
    But He will we trosten that He is lestyngly with us, and that in three manner.

2079–80 medlur bothen, mixture both. **2081 mischefe,** harm, damage; **deyand,** dying.
2085 onethys, scarcely. **2090 medle,** mixture. **2092 ilke,** same. **2096 falyn,** fall. **2099
grutchin ther agen,** complain against it. **2100 duryin,** endure. **2101 medlur,** mixed state.

He is with us in Hevyn, very man in His owne person, us updrawand, and that was shewid in the gostly thrist. And He is with us in erth, us ledand, and that was shewid in the thrid wher I saw God in a poynte. And He is with us in our soule endlesly wonand, us reuland and yemand. And that was shewid in the sixteenth, as I shal sey. And thus in the servant was shewid the mischefe and blyndhede of Adams fallyng, and in the servant was shewid the wisdam and godeness of God Son. And in the lord was shewid the ruth and pite of Adams wo, and in the lord was shewid the hey noblyth and the endles worship that mankynde is cum to be the vertue of the passion and the deth of His derworthy Son. And therfore mytyly He enjoyeth in His fallyng, for the hey reysing and fullhede of bliss that mankynde is cum to, overpassing that we shuld have had if He had not fallen. And thus to se this overpassing nobleth was myn understondyng led into God in the same tyme that I saw the servant fallen. And thus we have now matter of morneing, for our synne is cause of Crists paynes. And we haive lestingly matter of joy, for endles love made hym to suffir.

And therfore the creature that seith and felith the werkyng of love be grace hatith nowte but synne. For of al thyng, to my syte, love and hate arn herdest and most onmesurable contraries. And notwithstondyng all this, I saw and understode in our Lord menyng that we may not in this life kepe us from synne as holy in ful clenes as we shal ben in Hevyn. But we may wele be grace kepe us from the synnes which will ledyn us to endles paynes, as Holy Church techith us, and eschewen venial resonable upon our myte. And if we be our blyndhede and our wretchedness ony tyme fallen, that we redily risen, knowand the swete touching of grace, and wilfully amenden us upon the techyng of Holy Chuirch, after that the synne is grevous, and gon forwith to God in love; and neither on the on syd fallen overlow enclynand to despeyr, ne on that other syd ben over rekles as if we gove no fors, but nakidly knowing our feblehede, witeand that we may not stond a twincklyng of an eye but be keping of grace, and reverently cleven to God, on Him only trostyng.

For otherwise is the beholdyng of God, and otherwise is the beholdyng of man. For it longyth to man mekely to accusen hymselfe. And it longith to the propir goodnes of our Lord God curtesly to excusen man. And these be two parties that

2103 **us updrawand**, drawing us up. 2106 **wonand**, dwelling; **yemand**, guiding, caring for. 2121 **in our Lord menyng**, in our Lord's view. 2124 **be**, by. 2127 **gon**, go. 2128–29 **on syd . . . feblehede**, one side falling too low, inclining to despair, nor on the other hand being too reckless, as if we did not care at all, but nakedly knowing our fragility. 2132 **For otherwise . . . man**, For the vision of God differs from the vision of man, and the vision of man, from the vision of God.

111

2135 were shewid in the double chere in which the lord beheld the fallyng of his
lovid servant. That one was shewid outward, wel mekely and myldly with gret
ruth and pite, and that of endless love. And ryth thus will our Lord that we
accusen ourselfe, wilfully and sothly seand and knowand our fallyng and all the
harmes that cum thereof, seand and witand that we may never restoren it, and

2140 therwith that we wilfully and truly sen and knowen His everlasting love that He
hath us, and His plenteous mercy. And thus graciously to sen and knowen both
togeder is the meke accusyng that our Lord askyth of us. And Hymselfe werkith
it; then it is.

And this is the lowor parte of manys life, and it was shewed in the outward

2145 chere, in which shewing I saw two partes. That on is the reufull falling of man;
that other is the worshipfull asseth that our Lord hath made for man. The other
cher was shewid inward, and that was mor heyly and al on. For the life and the
vertue that we have in the lower parte is of the heyer, and it cummith downe to
us of the kinde love of the selfe be grace. Atwixen that on and that other is ryte

2150 nowte, for it is all one love, which on blissid love hath now in us double werking.
For in the lower part arn peynes and passions, ruthes and pites, mercies and
forgevenes, and swich other that arn profitable. But in the higer parte are none of
these, but al on hey love and mervelous joye, in which mervelous joy all peynis
are heyly restorid. And in this our good Lord shewid not only our excuseing,

2155 but also the worshipfull nobleth that He shall bring us to, turnand al our blame
into endles worshippe.

LIII

**The kindness of God assigneth no blame to His chosen, for in these is a godly will that
never consent to synne. For it behovyth the ruthfulhede of God so to be knitt to these
that ther be a substance kept that may never be departid from Hym. Fifty-third chapter.**

And I saw that He will we wettynn He takith not herder the fallyng of
any creatur that shall be save than He to toke the fallyng of Adam which we
knowen was endlesly lovid and sekirly kept in the tyme of all His nede, and now

2160 is blisfully restorid in hey, overpassing joyes. For our Lord God is so good, so
gentill, and so curtes that He may never assigne defaute in whom He shall ever
be blissid and praysid. And in this that I have now seyd was my desire in partie

2146 **asseth,** atonement.

answerid, and myn grete awer sumdele esid be the lovely gracious shewing of
our good Lord — in which shewing I saw and understode ful sekirly that in every
2165 soule that shal be save is a godly wille that never assent to synne, ne never
shall; which wille is so good that it may never willen ylle, but evermore continuly
it will good and werkyth good in the syte of God. Therefore our Lord will we
knowen it in the feith and the beleve, and namly and truly, that we have all this
blissid will hole and safe in our Lord Jesus Christe. For that ilke kind that Hevyn
2170 shall be fulfillid with behovith nedes, of Gods rythfulhede, so to be knitt and
onyd to Him that therin were kept a substance which myte never, ne shuld, be
partid from Him, and that throw His owne good will in His endles forseing
purpos. And notwithstonding this rythfull knitting and this endles onyng, yet
the redemption and the ageyn byeng of mankynd is nedefull and spedefull in
2175 everything, as it is don for the same entent and to the same end that Holy
Church in our feith us techith.

For I saw that God began never to loven mankynd. For ryte the same that
mankynde shal ben in endles bliss fulfilland the joye of God as anempts His
werks, ryte so the same mankynd hath ben, in the forsyte of God, knowen and
2180 lovid from without begynnyng in His rytefull entent and be the endles assent of
the full accord of al the Trinite. The Mid-Person would be ground and hede of
this fair kinde, out of whom we be al cum, in whom we be all inclosid, into
whome we shall all wyndyn, in Him fynding our full Hevyn in everlestand joye be
the forseing purpos of all the blissid Trinite from without begynnyng. For er that
2185 He mad us, He lovid us; and whan we were made we lovid Hym; and this is a
love made of the kindly substantial goodnes of the Holy Gost, mytye in reson of
the myte of the myte of the Fadir, and wise in mend of the wisdam of the Son.
And thus is man soule made of God, and in the same poynte knitt to God.

And thus I understond that mannys soule is made of nought — that is to sey,
2190 it is made, but of nought that is made, as thus: Whan God shuld make mans
body, He tooke the slyppe of erth, which is a matter medlid and gaderid of all
bodily things, and therof He made mannys bodye. But to the makyng of manys
soule, He wold take ryte nought, but made it. And thus is the kynd made ryte-
fully onyd to the maker, which is substantial kynd onmade, that is God. And
2195 therefor it is that ther may, ne shall, be ryte nowte atwix God and mannys soule.
And in this endles love mans soule is kept hole as the matter of the revelations
menyth and shewith, in which endless love we be led and kept of God, and
never shall be lost. For He will we wetyn that our soule is a lif, which lif, of His

2163 awer, concern (see note 1779). **2174 ageyn byeng**, redemption. **2191 slyppe**, slime; **medlid and gaderid**, mingled and gathered.

goodnes and His grace, shall lestin in Hevyn without end, Him loveand, Him thank-
2200 and, Him praysand. And ryte the same we shall be withoute end, the same we were
tresurid in God, and hidde, knowen, and lovid from withoute begynnyng. Wherfore He will we wettyn that the noblest thing that ever He made is mankynd.
And the fullest substance and the heyest vertue is the blissid soule of Criste.
And furthermore, He will we wettyn that His derworthy soule was preciousley
2205 knitt to Him in the makeing, which knott is sotil, and so myty that it is onyd
into God, in which onyng it is made endlesly holy. Furthermore, He will we
wettyn that al the soules that shall be savid in Hevyn without end ar knitt and
onyd in this onyng, and made holy in this holyhede.

LIV

**We ought to enjoye that God wonyth in our soule and our soule in God, so that atwix
God and our soule is nothing, but as it were al God; and how feith is ground of al vertue in our soule be the Holy Gost. Fifty-fourth chapter.**

And for the grete endless love that God hath to al mankynde, He makith no
2210 departing in love betwix the blissid soule of Crist and the lest soule that shal be
savid. For it is full hesy to leven and to trowen that the wonyng of the blissid
soule of Criste is full hey in the glorious Godhede; and sothly, as I understond
in our Lord menyng, wher the blissid soule of Crist is, ther is the substans of al
the soules that shal be savid be Crist. Heyly owe we to enjoyen that God wonyth
2215 in our soule, and mekil more heyly owe enjoyen that our soule wonyth in God.
Our soule is made to be Gods wonyng place, and the wonyng place of the soule
is God, which is onmade. And hey understonding it is inwardly to sen and to
knowen that God, which is our maker, wonyth in our soule. And an heyer
understondyng it is inwardly to sen and to knowen our soule, that is made, wonyth
2220 in Gods substance, of which substance, God, we arn that we arn.
And I saw no difference atwix God and our substance, but as it were al God; and
yet myn understondyng toke that our substance is in God; that is to sey, that God
is God, and our substance is a creture in God. For the almyty truth of the Trinite
is our fader, for He made us and kepith us in Him. And the depe wisdam of the
2225 Trinite is our moder in whom we arn al beclosid. The hey goodnes of the Trinite
is our lord, and in Him we arn beclosid, and He in us. We arn beclosid in the

2205 sotil, subtle. **2210 departing**, division, separation. **2211 hesy**, easy; **trowen**, believe.
2214 owe, ought.

Fadir, and we arn beclosid in the Son, and we arn beclosid in the Holy Gost; and the Fader is beclosid in us, and the Son is beclosid in us, and the Holy Gost is beclosid in us — Almytyhede, Alwisdam, Al goodnes: on God, on Lord.

2230 And our feith is a vertue that comith of our kynd substance into our sensual soule be the Holy Gost in which all our vertuys comith to us, for without that no man may receive vertue. For it is not ell but a rythe understondyng with trew beleve and sekir troste of our beyng that we arn in God, and God in us, which we se not. And this vertue, with al other that God hat ordeynid to us command

2235 therin, werkith in us grete things. For Crists mercifull werking is in us, and we graciosly accordand to Him throw the gefts and the vertues of the Holy Gost. This werkyng makith that we arn Crists children and Cristen in liveing.

LV

Christ is our wey, ledand and presenting us to the Fader; and forwith as the soule is infusid in the body, mercy and grace werkyn. And how the Second Person toke our sensualite to deliver us from duble deth. Fifty-fifth chapter.

And thus Criste is our wey, us sekirly ledand in His lawes, and Criste in His body mytyly berith us up into Hevyn. For I saw that Crist, us al havand in Him

2240 that shal be savid be Him, worshipfully presentith His Fader in Hevyn with us; which present ful thankfully His Fader receivith and curtesly gevith it to His Son Jesus Criste, which geft and werkyng is joye to the Fader and bliss to the Son and likyng to the Holy Gost. And of althyng that to us longith, it is most likyng to our Lord that we enjoyen in this joy which is in the blisfull Trinite of

2245 our salvation. And this was sen in the ninth shewing, wher it spekith more of this matter.

And notwithstanding al our feling, wo or wele, God will we understond and feithyn that we arn more verily in Hevyn than in erth. Our feith cummith of the kynd love of our soule, and of the cler lyte of our reson, and of the stedfast mend

2250 which we have of God in our first makyng. And what tyme that our soule is inspirid into our body, in which we arn made sensual, as swithe mercy and grace begynyth to werkyng, haveing of us cure and keping with pite and love; in

---

2234 command, coming. **2239 berith**, carries. **2248 feithyn**, believe. **2251 we . . . sensual**, we are made a physical, living being; **as swithe**, just as quickly. **2252 cure**, care.

which werkyng the Holy Gost formyth in our feith hope that we shal cum agen up aboven to our substance, into the vertue of Criste, incresid and fulfillid throw

2255 the Holy Ghost. Thus I understond that the sensualite is groundid in kind, in mercy, and in grace, which ground abylith us to receive gefts that leden us to endles life. For I saw full sekirly that our substance is in God. And also I saw that in our sensualite, God is; for the selfe poynte that our soule is mad sensual, in the selfe poynt is the cite of God, ordeynid to Him from withouten begynnyng,

2260 in which se He commith and never shall remove it. For God is never out of the soule in which He wonen blisfully without end. And this was sen in the six-teenth shewing wher it seith, the place that Jesus takith in our soule, He shal never remov it. And all the gefts that God may geve to cretures, He hath geven to His Son, Jesus, for us, which gefts he, wonand in us, hath beclosid in Him into

2265 the time that we be waxen and growne — our soule with our body, and our body with our soule, neyther of hem takeing help of other, till we be browte up into stature as kynd werkyth. And than in the ground of kind, with werkyng of mercy, the Holy Gost graciously inspirith into us gifts ledand to endless life.

And thus was my understondyng led of God to sen in Him and to understonden,

2270 to weten and to knowen, that our soule is made trinite — like to the onmade blisfull Trinite, knowen and lovid fro without begynnyng, and in the makyng unyd to the Maker, as it is afornseid. This syte was full swete and mervelous to beholden, pesible and restfull, sekir and delectabil. And for the worshipfull onyng that was thus made of God betwix the soule and body, it behovith needs

2275 to ben that mankynd shal be restorid from duble deth, which restoring might never be into the time that the Second Person in the Trinite had takyn the lower party of mankynde to whom the heyest was onyd in the first makyng. And these two partes were in Criste, the heyer and the lower, which is but on soule. The heyer part was on in peace with God in full joy and bliss. The lower partie, which

2280 is sensualite, suffrid for the salvation of mankynd. And these two partes were seene and felt in the eighth shewing in which my body was fulfillid of feling and mynd of Crists passion and His deth. And ferthermore, with this was a sotil feling and privy inward syte of the hey parte that I was shewed in the same tyme, wher I myte not, for the mene profir, lokyn up onto Hevyn, and that was

2285 for that mytye beholdyng of the inward lif, which inward lif is that hey sub-stance, that pretious soule, which is endlesly enjoyand in the Godhede.

2256 abylith, enables. **2258 sensualite,** concrete and bodily existence (see note 2250-51). **2259 cite,** city. **2260 se,** see, official domain. **2282 sotil,** subtle. **2284 for the mene profir,** on the basis of the intermediary's suggestion.

LVI

It is esier to know God than our soule, for God is to us nerer than that, and therfore if we will have knowing of it, we must seke into God; and He will we desir to have knowledge of kynde, mercy, and grace. Fifty-sixth chapter.

And thuss I saw full sekirly that it is ridier to us to cum to the knowyng of God than to knowen our owne soule, for our soule is so deepe groundid in God and so endlesly tresurid that we may not cum to the knowing therof till we have
2290 first knowing of God which is the maker to whom it is onyd. But notwithstondyng, I saw that we have of fulhede to desiren wisely and treuly to knowen our owne soule, wherby we are lernid to sekyn it wher it is, and that is in God. And thus be gracious ledyng of the Holy Gost, we should knowen hem both in on. Whither and we be sterid to knowen God or our soule, they arn both good and trew. God
2295 is nerer to us than our owen soule, for He is ground in whom our soule stondith, and He is mene that kepith the substance and the sensualite to God so that thai shall never departyn.

For our soule sittith in God in very rest, and our soule stondith in God in very strength, and our soule is kindly rotid in God in endles love. And therfore
2300 if we wil have knowlidge of our soule and comenyng and daliance therwith, it behovith to sekyn into our Lord God in whom it is inclosid. And of this inclos I saw and understode more in the sixteenth shewing, as I shall sey. And anempts our substaunce and sensualite, it may rytely be clepid our soule, and that is be the onyng that it hath in God. The worshipfull cyte that our Lord Jesus sittith
2305 in, it is our sensualite, in which He is inclosid; and our kindly substance is beclosid in Jesus with the blissid soule of Criste sitting in rest in the Godhede.

And I saw full sekirly that it behovith neds to be that we shuld ben in longyng and in penance into the time that we be led so depe into God that we verily and trewly knowen our own soule. And sothly I saw that into this hey depenes, our
2310 good Lord Himselfe ledith us in the same love that He made us, and in the same love that He bowte us be mercy and grace throw vertue of His blissid passion. And notwithstondyng al this, we may never come to full knowyng of God till we know first clerely our owne soule. For into the tyme that it is in the

2287 ridier to us, more easy for us. **2291 of fulhede,** for complete [understanding]. **2293–94 Whither and,** Whether if. **2296 mene,** the medium. **2299 rotid,** rooted. **2300 comenyng and daliance,** mutuality and communion, i.e., familiar conversation. **2303 clepid,** called, designated. **2304 cyte,** city.

2315 full myts we may not be al ful holy, and that is that our sensualite be the vertue of Crists passion be browte up to the substance, with al the profitts of our tribulation that our Lord shall make us to gettyn be mercy and grace. I had in partie touching; and it is grounded in kynde. That is to sey, our reson is groundid in God which is substantial heyhede. Of this substantial kindhede mercy and grace springith and spredith into us, werking al things in fulfilling of our joy. These arn

2320 our grounds in which we have our incres and our fulfilling. For in kind we have our life and our beyng; and in mercy and grace we have our incres and our fulfilling. These be three propertes in on goodnes, and wher on werkith, all werkyn in the things which be now longyng to us. God will we onderstond, desirand of al our hert and al our strength to have knowing of hem more and mor into the time

2325 that we ben fulfillid. For fully to knowen hem and clerely to sen hem is not ell but endless joy and bliss that we shall have in Hevyn, which God will they ben begun here in knowing of His love. For only be our reson we may not profitteyn, but if we have verily therwith mynd and love; ne only in our kindly ground that we have in God we may not be savid, but if we have connyng of the same

2330 ground, mercy, and grace. For of these three werkynges altogeder we receive all our goodnes, of the which the first arn goods of kynd. For in our first makyng God gaf us as ful goods and also greter godes as we myte receivin only in our spirite. But His forseing purpos in His endles wisdam wold that we wern duble.

LVII

In our substance we aren full; in our sensualite we faylyn, which God will restore be mercy and grace. And how our kinde which is the heyer part is knitt to God in the makyng, and God, Jesus, is knitt to our kind in the lower part in our flesh takyng. And of feith spryngyn other vertues; and Mary is our Moder. Fifty-seventh chapter.

2335 And anempts our substance, He made us nobil and so rich that evermore we werkyn His will and His worship. There I say "we," it menith man that shall be

---

2313–15 **For . . . substance,** For until our soul has its full power, we cannot be entirely holy, and that is [can happen then] because our psycho-physical being by the power of Christ's passion is [then] brought up to the substance. **2318 heyhede,** elevation; **kindhede,** natural placement. See note 2318. **2320 incres,** increase. **2329 connyng of,** knowledge of. **233133 For. . . spirite,** For in our first creation, God gave us fully all we need [in this life], and also greater goods such as we may receive only in our spirit. **2335 There,** Where.

savid. For sothly I saw that we arn that He lovith and don that He lekyth lestingly withouten ony stynting. And of the gret riches and of the hey noble, vertues be mesur come to our soule what tyme it is knitt to our body, in which knitting we arn made sensual. And thus in our substance we arn full and in our
2340 sensualite we faylyn, which faylyng God will restore and fulfill be werkyng mercy and grace plenteously flowand into us of His owne kynd godhede. And thus His kinde godhede makith that mercy and grace werkyn in us, and the kind godhede that we have of Him abilith us to receive the werking of mercy and grace.

I saw that our kind is in God hole, in which He makyth diverssetis flowand out
2345 of Him to werkyn His will, whom kind kepith, and mercy and grace restorith and fulfillith. And of these non shall perishen. For our kind which is the heyer part is knitt to God in the makyng, and God is knitt to our kinde, which is the lower partie in our flesh takyng, and thus in Crist our two kinds are onyd. For the Trinite is comprehendid in Criste in whome our heyer partie is groundid and
2350 rotid; and our lower partie, the Second Person hath taken, which kynd first to Him was adyte. For I saw full sekirly that all the workes that God hath done, or ever shall, wer ful knowen to Him and afornseen from without begynning. And for love He made mankynd, and for the same love Himself wold be man.

The next good that we receive is our feith, in which our profittyng begynnyth;
2355 and it commith of the hey riches of our kinde substance into our sensual soule. And it is groundid in us, and we in that, throw the kynde goodness of God be the werking of mercy and grace; and therof commen al other goods be which we arn led and savid. For the commandements of God commen therein, in which we owe to have two manner of understondyng, which are His bidding, to love
2360 them and to kepyn. That other is that we owe to knowen His forbyddings, to haten and to refusen. For in these two is all our werkyn comprehendid. Also in our feith commen the seven sacraments, ech folowing other in order as God hath ordeyned hem to us, and al manner of vertues. For the same vertues that we have receivid of our substance, gevyn to us in kinde be the goodness of God,
2365 the same vertues be the werkyng of mercy arn geven to us in grace throw the Holy Gost renued, which vertues and gyfts are tresurd to us in Jesus Christ. For in that ilk tyme that God knitted Him to our body in the Maydens womb, He toke our sensual soule; in which takyng, He us al haveyng beclosid in Him, He onyd it to our substance, in which onyng He was perfect man. For Criste, havyng
2370 knitt in Him ilk man that shall be savid, is perfit man.

Thus our Lady is our Moder in whome we are all beclosid and of hir borne in

---

2344 diverssetis, diversity. **2351 adyte**, assigned. **2366 renued**, renewed.

Christe, for she that is moder of our Savior, is moder of all that shall be savid in our Savior. And our Savior is our very moder in whom we be endlesly borne and never shall come out of Him. Plenteously and fully and swetely was this
2375 shewid. And it is spoken of in the first wher he seith we arn all in Him beclosid and He is beclosid in us, and that is spoken of in the sixteenth shewing wher it seith He sittith in our soule. For it is His likeyng to reygne in our understonding blisfully, and sitten in our soule restfully, and to wonen in our soule endlesly, us al werkeng into Hym, in which werkyng He will we ben His helpers, gevyng to
2380 Him al our entendyng, lerand His loris, kepyng His lawes, desirand that al be done that He doith, truely trosting in Hym. For sothly I saw that our substance is in God.

LVIII

God was never displesid with His chosin wif; and of three properties in the Trinite, faderhede, Moderhede, and lordhede; and how our substance is in every person, but our sensualite is in Criste alone. Fifty-eighth chapter.

God, the blisful Trinite which is everlestand beyng, ryte as He is endless from without begynning, ryte so it was in His purpose endles to maken mankynd, which
2385 fair kynd first was adyte to His owen Son, the Second Person. And whan He wold, be full accord of all the Trinite, He made us all at onys; and in our makyng He knitt us and onyd us to Hymself, be which onyng we arn kept as clene and as noble as we were made. Be the vertue of the ilke pretious onyng we loven our Maker and liken Him, praysen Him and thankyng Him and endlesly
2390 enjoyen in Him. And this is the werke which is wrought continuly in every soule that shal be save, which is the godly will afornsaid. And thus in our makeyng God almigty is our kindely fader, and God alwisdam is our kindly Moder, with the love and the goodnes of the Holy Gost, which is al one God, on Lord. And in the knittyng and in the onyng He is our very trewe spouse, and we His lovid
2395 wif and His fair maiden with which wif He is never displesid. For He seith, *I love the, and thou lovist me, and our love shal never be departid on to.*
 I beheld the werking of all the blissid Trinite, in which beholdyng I saw and understode these three properties: the properte of the faderhede, the properte of the moderhede, and the properte of the lordhede in one God. In our Fader

2380 lerand His loris, learning His lore. **2386 at onys**, at once.

2400 Almyty we have our keping and our bliss as anemts our kyndly substance, which is to us be our makyng without begynnyng. And in the Second Person, in witt and wisdam, we have our keping as anempts our sensualite, our restoryng, and our savyng. For He is our Moder, brother, and savior. And in our good Lord the Holy Gost we have our rewarding and our yeldyng for our lifyng and our

2405 travel; and endless overpassing all that we desiren, in His mervelous curtesy, of His hey plentiuous grace. For al our life is in thre. In the first we have our beyng, and in the second we have our encresyng, and in the thrid we hav our fulfilling. The first is kinde, the second is mercy, the thred is grace. For the first, I saw and understod that the hey myte of the Trinite is our fader, and the

2410 depe wisdam of the Trinite is our Moder, and the grete love of the Trinite is our Lord; and al this have we in kynd and in our substantial makyng.

 And ferthermore I saw that the Second Person, which is our Moder substantial, that same derworthy person is become our Moder sensual. For we arn duble of Gods makyng, that is to say, substantiall and sensual. Our substance is

2415 the heyer parte, which we have in our fader God Almyty. And the Second Person of the Trinite is our Moder in kynde in our substantiall makeyng, in whome we arn groundid and rotid, and He is our Moder in mercy in our sensualite, takyng flesh. And thus our Moder is to us dyvers manner werkyng, in whom our parties are kepid ondepartid. For in our Moder Criste we profitten and encresin, and in

2420 mercy He reformith us and restorith; and, be the vertue of His passion and His deth and uprisyng, onyth us to our substance. Thus werkith our Moder in mercy to all His children which arn to Him buxum and obedient.

 And grace werkyth with mercy, and namely in two propertes, as it was shewid, which werkyng longyth to the thred person, the Holy Gost. He werkith rewardyng

2425 and gefyng. Rewardyng is large gevyng of trewth that the Lord doth to hym that hath travellid; and gevyng is a curtes workyng which He doith, frely of grace fulfill, and overpassand al that is deservid of cretures. Thus in our fader God almyty we have our beyng; and in our Moder of mercy we have our reformyng and restoryng in whome our partes are onyd and all made perfitt man; and be

2430 yeldyng and gevyng in grace of the Holy Gost, we arn fulfillid. And our substance is our fader, God Almyty, and our substance is our Moder, God alwisdamm, and our substance is in our Lord the Holy Gost, God al goodnes. For our substance is hole in ilke person of the Trinite which is on God. And our sensualite is only in the second person, Crist Jesu in whom is the Fader and the

2435 Holy Gost; and in Him and be Him we arn mytyly taken out of Helle and out of

2404 yeldyng, repayment, harvest. **2419 kepid ondepartid**, kept together. **2424 thred**, third. **2429 perfitt**, perfect.

the wretchidnes in erth and worshipfully browte up into Hevyn, and blisfully onyd to our substance, incresid in riches and noblith be al the vertue of Criste, and be the grace and werkyng of the Holy Gost.

LIX

Wickednes is turnyd to bliss be mercy and grace in the chosyn, for the properte of God is to do good ageyn ille be Jesus our Moder in kynd grace; and the heyest soule in vertue is mekest, of which ground we have other vertues. Fifty-ninth chapter.

2440

2445

And all this bliss we have be mercy and grace, which manner of bliss we myte never had ne knowen, but if that propertes of goodness which is God had ben contraried, wherby we have this bliss. For wickednes hath ben suffrid to rysen contrarye to the goodnes, and the goodnes of mercy and grace contraried ageyn the wickidnes, and turnyd al to goodness and to worship to al these that shal be savid. For it is the properte in God which doith good agen evil. Thus, Jesus Criste, that doith good agen evill, is our very Moder. We have our beyng of Him wher the ground of moderhed begynnyth, with al the swete kepyng of love that endlessly folowith.

As veryly as God is our fader, as verily God is our Moder; and that shewid He in all, and namely in these swete words where He seith, *I it am.* That is to seyen,
2450 *I it am, the myte and the goodnes of the faderhed. I it am, the wisdam of the Moderhede. I it am, the lyte and the grace that is al blissid love. I it am, the Trinite; I it am, the Unite. I am the sovereyne goodness of all manner of thyngs. I am that makyth the to loven. I am that makyth the to longen. I it am, the endles fulfilling of al trew desires.* For then the soule is heyest, noblist, and worthyest
2455 when it is lowest, mekest, and myldhest; and of this substantial ground, we have al our vertues and our sensualite be geft of kynd and be helpyng and spedyng of mercy and grace, without the which we may not profitten. Our hey fader, God Almyty, which is beyng, He knew us and lovid us fro aforn any tyme; of which knoweing, in His mervelous depe charite be the forseing endless councel of all the
2460 blissid Trinite, He wold that the Second Person shuld becom our Moder, our brother, and our savior. Wherof it folowith that as verily as God is our fader, as verily God is our Moder. Our fader wyllyth, our Moder werkyth, our good Lord the Holy Gost confirmith. And therfore it longyth to us to loven our God in whom we have our being, Him reverently thankyng and praiseyng of our makyng,
2465 mytily prayeing to our Moder of mercy and pite, and to our Lord the Holy Gost of helpe and grace.

For in these three is all our life — kynde, mercy, and grace; whereof we have mekehede, myldhede, patiens, and pite, and hatyng of synne and wickidnes, for it longith properly to vertues to haten synne and wickidness. And thus is Jesus our
2470   very Moder in kynde, of our first makyng; and He is our very Moder in grace, be takyng of our kynde made. All the fair werkyng and all the swete kindly office of dereworthy moderhede is impropried to the Second Person, for in Him we have this godly will hole and save without ende, both in kinde and in grace, of His owne proper goodnes. I understode three manner of beholdyng of Moder-
2475   hede in God. The first is groundid of our kinde makeying. The second is taken of our kinde, and there begynnyth the Moderhede of grace. The thrid is Moder-hede of werkyng, and therin is a forthspreadyng, be the same grace, of length, and bredth, and of heyth, and of depenes withouten end — and al His own luf.

LX

How we be bowte ageyn and forthspred be mercy and grace of our swete, kynde, and ever lovyng Moder Jesus; and of the propertes of Moderhede. But Jesus is our very Moder, not fedyng us with mylke but with Himselfe, opening His syde onto us and chalengyng al our love. Sixtieth chapter.

But now behovyth to sey a litil mor of this forthspredyng, as I understond in
2480   the menyng of our Lord, how that we be bowte agen be the Moderhede of mercy and grace into our kyndly stede, wher that we were made be the Moderhede of kynd love; which kynd love, it never levyth us. Our kynd Moder, our gracious Moder — for He wold al holy become our Moder in al thyng — He toke the ground of His werke full low and ful myldely in the maydens womb. And that He
2485   shewid in the first where he browte that meke mayde aforn the eye of myn understondyng in the simple statur as she was whan she conceivid.

That is to sey, our hey God is sovereyn wisdom of all. In this low place, He rayhid Him and dyte Him ful redy in our pore flesh, Himselfe to don the service and the office of Moderhede in all thyng. The Moders service is nerest, redyest,
2490   and sekirest, for it is most of trueth. This office ne myte ne couthe ne never non don to the full but He alone. We wetyn that all our Moders beryng is us to peyne and to deyeng. And what is that but our very Moder Jesus? He, al love,

2472 **impropried to**, embodied in. 2477 **forthspreadyng**, amplification. 2488 **rayhid Him and dyte Him**, arrayed and prepared Himself.

beryth us to joye and to endles lyving. Blissid mot He be. Thus He susteynith us within Himselfe in love and traveled into the full tyme that He wold suffre the
2495 sharpist throwes and the grevousest peynes that ever were or ever shall be, and dyed at the last. And whan He had don, and so born us to bliss, yet myte not al this makyn aseth to His mervelous love, and that shewid He in these hey over-passing wordes of love: *If I myte suffre more, I wold suffre more.* He myte no more dyen, but He wold not stynten of werkyng. Wherfore than Him behovyth
2500 to fedyn us, for the dereworthy love of moderhede hath made Him dettor to us. The Moder may geven hir child soken her mylke, but our pretious Moder Jesus, He may fedyn us with Himselfe, and doith full curtesly and full tenderly with the blissid sacrament that is pretious fode of very lif.

And with al the swete sacraments He susteynith us ful mercifully and graciously.
2505 And so ment He in this blissid word wher that He seid, *I it am that Holy Church prechith the and techith the.* That is to sey, all the helth and lif of sacraments, al the vertue and grace of my word, all that godness that is ordeynid in Holy Church for the, I it am. The moder may leyn the child tenderly to her brest, but our tender Moder Jesus, He may homely leden us into His blissid brest be His
2510 swete open syde and shewyn therin party of the Godhede and the joyes of Hevyn with gostly sekirnes of endless bliss. And that He shewid in the tenth, gevyng the same understondyng in this swete word wher He seith, *Lo, how I lovid the,* beholdand into His syde, enjoyand.

This fair, lovely word *Modir*, it is so swete and so kynd of the self that it may
2515 ne verily be seid of none but of Him and to hir that is very Moder of Hym and of all. To the properte of Moderhede longyth kinde love, wisdam, and knowing, and it is good; for thow it be so that our bodily forthbrynging be but litil, low, and simple in regard of our gostly forthbringing, yet it is He that doth it in the creatures be whom that it is done. The kynde, Loveand Moder that wote and know-
2520 ith the nede of hir child, she kepith it ful tenderly as the kind and condition of moderhede will. And as it wexith in age, she chongith hir werking but not hir love. And whan it is waxen of more age, she suffrid that it be bristinid in brekyng downe of vices to makyn the child to receivyn virtues and graces. This werkyng with al that be fair and good, our Lord doith it in hem be whom it is done. Thus
2525 He is our Moder in kynde be the werkyng of grace in the lower parte for love of the heyer parte, and He will that we know it. For He will have al our love festynyd to Him. And in this I saw that all our dett that we owen, be Gods biddyng, be faderhede and Moderhede, for Gods faderhede and Moderhede is

2495 throwes, times, torments. **2497 makyn aseth to**, fully satisfy. **2522 bristinid**, broken, beaten severely.

fulfillid in trew lovyng of God, which blissid love Christ werkyth in us; and this
2530 was shewid in all, and namly in the hey plentiuous words wher He seith, *I it am
that thou lovest.*

LXI

**Jesus usith more tenderness in our gostly bringing forth; thow He suffrith us to fallyn
in knowing of our wretchidness, He hastily resysith us, not brekyng His love for our
trespass, for He may not suffre His Child to perish. For He will that we have the properte of a Child fleing to Him alway in our necessite. Sixty-first chapter.**

And in our gostly forthbringyng, He usith mor tenderness of keping without
ony likenes, be as mech as our soule is of more price in His syte. He kyndelyth
our understondyng, He directith our weys, He esith our consciens, He comfortith
2535 our soule, He lightith our herte, and gevith us in parte knowyng and lovyng in
His blisful Godhede, with gracious mynd in His swete Manhede and His blissid
passion, with curtes mervelyng in His hey, overpassyng goodnes, and makith us
to loven al that He loveth for His love, and to bend payd with Him and all His
werkes. And we fallen, hastily He reysith us be His lovely clepyng and gracious
2540 touchyng; and whan we be thus strenthyd be His swete werkyng, than we wilfully
chesyn Him, be His swete grace, to be His servants and His lovers lestingly
without end.

And after this He suffrith sum of us to fallen more hard and more grevously
than ever we diden afore, as us thynkyth. And than wene we, that be not al wyse,
2545 that al wer nowte that we have begun; but it is no so. For it nedith us to fallen,
and it nedith us to sen it, for if we felle nowte, we should not knowen how febil
and how wretchid we arn of ourselfe. Ne also we shuld not fulsomely so knowen
the mervelous love of our maker. For we shal sen verily in Hevyn withouten end
that we have grevously synned in this life, and notwithstondyng this, we shal sen
2550 that we were never hurt in His love, ne were never the less of price in His syte.
And be the assay of this fallyng we shall have an hey, mervelous knoweing of
love in God without end. For herd and mervelous is that love which may nowte,
ne will not, be brokin for trespas. And this is one understonding of profite.
Another is the lownes and mekenes that we shal gettyn be the syte of our fal-
2555 lyng. For therby we shal heyly ben raysid in Hevyn, to which reysing we might
never a come withoute that mekeness; and therfore it nedyth us to sen it, and if

2538 bend payd, be satisfied (or, yield, pleased). **2539 And**, If. **2551 assay**, trial.

we sen it not, thow we fellyn, it shuld not profitt us. And commenly, first we fallen, and syth we sen it, and both of the mercy of God. The Moder may suffre the child to fallen sumtyme, and be disesid in dyvers manners for the owen profitt, but she may never suffre that ony maner of peril cum to the child, for love. And thow our erthly moder may suffre hir Child to perishen, our hevynly Moder, Jesus, may not suffre us that arn His children to perishen. For He is almyty, all wisdom, and al love, and so is non but He. Blissid mot He ben.

But oftentymes whan our fallyn and our wretchidnes is shewid us, we arn so sore adred and so gretly ashamid of ourselfe, that onethys we wettyn where that we may holden us. But than will not our curtes Moder that we fle awey, for Him wer nothing lother. But He will than that we usen the condition of a child, for whan it is disesid or dred, it rennith hastely to the Moder for helpe with al the myte. So wil He that we don as a meke child, seyand thus: "My kind Moder, my gracious Moder, my dereworthy Moder, have mercy on me. I have made myselfe foul and onlike to the, and I ne may ne can amenden it but with prive helpe and grace." And if we fele us not than esyd al swithe, be we sekir that He usith the condition of a wise moder. For if He sen that it be more profitt to us to morne and to wepen, He suffrith it, with ruth and pite, into the best tyme, for love. And He will than that we usen the propertie of a child that evermor kindly trosteth to the love of the Moder in wele and in wo.

And He will that we taken us mytyly to the feith of Holy Church, and fyndyn there our dereworthy Moder in solace of trew understonding with al the blissid common. For on singler person may oftentymes be broken, as it semyth to selfe, but the hole body of Holy Church was never broken, ne never shall, withouten end. And therfore a sekir thing it is, a good and a gracious, to willen mekely and mytyly ben susteynd and onyd to our Moder, Holy Church, that is Crist Jesus. For the foode of mercy that is His dereworthy blood and pretious water is plentious to make us faire and clene. The blissid wound of our Savior ben open and enjoyen to helyn us. The swete gracious hands of our Moder be redy and diligently aboute us. For He in al this werkyng usith the office of a kinde nurse, and hath not all to don but to entendyn abouten the salvation of hir Child. It is His office to saven us. It is His worship to don it, and it is His will we knowen it, for He will we loven Him swetely and trosten in Him mekely and mytyly. And this shewid He in these gracious words: *I kepe the ful sekirly.*

2572 **al swithe**, at once. 2578–79 **blissid comon**, blessed community. 2587 **not . . . Child**, nothing to do at all but see about the salvation of her child.

LXII

The love of God suffrith never His chosen to lose tyme, for all their troble is turnyd into endless joye; and how we arn al bownden to God for kindness and for grace. For every kind is in man, and us nedyth not to seke out to know sondry kindes, but to Holy Church. Sixty-second chapter.

For in that tyme He shewid our frelte and our fallyngs, our brekyngs and our nowtyngs, our dispits and our outcastings, and all our wo so ferforth as methowte it myght fallen in this life. And therwith He shewid His blissid myte, His blissid wisdam, His blissid love, that He kepyth us in this tyme as tenderly 2595 and as swetely to His worship and as sekirly to our salvation, as He doith whan we are in most solace and comfort. And therto He resysith us gostly and heyly in Hevyn, and turnith it al to His worship and to our joye withoute end. For His love suffrith us never to lose tyme. And all this is of the kind goodnes of God be the werkyng of grace.

2600 God is kynde in His being; that is to sey, that goodnes that is kind, it is God. He is the ground, He is the substance, He is the same thing that is kindhede; and He is very fader and very Moder of kinde; and all kindes that He hath made to flowen out of Him to werkyn His will, it shall be restorid and browte ageyn into Him be the salvation of man throw the werking of grace.

2605 For of all kyndes that He hath set in dyvers creatures be parte, in man is all the hole — in fulhede and in vertue, in fairhede and in goodhede, in rialtie and nobley, in al manner of solemnite of pretioushede and worshipp. Here may we sen that we arn al bound to God for kinde, and we arn al bound to God for grace. Here may we sen us nedith not gretly to seken fer out to knowen sundry 2610 kindes, but to Holy Church, into our Moder brest, that is to sey, into our owen soule wher our Lord wonnyth; and ther shall we fynde all; now, in feith and in understondyng, and after, verily in Himselfe, clerely, in bliss. But no man ne woman take this singler to himselfe, for it is not so; it is general. For it is our pretious Criste, and to Him was this fair kind dyte for the worship and noblyth 2615 of mannys makyng and for the joye and the bliss of mannys salvation ryte as He saw, wiste, and knew from without begynnyng.

2592 **dispits**, humiliations. 2606 **rialtie**, royalty.

LXIII

Synne is more peynfull than Hell, and vile, and hurting kinde; but grace savith kinde and destroyith synne. The children of Jesus be not yet all borne, which pass not the stature of childhood livying in febilnes till thei come to Hevyn wher joys arn ever new begynnand without end. Sixty-third chapter.

Here may we sen that we have verily of kinde to haten synne, and we have verily of grace to haten synne. For kinde is al good and faire in the selfe; and grace was sent out to saven kind and destroyen synne, and bryngen ageyn fair
2620 kinde to the blissid poynt fro whens it came, that is God, with mor noble and worshipp be the vertuous werkeyng of grace. For it shal be sen afor God of al His holy in joye without end that kind hath ben assayed in the fire of tribulation, and therin founden no lak, no defaut. Thus is kind and grace of one accord, for grace is God, as kind is God. He is two in manner werkyng, and one
2625 in love, and neyther of hem werkyth without other, non be departid.

And whan we be mercy of God and with His helpe accorden us to kynde and grace, we shall seen verily that synne is very viler and peynfuller than Helle; without likenes, for it is contrarious to our fair kinde. For as sothly as synne is onclene, as sothly is it onkinde, and thus an horrible thing to sen to the lovid
2630 soule that wold be al faire and shynand in the syte of God, as kinde and grace techyth. But be we not adred of this, but inasmuch as drede may spede us; but mekely make we our mone to our dereworthy Moder, and He shal al besprinkle us in His precious blode, and make our soule ful soft and ful myld, and hele us ful faire be proces of tyme, ryte as it is most worship to Him and joy to us with-
2635 out end. And of this swete, fair werkyng He shall never cesyn ne stintin till all His derworthy children be born and forth browte, and that shewid He wher He shewid understonding of gostly threst, that is, the lovelongyng that shal lestin till domys day.

Thus in very Moder Jesus our life is groundid in the forseing wisdam of Himselfe
2640 from without begynnyng, with the hey myte of the Fader and the hey, sovereyn goodnes of the Holy Gost. And in the takyng of our kinde, He quicknid us; in his blissid deying upon the Cross, He bare us to endless life; and fro that time and now, and ever shall onto domysday, He fedith us and fordreth us, and ryte as that hey sovereign kindness of Moderhede and as kindly nede of childhede askith.
2645 Faire and swete is our hevenly Moder in the syte of our soule; precious and lovely arn the gracious children in the syte of our hevinly moder, with myldhede

2628 **sothly,** truly. 2630 **shynand,** shining. 2632 **mone,** lament. 2643 **fordreth,** fosters, helps.

and mekeness and all the fair vertues that long to children in kynde. For kindly the Child dispeirith not of the Moder love; kindly the Child presumith not of the selfe; kindly the Child lovith the Moder, and ilke on of the other. These arn

2650 the fair vertues, with all other that ben like, wherwith our hevenly Moder is servid and plesyd.

And I understode non heyer stature in this life than childhode in febilness and fayleing of myte and of witte into the tyme that our gracious Moder hath browte us up to our Faders bliss. And than shall it verily be made knowen to us

2655 His menyng in these swete words wher He seith, *Al shall be wele, and thou shalt sen thyselfe that al maner thyng shal ben wele.* And than shall the bliss of our Moder in Criste be new to begynnen in the joyes of our God, which new begynnyng shal lesten without end, new begynnand. Thus I understode that al His blissid children which ben comen out of Him be kinde shall be bowte ageyn into

2660 Him be grace.

LXIV

The fifteenth Revelation is as it shewid etc. The absense of God in this lif is our ful gret peyne, besyde other travel, but we shal sodenly be taken fro all peyne, having Jesus to our Moder; and our patient abyding is gretly plesyng to God. And God wil we take our disese lightly, for love, thinkand us alwey at the poynte to be delivirid. Sixty-fourth chapter.

Aforn this tyme I had gret longyng and desire of Goddis gifte to be deliverid of this world and of this lif. For oftentimes I beheld the wo that is here, and the wele and the bliss that is beyng there. And if ther had ben no peyn in this lif but the absens of our Lord, methowte it was sumtime mor than I myte baren, and

2665 this made me to morn and besyly to longen. And also of myn owen wretchidnes, slawth, and wekehede, that me lekid not to leveyn and to travelyn as me fel to don. And to all this our curtes Lord answerid for comfort and patiens, and said these words: *Sodenly thou shal be taken fro al thy peyne, fro al thi sekeness, fro al thi disese, and fro al thi wo. And thou shalt commen up aboven, and thou shalt have*

2670 *me to thi mede. And thou shal be fulfillid of love and of bliss. And thou shal never have no maner of peyne, no manner of mislekyn, no wanting of will, but ever joye and bliss withouten ende. What shuld it than agrevyn the to suffre a while sen that it is my will and my worship?* And in this word, *Sodenly thou shal be taken,* I saw

2663 beyng, being, existence.

2675 that God rewardith man of the patiens that he hath in abyding Gods will and of his tyme, and that man lengith his patiens over the tyme of his living.

For onknowing of his tyme of passing, that is a gret profitt. For if a man knew his time, he shuld not have patience over that tyme. And as God will while the soule is in the body, it semyt to the selfe that it is ever at the poynt to be takyn. For al this life and this langor that we have here is but a poynte, and 2680 whan we arn taken sodenly out of peyn into bliss, than peyn shall be nowte.

And in this tyme I saw a body lyand on the erth, which body shewid hevy and oggley withoute shappe and forme, as it were a bolned quave of styngand myre; and sodenly out of this body sprang a ful fair creature, a little childe, ful shapen and formid, swyft and lively, whiter than lilly, which sharpely glode up on to Hevyn. 2685 And the bolnehede of the body betokenith gret wretchidnes of our dedly flesh, and the littlehede of the child betokenith the clenes of purity in the soule. And I thowte: With this body belevith no fairehede of this child, no on this child dwellith no foulehede of this body. It is ful blisfull, man to be taken fro peyne, mor than peyne to be taken fro man; for if peyn be taken fro us it may commen 2690 agen. Therfore it is a severen comfort and blissfull beholdyng in a lovand soule yf we shal be taken fro peyne. For in this behest I saw a mervelous compassion that our Lord hath in us for our wo and a curtes behoting of clene deliverance.

For He will that we be comforted in the overpassing, and that He shewid in these words: *And thou shalt come up aboven, and thou shal have me to thi mede,* 2695 *and thou shall be fullfillid of joye and bliss.* It is God will that we setten the poynte of our thowte in this blisfull beholdyng as often as we may, and as long tyme kepen us therin with His grace. For this is a blissid contemplation to the soule that is led of God and full mekil to His worship for the time that it lestith. And we falyn ageyn to our hevynis and gostly blyndhede, and felyng of 2700 peyens, gostly and bodily, be our frelty, it is God will that we knowen that He hath not forgetten us, and so menith He in thes words and seith for comfort: *And thou shall never more have peyne, no manner sekenes, no maner mislekyng, non wanting of will but over joy and bliss withouten ende. What shuld it than agrevyn the to suffre a while, seing it is my will and my worshippe?* It is God will 2705 we taken His behests and His comfortings as largely and as mytyly as we may taken hem. And also He will that we taken our abiding and our diseses as lytely as we may taken hem, and set hem at nowte. For the lyter we taken hem, and the less price we setten at hem for love, the less peyne shall we have in the feling of hem, and the more thanke and mede shal we have for hem.

2678 **semyt**, seems. 2682 **oggley**, ugly; **bolned quave of styngand myre**, swollen heaving of stinking mire. 2685 **bolnehede**, swelling. 2687 **belevith**, stays, is left. 2690 **severen**, sovereign, the greatest possible. 2691 **behest**, promise. 2692 **behoting**, promise. 2705 **behests**, promises.

LXV

He that chesith God for love with reverent mekeness is sekir to be savid, which reverent mekenes seith the Lord mervelous grete and the selfe mervelous litil. And it is God will we drede nothing but Him, for the power of our enemy is taken in our freinds hand. And therfore al that God doith shall be gret likyng to us. Sixty-fifth chapter.

2710   And thus I understode that what man or woman wilfully chesith God in this life for love, he may be sekir that he is lovid without end, which endless love werkith in him that grace. For He will that we kepe this trosty, that we be all sekir in hope, in hope of the bliss of Hevyn whil we arn here, as we shall be in sekirnes whan we arn there. And ever the more likyng and joy that we taken in 2715   this sekirness with reverens and mekenes, the better likyth Him, as it was shewid.

This reverens that I mene is a holy, curtes drede of our Lord, to which mekeness is knitt. And that is, that a creture seith the Lord mervelous grete, and the selfe mervelous litil. For these vertues arn had endlesly to the lovid of God, and it mon now ben sen and felt in mesure be the gracious presence of our Lord whan 2720   it is; which presens in althing is most desirid, for it werkith mervelous sekirness in trew feith and sekir hope be gretness of charite, in drede that is swete and delectable. It is God will that I se myselfe as mekil bounden to Him in love, as if He had don for me al that He hath don. And thus should every soule thinkyn in reward of his lover. That is to seyn, the charite of God makyth in us such a 2725   unite that whan it is trewly seen, no man can parten himselfe fro other. And thus oweth our soule to thinken that God hath don for him al that He hath don; and this shewith He to maken us to loven Him and nowte drede but Him.

For it is His will that we wetyn that al the myte of our enemy is token into our frends hand, and therfore the soule that wott sekirly this, he shall not dredyn but 2730   Him that he lovith. All our dreds He setteth among passions and bodely sekenes and imaginations; and therfore thow we be in so mech payne, wo, and disese that us thinkith we can thynke ryte nowte but that we arn in or that we felyn, as sone as we may, pass we lytely over and sett we it at nowte. And why? For God will we knowen; if we knowen Him, and loven Him, and reverently dredyn Him, 2735   we shall have peas and ben in great rest, and it shall be great lykyng to us, all that He doith. And this shewid our Lord in these words: *What shuld it than agrevyn the to suffre a while, sith it is my will and my worshippe?*

Now have I told you of fifteen Revelations, as God vouchsafe to ministren

2712 trosty, in trust, without doubt. **2718 had . . . lovid of God,** possessed infinitely by those whom God loves. **2719 mon,** may.

131

2740 hem to mynd, renewid by lyghtings and tuchyngs, I hope of the same spirite that shewid hem all. Of which fifteen shewings, the first beganne erly on the morne aboute the howre of fowre, and it lestid, shewing be process ful faire and sekirly ich folowand other, till it was none of the day overpassid.

LXVI

The sixteenth Revelation etc. And it is conclusion and confirmation to all fifteen. And of hir frelty and morning in disese and lyte speking after the gret comfort of Jesus, seying she had ravid; which, being hir gret sekeness, I suppose was but venial synne. But yet the Devil after that had gret power to vexin hir ner to deth. Sixty-sixth chapter.

And after this the good Lord shewid the sixteen on the night folowing, as I shall seyn after; which sixteen was conclusion and confirmation to all fifteen.
2745 But first me behovith to tellen you as anempt my febilnes, wretchidnes, and blindness. I have seid in the begynnyng, "And in this al my peine was sodenly taken from me," of which peyne I had no greife ne disese, as long as the fifteen shewings lestid folowand. And at the end al was close, and I saw no more. And sone I felt that I shuld liven and langiren, and anon my sekenes cam agen, first
2750 in my hede with a sound and a dynne; and sodenly all my body was fulfillid with sekeness like as it was aforn, and I was as baren and as drye as I never had comfort but litil. And as a wretch I moned and hevyed for felyng of my bodily peynes and for fayling of comfort, gostly and bodily.
Than cam a religious person to me and askid me how I ferid. I seyd I had ravid
2755 today, and he leuhe loud and inderly. And I seyd, "The cross that stod afor my face, methowte it blode fast." And with this word, the person that I spake to waxid al sad and mervelid, and anon I was sor ashamid and astonyed for my recleshede. And I thowte, this man takith sadly the lest word that I myte seyen, that sawe no mor therof; and whan I saw that he toke it sadly and with so gret
2760 reverens, I wepid, ful gretly ashamid, and wold have ben shrevyn. But at that tyme I cowde tell it no preist. For I thowte, how should a preist levyn me? I leve not our Lord God. This I levid sothfastly for the tyme that I saw Him, and so was than my will and my menyng ever for done without end, but as a fole, I let it passyn fro my mynd. A, lo I, wretch, this was a gret synne, grete onkindness,

2742 ich, each. **2748 lestid folowand,** were going on consecutively; or, were perpetually in my mind. **2749 langiren,** languish. **2752 hevyed,** heaved, tossed. **2754 ferid,** fared. **2755 leuhe . . . inderly,** laughed loud and heartily. **2756 blode fast,** bled profusely. **2758 recleshede,** recklessness. **2760 shrevyn,** absolved, shriven. **2761 levyn,** believe. **2763 fole,** fool.

2765   that I, for foly of feling of a littil bodily peyne, so onwisely lost for the time the comfort of all this blissid shewing of our Lord God. Here may you sene what I am of myselfe, but herein wold our curtes Lord not leve me; and I lay still till night trosting in His mercy, and than I gan to slepyn.

     And in the slepe at the begynnyng, methowte the fend set him in my throte
2770   puttand forth a visage ful nere my face like a yong man, and it was longe and wonder lene. I saw never none such. The color was rede like the tilestone whan it is new brent, with blak spots therin like blak steknes fouler than the tile stone. His here was rode as rust evisid aforn with syde lokks hongyng on the thounys. He grynnid on me with a shrewd semelant, shewing white teeth, and so
2775   mekil methowte it the more oggley. Body ne honds had he none shaply, but with his pawes he held me in the throte and wold have stranglid me, but he myte not.

     This oggley shewing was made slepyng, and so was non other. And in all this time I trostid to be savid and kepid be the mercy of God. And our curtes Lord
2780   gave me grace to waken, and onethis had I my lif. The persons that wer with me beheld me and wet my temples, and my herte began to comforten. And anon a lyte smoke came in the dore with a grete hete and a foule stinke. I said, "Benedicite domine, it is al on fire that is here"; and I wened it had ben a bodily fire that shuld a brent us al to dede. I askid hem that wer with me if thei felt ony stynke.
2785   Thei seyd, nay, thei felt none. I said, "Blissid be God"; for that wist I wele it was the fend that was comen to tempest me. And anon I toke to that our Lord had shewid me on the same day with al the feith of Holy Church. For I beheld it is bothen one, and fled therto as to my comforte. And anone al vanishid away, and I was browte to gret rest and peas withouten sekenes of body or drede of
2790   conscience.

LXVII

Of the worshipfull syte of the soule which is so nobly create that it myte no better a be made, in which the Trinite joyeth everlastingly; and the soule may have rest in nothing but in God, which sittith therin reuling al things. Sixty-seventh chapter.

     And than our Lord opened my gostly eye and shewid me my soule in midds of my herte. I saw the soule so large as it were an endles world and as it were a blisfull kyngdom; and be the conditions I saw therin, I understode that it is a

2768 **gan to slepyn,** went to sleep. 2772 **steknes,** speckles, stitches (see note). 2773 **rode,** red; **evisid,** clipped. 2774 **thounys,** temples; **shrewd,** wicked.

worshipful syte. In the midds of that syte sitts our Lord Jesus, God and man, a
2795 faire person and of large stature, heyest bishopp, solemnest kinge, worshipful-
liest Lord. And I saw Him clad solemnly, and worshiply He sitteth in the soule
even ryte in peace and rest. And the Godhede ruleth and gemeth Hevyn and erth
and all that is — sovereyn myte, sovereyn wisedom, and sovereyn goodnes. The
place that Jesus takith in our soule, He shal never removen it without end, as to
2800 my syte. For in us is His homliest home and His endles wonyng, and in this He
shewid the lekyng that He hath of the makyng of manys soule. For as wele as
the Fader might make a creature and as wele as the Son couth make a creature, so
wele wold the Holy Gost that manys soule were made, and so it was don; and
therfore the blissid Trinite enjoyeth withouten end in the makyng of manys soule.
2805 For He saw fro without begynnyng what shuld liken Him without end.

Althing that He hath made shewith His Lordship, as understonding was geven at
the same tyme be example of a creature that is to sen gret noblyes and king-
domes longand to a Lord. And whan it had sen al the noblyth beneathyn, then,
merveling, it was sterid to seeke aboven to the hey place where the lord wonnyth,
2810 knowing be reason that his dwelling is in the worthyest place. And thus I
understode sothly that our soule may never have rest in things that is beneathin
itselfe; and whan it cometh aboven all creatures into the selfe, yet may it not
abyden in the beholdyng of itselfe, but all the beholding is blisfully sett in God
that is the makar wonand therinn. For in manys soule is his very wonyng. And
2815 the heyest lyte and the brightest shynyng of the cite is the glorious love of our
Lord, as to my syte. And what may maken us more to enjoyen in God than to
sen in Hym that He enjoyeth heghest of al his werkes? For I saw in the same
shewing that if the blisfull Trinite myte have made manys soule ony better, ony
fairer, ony noblyer than it was made, He shuld not have be full plesid with the
2820 makyng of manys soule. And He will that our herts ben mytyly reysid above the
depeness of the erth and al vayne sorows, and enjoyen in Him.

LXVIII

**Of sothfast knowing that it is Jesus that shewid all this, and it was no ravyng; and how
we owen to have sekir troste in all our tribulation that we shall not be overcome. Sixty-
eighth chapter.**

This was a delectable syte and a restfull shewyng, that it is so withouten end.
And the beholding of this while we arn here, it is ful plesant to God, and full

2797 gemeth, guides. **2814 makar,** maker. **2815 cite,** city.

2825 gret spede to us. And the soule that thus beholdyth, it makith it like to Him that is behaldyn and onyth it in rest and peas be His grace. And this was a singlar joy and bliss to me, that I saw Him sitten. For the sekirnes of sitting shewith endles dwelling. And He gave me knowing sothfastly that it was He ᵗhat shewid me al aforn. And whan I had beholden this with avisement, than shewid our good Lord words full mekely, withouten voice and withouten openyng of lipps,

2830 ryte as He had done, and said full swetely: *Wete it now wele that it was no raveing that thou saw today, but take it and leve it, and kepe the therin and comfort the therwith and troste thou therto, and thou shalt not be overcome.* These last words wer seid for leryng of trew sekirness that it is our Lord Jesus that shewid me all, and ryte as in the first worde that our good Lord shewid, menyng His bliss-

2835 full passion, *Herwith is the devill overcome,* ryte so He seid in the last word with full trew sekirness, menand us all, *Thou shalt not ben overcommen.* And all this leryng in this trew comfort, it is generall to all myn even Cristen as it is afornseid, and so is Gods will. And these words, *Thou shalt not ben overcome,* was seid full sharply, and full mightily, for sekirness and comfort agens all tribula-

2840 tions that may comen.

He seid not, Thou shalt not be tempestid, thou shalt not be travelled, thou shalt not be disesid, but He seid, *Thou shalt not be overcome.* God will that we taken heede at these words, and that we be ever myty in sekir troste in wele and wo, for He lovith and lekyth us, and so will he that we love Him and lekin Him,

2845 and mytily trosten in Him, and al shal be wele. And sone after al was close, and I sow no more.

LXIX

Of the second long temptation of the devill to despeir; but she mytyly trosted to God and to the feith of Holy Church, rehersing the passion of Christe be the which she was deliverid. Sixty-ninth chapter.

After this the fend came agen with his hete and with his stinke and made me full besy. The stinke was so vile and so peynfull, and also dredfull and travellous. Also I heard a bodily jangeling as it had be of two bodies, and both, to my

2850 thynkyng, janglyd at one time as if they had holden a parlement with a gret bysynes. And al was soft muttering, as I understode nowte what they seid. And

2831 leve, believe. **2845–46 And . . . more,** And soon after all was closed, and I saw no more. **2850 parlement,** debate.

al this was to stirre me to dispeir, as methowte, semand to me as thei scornyd bidding of beds, which arn seid boistrosly with mouth, failing devowte entending and wise diligens the which we owen to God in our prayors. And our Lord God

2855 gave me grace mytyly for to trosten in Him, and to comforten my soule with bodily spech as I shuld have don to another person that had ben travelled. Methowte that bysynis myte not be likenyd to no bodily bysynes.

My bodily eye I sett in the same cross wher I had ben in comfort aforn that tyme; my tonge with speech of Crists passion, and rehersing the feith of Holy
2860 Church; and myn hert to festen on God with al the trost and the myte. And I thowte to myselfe, menand: Thou hast now grete bysynes to kepe the in the feith, for thou shuldst not be taken of thi enemy; woldst thou now for this time evermore be so bysy to kepe the fro synne, this were a good and a soverain occupation. For I thowte sothly, were I saf fro synne, I wer full saf fro all the
2865 fends of Helle and enemys of my soule. And thus he occupyed me al that nyte, and on the morne till it was about prime day. And anon they wer all gone and all passid, and then left nothing but stinke, and that lestid still awhile. And I scornyd him, and thus was I deliverd of hem be the vertue of Christ passion. For therwith is the fend overcome, as our Lord Jesus Criste seid aforn.

LXX

In all tribulation we owe to be stedfast in the feith trosting mytyly in God. For if our faith had no enimyte it should deserve no mede; and how all these shewings arn in the faith. Seventieth chapter.

2870 In all this blissid shewing our good Lord gave understondyng that the syte shuld passyn, which blissid shewing the feith kepith with His owne good will and His grace. For He left with me neyther signe nor token wherby I myte knowen it, but He left with me His owne blissid worde in true understondyng, byddand me full mytyly that I shuld leven it, and so I do; blissied mot He ben. I
2875 beleve that He is our Savior that shewid it, and that it is the feith that He shewid; and therfore I leve it, enjoyand, and therto I am bounden be al His own menyng with the next words that folowen: *Kepe the therein, and comfort the therewith, and trost thou therto.* Thus I am bounden to kepen it in my feith. For on the selfe day that it was shewid, what time that the syte was passid, as a wretch
2880 I forsoke it, and openly I seid that I had ravid.

2853 bidding of beds, praying of beads, i.e., saying the rosary. **2863 soverain**, sovereign, the best possible. **2874 byddand**, commanding.

Than our Lord Jesus of His mercy wold not letten it perish, but He shewid it al agen within, in my soule, with mor fulhede with the blissid lyte of His pretious love, seyand these word full mytyly and full mekely: *Witt it now wele, it was no raving that thou saw this day*; as if He had seid, "For the syte was passid fro, thee 2885 lestist it and couthest not kepe it, but witt it now; that is to sey, now that thou seest it." This was seid not only for the same time, but also to setten thereupon the ground of my feith, where He seith anon folowing, *But take it, leve it, and kepe the therin, and comfort the therwith, and trost thou therto, and thou shalt not be overcome.* In these six words that folowen "take it," His menyng is to festyn 2890 it feyfully in our herte, for He will that it dwell with us in feith to our lifes end, and after in fulhede of joy, willand that we have ever sekir trost in His blisfull behests knowyng His goodnes. For our feith is contried in divers manners be our owne blindhede and our gostly enemy within and without. And therfore our pretious lover helpith us with gostly syte and trew teching on sundry manners, 2895 within and without, wereby that we may know Him. And therfore in what manner He techith us, He will we persivyn Him wisely, receivyn Him swetely, and kepin us in Hym feithfully. For aboven the feith is no goodnes kept in this life, as to my sight, and beneath the faith is no helpe of soule. But in the feith, there will the Lord that we kepe us. For we have be His goodnes and His owne werkeing 2900 to kepe us in the feith, and, be His suffrance, be gostly enmyte we are assayed in the feith and made myty. For if our feith had none enmyte it should deserve no mede, as to the understondyng that I hav in all our Lords menyng.

LXXI

Jesus will our soules be in glad cher to Hym, for His cher is to us mery and lovely; and how He shewith to us three manner cher, of passion, compassion, and blisfull cher. Seventy-first chapter.

Glad and mery and sweete is the blisfull lovely cher of our Lord to our souleis. For He havith us ever lifand in lovelongeing, and He will our soule be in 2905 glad chere to Him to gevin Him His mede. And thus I hope with His grace He hath, and more shall, draw in the utter chere to the inner cher, and maken us all at one with Him, and ech of us with other in trew lestand joye that is Jhesus.

2889-90 festyn it feyfully, fasten it faithfully. **2896 persivyn**, understand. **2906 utter**, outer.

I have menyng of three manner of cheres of our Lord. The first is cher of passion, as He shewid while He was here in this lif, deyand. Thow this beholdyng be mornyng and swemful, yet it is glad and mery, for He is God. The second manner of chere is pite and ruth and compassion, and this shewith He to all His lovers with sekirnes of keping that have nede to His mercy. The third is the blisfull cher as it shal be without end; and this was oftenest and longest continuid. And thus in the time of our peyne and our wo He shewith us chere of His passion and of His cross, helpand us to beer by His owne blissid vertue. And in the time of our synnyng He shewith to us chere of ruth and pite, mytily kepand us and defending agaynst all our enemies.

2910

2915

And these two be the common cher which He shewith to us in this life. Therewith medlarid the thord, and that is His blisfull chere like in parte as it shall be in Hevyn. And that is be gracious touchyng and swete lyteyng of the gostly life wherby that we arn kept in sekir feith, hope, and charite, with contrition and devotion, and also with contemplation and alle manner of true solace and swete comforts. The blisfull cher of our Lord God werkith it in us be grace.

2920

LXXII

Synne in the chosen soulis is dedly for a time, but thei be not ded in the syght of God; and how we have here matter of joy and moneing, and that for our blindhede and weyte of flesh; and of the most comfortable chere of God; and why these shewings were made. Seventy-second chapter.

But now behovyth me to tellen in what manner I saw synne dedly in the creatures which shall not dyen for synne, but livyn in the joy of God withouten end. I saw that two contrareties should never be to God in one stede. The most contrious that arn is the heyest bliss and the depest peyne. The heyest bliss that is, is to have Him in cleerty of endless life, Him verily seand, Him swetely feland, all perfectly haveand in fulhede of joy. And thus was the blisfull cheere of our Lord shewid in pite, in which shewing I saw that synne is most contrarie; so ferforth, that as long as we be medled with ony part of synne, we shall never see cleerly the blisfull cheere of our Lord. And the horibler and the greivouser that our synnes bene, the deeper are we for that time fro this blisfull syte. And therfore it semith to us oftentimes as we wern in peril of deth, in a party of Hell, for the sorow and peyne that the synne is to us.

2925

2930

2935

2908 **cheres,** countenances. 2915 **beer,** endure. 2919 **medlarid the thord,** mingles the third. 2928 **cleerty,** clarity; **feland,** feeling. 2931 **medled with ony,** mixed with any.

And thus we arn ded for the tyme fro the very syte of our blisfull life. But in all this I saw sothfastly that we be not dede in the syte of God, ne He passith never fro us. But He shall never have His full bliss in us till we have our full bliss in Him, verily seand His faire blisfull chere. For we arn ordeynid therto in
2940 kinde, and gettyn therto be grace. Thus I saw how synne is dedly for a short time in the blissid creatures of endless life. And ever the more clerely that the soule seith this blisfull chere be grace of loveyng, the more it longyth to seen it in fullhede. For notwithstonding that our Lord God wonnyth in us and is here with us, and al He halsith us and beclosith us for tender love that He may never levyn
2945 us, and is more nere to us than tongue can tellen or herte can thynke, yet may we never stint of moning nor of weping ne of longyng til whan we see Him cleerly in His blissfull chere. For in that pretious blisfull syte there may no wo abiden, ne no wele failen.

And in this I saw matter of myrth and matter of monyng. Matter of myrthe,
2950 for our Lord, our Maker, is so nere to us and in us, and we in Him be sekirness of keping of His grete goodnes; matter of monyng for our gostly eye is so blinde and we be so born downe be weyte of our dedly flesh and derkhede of synne that we may not sen our Lord God clerly in His faire blisful chere. No, and because of this myrkehede unethes we can leven and trowen His grete love, our
2955 sekirness of keping; and therefore it is that I sey we may never stinten of moning ne of wepyng.

This weping meneth not al in poryng out of teares by our bodily eye, but also to more gostly understondyng. For the kindly desire of our soule is so gret and so onmesurable, that if it were goven us to our solace and to our comfort al the
2960 noblyth that ever God made in Hevyn and in erth, and we saw not the fair blissfull chere of Hymselfe, yet we shuld not stynten of moning ne of gostly weping, that is to sey, of peynfull longing, till whan we sen verily the faire blisfull chere of our Maker. And if we were in all the peyne that herte can thynke and tongue may tell, if we myten in that time sen his faire blisfull chere, all this peyn shuld
2965 us not agrevin. Thus is that blisfull syte end of all manner of peyne to lovand soule, and fulfilling all manner of joy and bliss. And that shewid He in the hey, mervelous words wher He seyd, *I it am that is heyest; I it am that is lowist; I it am that is all.*

It longith to us to have three manner of knowyngs. The first is that we knowen
2970 our Lord God. The second, that we knowen ourselfe, what we arn be Him in kinde and grace. The third that we knowen mekely what our selfe is anempts our synne and febilness. And for these three was all the shewing made, as to myn understondyng.

2944 al He halsith us, He embraces us entirely. **2954 myrkehede**, darkness.

LXXIII

These Revelations were shewid three wises. And of two gostly sekenes, of which God will we amend us, remembring His passion, knowing also He is al love; for He will we have sekirnes and liking in love, not takyng onskilfull hevyness for our synnes past. Seventy-third chapter.

2975

2980

2985

2990

2995

3000

All the blissid teching of our Lord God was shewid be three partes, that is to sey, by bodily syte and by word formyd in myn understondyng, and be gostly sight. For the bodily sygte, I have seid as I saw as trewly as I can. And for the words, I have seid them rith as our Lord shewid hem to me. And for the gostly syght, I have seyd sumdele, but I may never full tellen it, and therefore of this syght I am sterrid to sey more, as God will give me grace.

God shewid two manner of sekenes that we have. That on is onpatience or slaith, for we bere our trevell and our peynes hevily. That other is dispeir or doubtfull drede, as I shall seyen after. Generally, He shewid synne, wherin that all is comprehendid. But in special He shewid not but thes two. And these two arn thei that most travelin and tempesten us, as be that our Lord shewid me, of which He will we be amendid. I speake of swich men and women that for God love haten synne and disposen hem to do Gods will. Than be our gostly blind-hede and bodily hevynes, we arn most enclinand to these. And therfore it is Gods will thei be knowen, and than shall we refusen hem as we don other synnes. And full helpe of this ful mekely our Lord shewid: the patience that He had in His herd passion and also the joyeing and the likyng that He hath of that passion for love. And this He shewid in example that we shuld gladly and wisely baren our peynes for that is gret plesing to Him and endless profitt to us. And the cause why we arn trevellid with them is for onknoweing of love. Thow the three persons in the Trinite ben all even in the selfe, the soule toke most under-stonding in love. Ya, and He will in all thing that we have our beholding and our enjoyeyng in love.

And of this knoweyng arn we most blynd. For som of us leven that God is almyty, and may don all, and that He is al wisdam, and can don all; but that He is all love, and will don all, there we astynten. And this unknowing — it is that that lettith most Gods lovers, as to my syte. For whan we begynnen to haten synne, and amenden us be the ordinance of Holy Church, yet ther dwellith a drede that lettith us, for the beholding of our selfe, and of our synnes aforn don,

2977 **rith**, exactly. 2978 **sumdele**, something. 2980–81 **on . . . hevily**, one is impatience or sloth, for we endure our trouble and pains heavily. 2999 **astynten**, stop.

and sum of us for our everydayly synnes. For we hold nor our covenants ne kepe not our cleness that our Lord settith us in, but fallen oftimes in so much wretchid-
3005 ness that shame it is to seen it. And the beholding of this makyth us so sorry and so hevy that onethis we can finde ony comfort. And this drede we taken sumtime for a mekness, but this is a foule blyndhed and a waykenes. And we cannot dispisen it as we don another synne that we knowen, for it commyth of enmite, and it is agens truth.
3010 For of all the propertes of the blisfull Trinite, it is God will that we have most sekirnes and likeing in love. For love makith myte and wisdam full meke to us. For ryte as be the curtesye of God He forgivith our synne atte the tyme that we repenten us, ryte so will He that we forgiven our synne as anempts our unskilfull hevyness and our doutfull dreds.

LXXIV

Ther ben four manner of drede, but reverent drede is a lovely true that never is without meke love; and yet thei be not both one; and how we should pray God for the same. Seventy-fourth chapter.

3015 For I understond four manner of dreds. One is the drede of afray that cum-mith to a man sodenly be frelte. This drede doith good, for it helpith to purge man as doeth bodily sekenes or swich other peyne that is not synne. For all swich peynys helpe man, if thei be patiently taken. The second is drede of peyne, wherby man is sterid and wakid fro sleepe of synne. He is not abil for the time
3020 to perceivyn the soft comfort of the Holy Gost, till he have understonding of this drede of peyne, of bodily deth, and of gostly enemyes. And this drede stirrith us to seken comfort and mercy of God, and thus this drede helpith us to sekyn comfort and mercy of God and abileth us to have contrition be the blisfull touching of the Holy Gost. The third is doubtfull drede. Doutfull drede, in as
3025 mech as it drawith to dispeir, God will have it turnyd in us into love be the knowing of love, that is to sey, that the bitternes of doubt be turnyd into swete-ness of kinde love be grace. For it may never plesyn our Lord that His servants douten in his goodnes.
The fourth is reverent drede. For there is no drede that fully plesith God in us
3030 but reverent drede, and that is full soft, for the more it is had, the less is it felt for swetenes of love. Love and drede are brethren, and thei arn rotid in us be the

3015 afray, sudden attack. **3031 thei arn rotid**, they are rooted.

goodnes of our makere; and thei shall never be taken fro us without end. We have of kinde to loven, and we have of grace to loven; and we have of kinde to dreden, and we have of grace to dreden. It longith to the lordshippe and to the

3035 faderhede to be dred, as it longith to the goodnes to be lovid. And it longith to us that arn His servants and His children to dreden Him for lordshipp and faderhede, as it longith to us to loven Him for goodhede. And thow this reverent drede and love be not partid asundre, yet thei arn not both one, but thei arn two in properte and in werking. And neither of them may be had without other.

3040 Therfore I am sekir, he that lovith, he dredith, thow that he fele it but a littil. All dreds other than reverent drede that arn proferid to us, thow they come under the collor of holyness, yet arn not so trew, and hereby may they be knowen asunder.

That drede that makith us hastily to fleen from all that is not good, and fallen

3045 into our Lords brest as the child into the moder barme, with all our entent and with all our mynd, knowand our febilness and our gret nede, knowing His ever-lesting goodnes and His blisfull love, only sekeing to Him for salvation, clevand to with sekir troste — that drede that bringith us into this werking — it is kinde, gracious, good, and true. And all that contraries to this, either it is wronge or it

3050 is medlid with wronge. Than is this the remedye: to knowen hem both and refusen the wrong. For the kinde profitt of drede which we have in this lif be the gracious werking of the Holy Gost, the same shall be in Hevyn aforn God, gentill, curtes, and ful delectabil.

And thus we shall in love be homley and nere to God, and we shall in drede

3055 be gentil and curtes to God, and both alike evyn. Desir we of our Lord God to dredin Him reverently and to love Him mekely and to trosten in Him mytyly. For whan we drede Him reverently and loven Him mekely our troste is never in vaine; for the more that we trosten, and the mytylier, the more we plesyn and worshippe our Lord that we trosten in. And if us feile this reverent drede and

3060 meke love (as God forbode we should), our trost shall sone be misrulid for the tyme. And therefore us nedith mekil for to prayen our Lord of grace that we may have this reverent drede and meke love, of his gift, in herte and in werke, for withouten this no man may plesyn God.

LXXV

Us nedith love, longing, and pite; and of three manner of longing in God which arn in us; and how in the day of dome the joy of the blissid shal ben incresid, seing verily the

3045 **moder barme**, mother's bosom. 3050 **medlid**, mixed. 3059 **us feile**, we fail in.

cause of all thyng that God hath don, dredfully tremeland, and thankand for joye, mervelyng the gretnes of God and littlenes of all that is made. Seventy-fifth chapter.

I saw that God may done all that us nedith. And these three that I shall seyen, neden: love, longing, pite. Pite in love kepith us in the time of our nede, and longing in the same love drawith us into Hevyn. For the threist of God is to have the general man into Him, in which thrist He hath drawyn His holy that be now in bliss; and gettand His lively members, ever He drawith and drinkith, and yet He thristith and longith.

I saw three manner of longing in God, and al to one end; of which we have the same in us, and of the same vertue, and for the same end. The first is for that He longyth to learn us to knowen Him and loven Him evermore, as it is convenient and spedefull to us. The second is that He longith to have us up to His bliss as soules arn whan thei arn taken out of peyne into Hevyn. The third is to fulfillen us in bliss, and that shall be on the last day fulfillid, ever to lesten. For I saw, as it is knowne in our feith, that the peyne and sorow shall be endid to all that shall be savid. And not only we shall recevyn the same bliss the soule aforne have had in Hevyn, but also we shall receive a new, which plenteously shall be flowing out of God into us, and fullfillen us. And this be the goods which He hath ordeynid to geve us from without begynnyng.

These goods are tresurid and hidde in Hymselfe. For into that time, creature is not myty ne worthy to receivin them. In this we shall seen verily the cause of all thyng He hat don. And evermore we shall seen the cause of all things that He hath suffrid. And the bliss and the fulfilling shall be so deepe and so hey that, for wonder and mervell, all creatures shall have to God so gret reverent drede, overpassing that hath been seen and felt beforn, that the pillers of Hevyn shall tremelyn and quakyn, but this manner of tremelyng and drede shall have no peyne.

But it longith to the worthy myte of God thus to be beholden of His creatures, dredfully tremeland and quakand for mekehede of joye, mervelyng at the greatnes of God the maker, and of the litilhede of all that is made. For the beholdyng of this makith the creature mervelous meke and mylde. Wherfore God will, and also it longith to us both in kynde and grace, to witten and knowen of this, desirand this syte and this werking. For it ledith us in ryte wey, and kepith us in true life, and onyth us to God. And as good as God is, as gret He is, and as mekil as it longith to His Godhede to be lovid, so mekill it longyth to His grethede to be dredid. For this reverent drede is the faire curtesie that is in Hevyn aforn

3065 neden, are needed. **3066 threist,** thirst. **3067 His holy,** His saints. **3068 lively,** living. **3087 tremelyn and quakyn,** tremble and quake. **3089 tremeland and quakand,** trembling and quaking.

Gods face. And as mekil as He shall than be knowen and lovid overpassing that
He is now, in so mekill He shall be dredid overpassing that He is now. Wherfore
it behovith needs to ben that all Hevyn and erth shall tremelyn and quaken when
3100 the pillars shall tremelyn and quaken.

LXXVI

**A loveand soule hatith synne for vilehede more than all the peyn of Hell; and how the
beholdyng of other mannys synne (but if it be with compassion), lettith the beholdyng
of God; and the devill, be putting in remembrans our writchidness, would letten for the
same; and of our slawth. Seventy-sixth Chapter.**

I speke but littil of reverent drede, for I hope it may be seen in this matter
afornseid. But wele I wot our Lord shewid me no soules but those that dred
Him. For wele I wott the soule that trewly takith the techyng of the Holy Gost,
it hatith more synne for vilehede and horibilite, than it doth all the peyne that
3105 is in Hell. For the soule that beholdith the kindenes of our Lord Jesus, it hatith
non helle but synne, as to my sygte. And therefore it is Goddis will that we
knowen synne, and prayen bysyly, and travellyn willfully, and sekyn teching
mekely, that we fall not blindly therin; and, if we fallen, that we risen redily.
For it is the most peyne that the soule may have, to turne fro God ony time be
3110 synne. The soule that will be in rest, whan other mannys synne commith to my
mynde, he shall fleen it as the peyne of Helle, seking into God for remedy, for
helpe agayne it. For the beholdyng of other mannys synnes, it makith, as it were,
a thick myst aforne the eye of the soule, and we may not for the tyme se the
fairehede of God — but if we may beholden hem with contrition with him, with
3115 compassion on him, and with holy desire to God for him. For withouten this it
noyeth and tempestith and lettith the soule that beholdith hem. For this I understode in the shewing of compassion.

In this blisfull shewing of our Lord, I have understondyng of two contaries.
That one is the most wisdam that ony creture may don in this life; that other is
3120 the most foly. The most wisdam is a creature to done after the wille and councell
of his heyest, sovereyn freind. This blissid freind is Jhesus, and it is His will and
His councell that we holden us with Him, and festyn us to Him, homley, evermore in what state so we ben, for whether so that we ben foule or clene we arn
al one in His loveing. For wele ne for wo, He will never we fleen Him.

3107 **travellyn**, work.

3125   But for the chongeabilitie that we arn in, in ourselfe we fallen often into synne. Than we have this be the stering of our enemy and be our owne foly and blyndhede. For they seien thus: Thou wittest wele thou art a wretch, a synner, and also ontrew, for thou kepist not the command; thou behotist oftentymes our Lord that thou shalt don better, and anon after, thou fallest agen in the same,

3130   namely in slauth, in lesyng of tyme. For that is the begynning of synne, as to my syghte, and namely to the creatures that have goven hem to serven our Lord with inward beholding of his blissid goodness. And this makith us adred to apear afore our curtes Lord. Than is it our enemy that will putt us on bakke with his false drede of our writchidnes, for peyne that he threatith us by, for it is his men-

3135   yng to make us so hevy and so wery in this that we shuld lettyn out of mende the fair, blisfull beholdyng of our everlasting freind.

LXXVII

Off the enmite of the fend which lesith more in our uprising than he winnith be our fallyng, and therfore he is scornyd. And how the scorge of God shuld be suffrid with mynde of His passion. For that is specially rewardid aboven penance be ourselfe chosen. And we must nedes hove wo, but curtes God is our leder, keper, and bliss. Seventy-seventh chapter.

    Our good Lord shewid the enmite of the fend, wherby I understode that all that is contrarious to love and to pece, it is the fend and of his parte. And we have of our febilnes and our foly to fallen, and we have of mercy and grace of

3140   the Holy Gost to risen to more joye. And if our eneme owte wynnith of us by our fallyng, for it is his likenes, he lesith manyfold more in our rising be charite and mekenes. And this glorious riseing, it is to him so gret sorow and peyne for the hate that he hath to our soule that he brynnyt continuly in envy. And al this sorow that he wold maken us to have, it shal turne to himselfe. And for this it

3145   was that our Lord scornyd him, and this made me mytyly to lauhen.

    Than is this the remedy — that we ben aknowen our writchidnes and flen to our Lord. For ever the mor nedier that we ben, the more spedefull it is to us to neyghen Him. And sey we thus in our mening: I know wele I have a shrewid

---

3128 behotist, promised. **3130 slauth**, sloth; **lesyng**, losing. **3143 brynnyt**, burns. **3146 flen**, flee. **3148 neyghen**, draw near to. **3148–49 shrewid peyne**, wicked, i.e., severe pain.

peyne, but our Lord is almyty and may punish me mytyly, and He is al wisdam
3150 and can punish me skilfully, and He is all goodnes and lovith me full tendirly.
And in this beholdyng it is necessarye for us to abeyden, for it is a lovely mekeness of a synfull soule, wroute be mercy and grace of the Holy Gost, whan we
will willfully and gladly taken the scorge and chastening of our Lord Himselfe
will geve us. And it shall be full tendir and full esy, if that we will onely holden
3155 us paid with Him and with all His werkes.

For the pennance that man taketh of himselfe was not shewid me, that is to
sey, it was not shewid specifyed; but it was shewid specialy and heyly and with
full lovely chere, that we shall mekely and patiently beryn and suffren the penance that God Himselfe gevith us with mynde in His blissid passion. For whan
3160 we have mend in His blissid passion with pite and love, than we suffren with
Him like as His freinds did that seen it. And this was shewid in the thirteenth
ner at the begynnyng wher it spekith of pite. For He seith, *Accuse not selfe*
overdon mekil, demandand that tribulation and thy wo is al for thy defaute, for I
will not that thou be hevye ne sorowfull undiscretly. For I tell the howso tho thou
3165 *do, thou shalt have wo, and therfore I will that thou wisely know thi penance and*
shalt then sothly seene that all thi living is penance profitable. This place is prison,
and this life is penance; and in the remedy He will we enjoyen. The remedy is
that our Lord is with us, kepand and ledand into the fulhede of joye. For this is
an endless joy to us in our Lords menyng, that He that shall ben our bliss whan
3170 we arn there, He is our keper while we arn here. Our wey and our Hevyn is trew
love and sekir troste, and of this He gaf understonding in al, and namly in the
shewing of His passion wher He made me mytyly to chesin Him for my Hevyn.

Fle we to our Lord, and we shall be comfortid; touch we Him, and we shull be
made clene; cleve to Him, and we shall be sekir and safe fro al maner of peril.
3175 For our curtes Lord will that we ben as homley with Him as herte may thinke or
soule may desiren. But beware that we taken not so reklesly this homleyhede
that we levyn curtesy. For our Lord Himselfe is sovereyn homleyhede, and as
homley as He is, as curtes He is, for He is very curtes. And the blissid creatures
that shall ben in Hevyn with Him without end, He will have hem like to Himselfe
3180 in all things. And to be like our Lord perfectly, it is our very salvation and our
full bliss. And if we wott not how we shall don all this, desire we of our Lord, and
He shal lerne us, for it is His owne likeing and His worship. Blissid mot He be.

3162–63 Accuse . . . demandand that, Do not accuse yourself too much, deciding that.
3171 gaf, gave.

LXXVIII

Our Lord will we know four manner of goodnes that He doith to us; and how we neede the lyte of grace to knowen our synne and febilnes, for we arn nothing of ourselfe but writchidnes, and we may not know the horribilnes of synne as it is. And how our enemy would we should never know our synne til the last day, wherfore we arn mekil bowndend to God that shewith it now. Seventy-eighth chapter.

Our Lord of His mercy shewith us our synne and our febilnes be the swete gracious lyte of Hymselfe, for our synne is so vile and so horrible that He of His
3185 curtesee will not shew it to us, but be the lyte of His grace and mercy. Of four things it is His will that we have knowing: The first is that He is our ground of whom we have all our life and our being. The second, that He kepith us mytyly and mercifully in the tyme that we arn in our synne and monge all our enemies that arn full fel upon us; and so mekil we arn in the more peril, for we geven
3190 hem occasion therto and kno not our owne nede. The third is how curtesly He kepith us and makith us to knowen that we gon amyss. The fourth is how sted-fastly He abidith us and chongith no chere, for He will that we be turnyd and onyd to Him in love as He is to us.

And thus be this gracious knoweing we may seen our synne profitably without
3195 despeir. For sothly us nedith to seen it, and be the syte we shall be made ashamd of ourselfe and broken downe as anempts our pride and presumtion. For us behov-ith verily to seen that of ourselfe we arn ryte nowte but synne and wretchiddnes. And thus be the syte of the less that our Lord shewith us, the more is wastid which we se not. For He of his curtesye mesurith the syte to us, for it is so vile
3200 and so horrible that we shuld not enduren to seen it as it is. And be this meke knowing, thus throw contrition and grace we shall be broken fro all things that is not our Lord, and than shall our blissid Saviour perfectly helyn us and one us to Him.

This breking and this helyng our Lord menith be the generall man. For he that
3205 is heyest and nerest with God, he may seen himselfe synnefull, and nedith, with me. And I that am the lest and lowest of those that shall be save, I may be comfortid with him that is heyest. So hath our Lord onyd us in charite whan He shewid me that I shuld synne. And for joy that I had in beholdyng of Him, I entend not redily to that shewing, and our curtis Lord stynte then, and wold not
3210 ferther tech me till that He gave me grace and will to entenden. And hereof was I lerid thow that we be heyly lifted up into contemplation be the special gift of our Lord, yet us behovith nedis therwith to have knoweing and syte of our synne and our febilnes. For withouten this knowing we may not have trew mekenes,

147

3215 and without this we may not be savid. And also I saw that we may not have this knowing of ourselfe, ne of none of all our gostly enemies, for thei will us not so mekil good. For if it wer be their will, we should not seen it into our endyng day. Than we be mekil bounden to God that He will Himselfe for love shewen it us in time of mercy and grace.

LXXIX

We are lernyd to our synne, and not to our neighbors, but for their helpe; and God will we know whatsomever stering we have contrary to this shewing, it comith of our enemy. For the gret love of God knowen, we should not ben the more reckles to fallen, and if we fallen, we must hastily risen or ell we are gretly onkind to God. Seventy-ninth chapter.

Also I had in this more understondyng. In that He shewid me that I should
3220 synne, I toke it nakidly to myne owne singular person, for I was none otherwise stirrid at that time. But be the hey, gracious comfort of our Lord that followid after, I saw that His menyng was for the general man, that is to sey, all man which is synfull and shall ben into the last day, of which man I am a member, as I hope, be the mercy of God. For the blissid comfort that I saw, it is large enow
3225 for us all. And here was I lerid that I shuld se myn owne synne and not other mens synns but if it may be for comfort and helpe of myn evin Cristen. And also in this same shewing where I saw that I shuld synne, then was I leryd to be dredfull for onsekirness of myselfe, for I wott not how I shall fallen, nor I know not the mesure ner the gretness of synne. For that wold I have wist dredfully;
3230 and therto, I had non answere. Also our curtes Lord, in the same tyme, He shewid full sekirly and mytyly the endleshede and the onchongeabilitie of His love. And alsa, be His grete goodnes and His grace inwardly keping, that the love of Him and our soule shal never be departid in two, without end. And thus in this drede I have matter of mekeness that savith me from presumption. And
3235 in the blissid shewing of love, I have matter of tru comfort and of joy that savith me fro dispeir.

All this homley shewing of our curtes Lord, it is a lovely lesson and a swete, gracious teching of Himselfe in comforting of our soule. For He will that we knowen be the swetenes and homley loveing of Him, that all that we seen or felyn,
3240 within or without, which is contrarious to this is of the enemy, and not of God. As thus: if we be stired to be the more recles of our living or of the keping of

3232 alsa, also. **3241 recles,** careless.

148

our herts be the cause that we have knowing of this plenteous love, than needs us gretly to beware. For this stering, if it come, it is ontrew, and gretly we owen to haten it, for it all hath no likeness of Gods will. And whan that we be fallen
3245 be frelte or blyndhede, than our curtes Lord touchith us, stireth us, and kepith us, and than will He that we seen our wretchidness and mekely ben it aknowen. But He will not we abiden thus, ne He will not that we beseyn us gretly about our accusing, nor He will not that we ben wretchfull of our selfe. But He will that we hastily entenden to Him, for He stondyth al alufe, and abideth us swemefully
3250 and monyngly till whan we come, and hath hast to have us to Him, for we arn His joy and His deligte, and He is our salve and our life. Tho I sey He stondyth al alone, I leve the speking of the blissid company of Hevyn, and speke of His office and His werking here on erth upon the condition of the shewyng.

LXXX

By three thyngs God is worshippid and we savid; and how our knowing now is but as an ABC. And swete Jhesus doith all, abyding and monyng with us, but whan we arn in synne, Christ monyth alone. Than it longith to us for kindness and reverens hastily to turne agen to Him. Eightieth chapter.

Be three things man stondith in this life, be which three God is worshippid and
3255 we be spedid, kept, and savid. The first is use of manys reason naturall. The second is commen teching of Holy Church. The thred is inward, gracious werking of the Holy Gost. And these three ben all of one God: God is the ground of our kindly reason, and God, the teaching of Holy Church, and God is the Holy Gost. And all ben sundry gifts to which He will we have gret regard and attenden us
3260 therto. For these werkyn in us continualy all to God, and these ben grete thyngs, of which gret things He will we have knowing here as it were in one ABC; that is to seyn, that we have a litill knoweing, whereof we shall have fullhede in Hevyn; and that is for to spede us.

We knowen in our feith that God alone toke our kinde, and non but He; and
3265 ferthermore that Criste allone did all the werks that longin to our salvation, and none but He; and ryte so He alone doith now in the last end. That is to sey, He wonnyth here with us and rulith us and governith us in this lifing and bringith us

3247 **beseyn us**, busy ourselves. 3249 **swemefully**, piteously. 3250 **hath hast**, has haste (i.e., is eager to).

to His bliss. And thus shall He doe as long as ony soule is in erth that shall come to Hevyn; and so ferforth that if ther were no suich soule but one, He shuld

3270 be, with all, alone, till He had browte it up to His bliss.

I leve and understond the ministration of angells, as clerks tellen, but it was not shewid me. For Himselfe is nerest and mekest, heyest and lowest, and doith all. And not only all that us neds, but also He doith all that is worshipfull to our joy in Hevyn. And wher I sey he abidith swemefully and monyng, it menyth all

3275 the trew felyng that we have in ourselfe in contrition and compassion, and all sweming and monyng that we are not onyd with our Lord. And all swich that is spedfull, it is Christ in us. And thow some of us fele it seldam, it passith never fro Criste till what tyme He hath browte us out of all our wo. For love suffrith never to be without pite.

3280 And what tyme that we fallen into synne and leve the mynd of Him and the keping of our own soule, than kepith Criste alone al the charge of us, and thus stondith He swemely and monyng. Than longith it to us for reverence and kindeness to turne us hastely to our Lord and levyen Him not alone. He is here alone with us all; that is to sey, only for us, He is here. And what tyme I am strange to

3285 Him be synne, dispeir, or slawth, than I let my Lord stonden alone in as mekill as it is in me. And thus it farith with us all which ben synners. But thow it be so that we do thus oftentimes, His goodnes suffrith us never to be alone, but lestingly He is with us, and tenderly He excusith us, and ever sheildith us fro blame in His syte.

LXXXI

This blissid woman saw God in divers manners, but she saw Him take no resting place but in manys soule. And He will we enjoyen more in His love then sorowen for often falling, remembring reward everlasting and liveing gladly in penance; and why God suffrith synne. Eighty-first chapter.

3290 Our good Lord shewid Him in dyvers manners, both in Hevyn, in erth; but I saw Him take no place but in mannys soule. He shewid Him in erth in the swete incarnation, and in His blissid passion. And in other manner He shewid Him in erth, wher I sey I saw God in a poynte. And in other manner He shewid Him in erth, thus as it were in pilegrimage, that is to sey, He is here with us, ledand us,

3274 **swemefully**, sorrowfully. 3280 **leve . . . Him**, fail to keep Him in mind. 3282 **swemely and monyng**, sorrowful and lamenting.

3295 and shul ben till whan He hath browte us all to His bliss in Hevyn. He shewid
Him dyvers tymes reynand, as it is afornseyd, but principally in mannys soule. He
hath taken there His resting place and His worshipfull cyte, out of which worshipfull see He shall never risen nor removen without end. Mervelous and solemne is the place wher the Lord wonnyth, and therefore He will that we redily
3300 entenden to His gracious touching, more enjoying in His hole love than sorow-
and in our often fallings.

For it is the most worshippe to Him of onything that we may don that we
leven gladly and meryly, for His love, in our penance. For He beholdith us so
tendirly that He seith all our liveing and penance. For kind loveand is to Him
3305 ay lestand penance in us, which penance He werkith in us, and mercifully He
helpith us to baren it. For His love makith Him to longyn, His wisdam and His
trewth with His rytfulhede makith Him to suffren us here; and in this manner
He will seene it in us. For this is our kindly penance and the heyest, as to my
syte. For this penance commith never fro us till what tyme that we be fullfilled
3310 whan we shal have Him to our mede. And therfore He will that we setten our
herts in the overpassing, that is to sey, fro the peyne that we felen into the bliss
that we trosten.

LXXXII

**God beholdith the monyng of the soule with pite and not with blame, and yet we do
nowte but synne, in the which we arn kept in solace and in drede. For He will we turne
us to Him, redy clevand to His love, seand that He is our medicyne. And so we must love
in longing and in enjoyeing, and whatsover is contrarie to this is not of God but of
enmity. Eighty-second chapter.**

But here shewid our curtes Lord the moneing and the morning of the soule,
menand thus: I wote wele thou wilt liven for My love, merily and gladly suffrand
3315 all the penance that may com to the. But inasmech as thow livest not without
synne, thou woldest suffre for My love all the wo, all the tribulation, and disese
that myte come to the. And it is soth, but be not mekill agreved with synne that
fallith to the agens thy will.

And here I understode that: that the Lord biholdith the servant with pitie and
3320 not with blame, for this passing lif askith not to liven al withoute blame and

3296 **reynand**, reigning.   3299 **wonnyth**, dwells.   3310 **mede**, reward.   3318 **the agens**, you
against.

synne. He loveith us endlesly, and we synne customably. And He shewith us full myldely; and than we sorow and mornen discretly, turnand us into the beholding of His mercy, clevand to His love and goodness, seand that He is our medicine, wittand that we doe nowte but synne. And thus be the mekeness that we getten
3325 be the syte of our synne, feythfully knowyng His everlasting love, Him thanking and prayseing, we plesyn Him. *I love the and thou lovist Me, and our love shall not be departid in two, and for thi profitt I suffre.* And all this was shewid in gostly understondyng, seyand these blissid words: *I kepe the full sekerly.*

And be gret desire that I have in our blissid Lord that we shal leven in this
3330 manner, that is to sey, in longing and enjoyeing as all this lesson of love shewith, therby I understode that all that is contrarious to us is not of Him, but of enmyte. And He will that we knowen it be the swete gracious lyt of His kynde love. If any swich lover be in erth which is continuly kept fro falling, I know it not, for it was not shewid me. But this was shewed, that in falling and in ryseing
3335 we arn ever preciously kept in one love. For in the beholding of God we fall not; in the beholding of selfe we stond not; and both these ben soth, as to my syte. But the beholdyng of our Lord God is the heyest sothnes.

Than arn we mekil bound to God, that He will in this living shewin us this hey sothness. And I understode that while we be in this life, it is full spedefull to us
3340 that we sen both these at onys. For the heyer beholding kepith us in gostly solace and trew enjoying in God. That other, that is the lower beholding, kepith us in drede and makith us ashamyd of ourselfe. But our good Lord will ever that we holden us mekil more in the beholdyng of the heyer, and not levyn the knowing of the lower, into the time that we be browte up above wher we shall have
3345 our Lord Jhesus onto our mede, and ben fulfillid of joy and bliss without ende.

LXXXIII

Of three properties in God — Life, Love and Light; and that our reason is in God, accordand. It is heyest gift; and how our feith is a light commeing of the Fadre mesurid to us, and in this night us ledand. And the end of our wo: Sodenly our eye shall be openid in full light and clarity of syte which is our maker, Fader, and Holy Gost, in Jhesus our Savior. Eighty-third chapter.

I had in parte touching, sight, and feling in three propertes of God in which the strength and effect of all the revelation stondith, and thei were seene in

3321 **customably,** customarily, habitually. 3323 **clevand,** cleaving; **seand,** seeing. 3324 **wittand,** knowing. 3332 **lyt,** light.

every shewing, and most propirly in the twelfth wher it seith oftentimes, *I it am.*
The propertees are these: lif, love, and ligte. In life is mervelous homlihede, and
3350 in love is gentil curtesye, and in lyte is endless kyndhede. These propertes were
in on goodness, into which goodnes my reason wold ben onyd and cleve to with
all the myte. I beheld with reverent drede, and heyly mervelyng in the syte and
in the feling of the swet accord, that our reason is in God, understondyng that it
is the heyest gifte that we have receivid, and it is groundid in kinde. Our feith is a
3355 light kindly command of our endles day that is our fader, God, in which light our
Moder, Criste, and our good lord, the Holy Gost, leidith us in this passand life.

This light is mesurid discretly, nedefully standand to us in the night. The light
is cause of our life, the night is cause of our peyne and of al our wo, in which we
diserven mede and thanks of God. For we, with mercy and grace, wilfuly knowen
3360 and leven our light, goeand therin wisely and mytyly. And at the end of wo,
sodenly our eye shall ben openyd, and in clerte of light our sight shall be full,
which light is God our Maker, and Holy Gost, in Christ Jhesus our savior. Thus
I saw and understode that our feith is oure light in our night, which light is God,
our endless day.

LXXXIV

Charite is this light which is not so litil but that it is nedefull with travel to deserven
endles worshipfull thanke of God. For feith and hope leden us to charite which is in
three manners. Eighty-fourth chapter.

3365 The light is charite, and the mesuring of this light is don to us profitably by
the wisdam of God. For neyther the light is so large that we may seen our blisfull day, ne it is sperid fro us, but it is suich a light in which we may liven mede-
fully with travel deservand the endless worship of God. And this was seen in the
sixth shewing where He seid, *I thanke the of thi service and of thi travell.* Thus
3370 charite kepith us in feith and in hope, and hope ledith us in charite. And at the
end, al shall be charite.

I had three manner of understonding in this light, charite. The first is chartite
onmade. The second is charite made. The third is charite goven. Charite onmade
is God. Charite made is our soule in God. Charite goven is vertue. And that is
3375 a gracious geft of werking in which we loven God for Himselfe and ourselves in
God, and that God lovith, for God.

3361 clerte, clarity. **3367 sperid,** closed off; **suich,** such.

LXXXV

God lovid His chosen fro without begynnyng, and He never suffrith them to be hurte, wherof their bliss might be lessid; and how privities now hidde in Hevyn shall be knowen, wherefore we shall bliss our Lord that everything is so wele ordeynid. Eighty-fifth chapter.

And in this sight I mervelid heyley. For notwithstondyng our simple liveing and our blindhede here, yet endlesly our curtes Lord beholdith us in this worke-ing, enjoyand. And of all thing we may plesin Him best wisely and truely to leven
3380 it and to enjoyen with Him and in Him. For as verily as we shall ben in the bliss of God withouten end, Him praysand and thankand, as verily we have ben in the foresight of God lovid and knowen in His endless purpose fro withouten begyn-ning, in which onbegunne love He made us, and in the same love He kepith us, and never suffrith us to be hurte be which our bliss myte be lesid. And therfore
3385 whan the dome is goven, and we ben al browte up above, than we cleerly se in God the privities which be now hidde to us. Than shall non of us be sterid to sey in onywise, "Lord if it had ben thus, than it had bene full wele"; but we shall seyn al without voice, "Lord, blissid mot thou ben, for it is thus, it is wele." And now se we verily that all thing is done as it was then ordeynd beforn that ony
3390 thing was made.

LXXXVI

The Good Lord shewid this booke shuld be otherwise performid than at the first writing. And for His werking He will we thus prey, Him thankand, trostand, and in Him enjoy-and. And how He made this shewing because He will have it knowen, in which knoweing He will give us grace to love Him. For fifteen yeere after it was answerid that the cause of all this shewing was love, which Jhesus mote grant us. Amen. Eighty-sixth chapter.

This booke is begunne be Gods gift and His grace, but it is not yet performid, as to my syte. For charite pray we all to God, with Godds werking, thankand, trostand, enjoyand. For thus will our good Lord be prayd, as be the understond-ing that I tooke in al His owne mening and in the swete words wher He seith full
3395 merrily, *I am ground of thi beseking.* For trewly I saw and understode in our Lords mening that He shewid it for He will have it knowen more than it is, in which knowing He will given us grace to loven Him and clevyn to Him. For He

3389 **beforn that,** before.

beholdith His hevenly tresure with so grete love on erth that He will give us more light and solace in hevenly joy, in drawing of our herts, for sorow and merk-

3400 ness which we arn in.

And fro that time that it was shewid I desired oftentimes to witten what was our Lords mening. And fifteen yer after and more I was answerid in gostly understonding, seyand thus: *Woldst thou wetten thi Lords mening in this thing? Wete it wele, love was His mening. Who shewid it the? Love. What shewid He the?*

3405 *Love. Wherfore shewid it He? For love. Hold the therin, and thou shalt witten and knowen more in the same. But thou shalt never knowen ne witten therein other thing without end.* Thus was I lerid that love was our Lords mening. And I saw full sekirly, in this and in all, that ere God made us, He lovid us, which love was never slakid, no, never shall. And in this love He hath don all his werks, and in

3410 this love He hath made all things profitable to us. And in this love our life is everlestand. In our making we had beginning. But the love wherin He made us was in Him from withoute begynning, in which love we have our beginning. And all this shall be seen in God without end, which Jhesus mot grant us. Amen.

Thus endith the Revelation of love of the blissid Trinite shewid by our Savior,

3415 Christ Jesu, for our endles comfort and solace and also to enjoyen in Him in this passand jorney of this life.

Amen. Jhesu. Amen.

I pray Almyty God that this booke com not but to the hands of them that will be His faithfull lovers, and to those that will submitt them to the feith of Holy

3420 Church, and obey the holesom understondying and teching of the men that be of vertuous life, sadde age, and profound lerning. For this Revelation is hey Divin-itye and hey wisdam, wherfore it may not dwelle with him that is thrall to synne and to the Devill. And beware thou take not on thing after thy affection and liking and leve another, for that is the condition of an heretique. But take every-

3425 thing with other, and trewly understonden all is according to holy scripture and growndid in the same, and that Jhesus, our very love, light, and truth, shall shew to all clen soules that with mekenes aske perseverantly this wisdom of Hym. And thou to whome this booke shall come, thanke heyly and hertely our Savior Crist Jhesu that He made these shewings and revelations for the, and to the, of

3430 His endles love, mercy, and goodnes, for thine and our save guide and conduct to everlestyng bliss; the which Jhesus mot grant us. Amen.

3399—3400 merkness, darkness. **3424 heretique**, heretic.

Notes

Abbreviations:

C&W   *A Book of Showings to the Anchoress Julian of Norwich*, ed. Edmund Colledge and James Walsh. Toronto: Pontifical Institute of Mediaeval Studies, 1978. [Includes both short and long versions.]

S1   London. British Library MS Sloane 2499. [Base text for this edition of the longer version.]

S2   London. British Library MS Sloane 3705.

P   Paris. Bibliothèque Nationale MS Fonds anglais 40. [Base text for the longer version in C&W.]

A   London. British Library MS Additional 37790. [Base text for the short version in C&W.]

Chapter I

The shorter version gives no preliminary summary. If not editorial, this outline supports other evidence that Julian not only added to her book but also reconsidered it as a whole. Internal references directing readers to past or future passages (e.g., in chapters 17 and 56) also indicate that she reviewed the whole work as a whole. The shorter version lacks such referrals.

4   *the Trinite.* S1 *thee.*

11   *pretious.* S1 barely legible. P *precious.*

16   *also.* S1 *aso.* P *also.*

26–27   *and of the pretious asseth that He hath made for man synne. Asseth,* "satisfaction," "compensation," or "amends," is both a legal and an ecclesiastical term. John A. Alford includes it in his *Piers Plowman: A Glossary of Legal Diction* (Cambridge: D. S. Brewer/Boydell & Brewer, 1988), pp. 10–11, directing readers to *English Wycliffite Sermons*, ed. Anne Hudson (Oxford: Clarendon Press, 1983), 1, 497–99, for an entire sermon on the place of *asseth* in the economy of salvation. Mona Logarbo in "Salvation Theology in Julian of Norwich: Sin, Forgiveness, and Redemption in the *Revelations*," *Thought* 61 (1986), 374, points to derivation from OF *assez* which had its roots in Latin *ad satis*; she defines *asseth* in Julian as "that which makes sufficient"; what is sufficient for Julian, Logarbo indicates, is Christ's achieved filling in of the breach between God and humanity caused by the "great harm" of Adam's sin.

29 *make wele.* S1 *make wle.*

38 *wonyth.* S1 marginal gloss: *dwelleth.*

Chapter II

Eight chapter headings refer to Julian in the third person, those for chapters 2, 8, 9, 50, 51, 66, 69, and 81. All headings may be editorial, and those for chapters 9 and 81 almost certainly are, referring, as they do, to "the mekenes of this woman" and "this blissid woman."

42 *the eighth day of May.* P gives May 13 as the date.

44–45 *three wounds.* The shorter text adds a reference to Saint Cecelia: "For the thirde, I harde a man telle of halye kyrke of the storye of Saynte Cecylle. In the whilke schewynge I undyrstode that sche hadde thre woundys with a swerde in the nekke, with the whilke sche pynede to the dede. By the styrrynge of this I conseyvede a myghty desyre, prayande oure lorde god that he wolde grawnte me thre woundys . . ." [For the third, I heard a man tell of holy church's story of Saint Cecelia, from which account I understood that she had three wounds with a sword in her neck, with which she suffered till death. By this inspiration I conceived a mighty desire, praying our Lord God that He would grant me three wounds] (fol. 97v). This single mention of a normal and specific mode of receiving information is of hearing, not reading. Riehle believes that the request for three wounds and for physical illness owes something to women mystics on the continent whose writings may have reached England; the parallels he gives are approximate (pp. 28–30).

50   *and suffer with Him.* The shorter version adds, "not withstandynge that I leevyd sadlye alle the peynes of cryste as halye kyrke schewys & techys, & also the payntyngys of crucyfexes that er made be the grace of god aftere the techynge of haly kyrke to the lyknes of crystes passyoun, als farfurthe as manys witte maye reche" [notwithstanding that I firmly believed all the pains of Christ just as holy church shows and teaches, and also the paintings of crucifixes that are made to the likeness of Christ's passion, as far as man's intelligence may reach, by the grace of God, and after the teaching of holy church] (fol. 97r). Commentators cite this passage as evidence that religious art affects the images of the showings. For the possibility that "payntyngys" may be a neo-Platonic term, see C&W, I, 202, and the article cited there by G. V. Smithers, "Two Typological Terms in the *Ancrene Riwle*," *Medium Aevum* 34 (1965), 126–28.

Julian's desire to be in effect a fellow witness of the Crucifixion would not be unusual in the affective piety of the fourteenth century. Richard Rolle, the earlier fourteenth-century mystic, wrote a "Meditations on the Passion" in which the speaker attempts to view the events of Christ's last hours from arrest to entombment as if they were unfolding before his eyes in sequence (*English Writings of Richard Rolle*, ed. Hope Emily Allen [Oxford: Clarendon Press, 1931], pp. 17–36). The popular pseudo-Bonaventuran *Meditationes vitae Christi* (13th century) initiated and sustained many similar devotions. See Jantzen for a sketch of precedents and the role of monastic reading technique as an influence upon the development of such devotion (pp. 56–58). What is unusual about Julian's petition is the form its granting took. For the theme of Christ's suffering as it figures in the writings of female mystics in particular, see Petroff, pp. 9–16. For the distinctive caste of Julian's treatment of this theme, see Bhattacharji, pp. 85–88.

64   *seying.* S2; S1 *sey.* P's syntax is too different to furnish the word.

69   *willfull longing to God.* In medieval psychology the will was the faculty which could choose and love. *Will* and *willful* are specific, weighted words in Julian, usually carrying the sense of a sustained intentionality, a fully conscious choosing. See lines 85, 167–68, 225–28, and 2710–12 as typical examples. Though the request for a critical illness to death is the one that startles, to a great extent this third part of her third request, the desired willful longing to God, constitutes the core subject of the *Shewings* which

also illustrates it. *Longing* may mean either yearning or belonging, and Julian's use frequently captures both definitions.

Chapter III

77   *sweeme.* S1 marginal gloss: *regret.*

89   *My curate was sent for.* A is more circumstantial: "thay that were with me sente for the persoun, my curette, to be atte myne endynge [the parson, my curate, to be at my end]. He come, and a childe with hym, and brought a crosse & be thanne I hadde sette myne eyenn [eyes], and myght nought speke. The persone sette the crosse before my face, and sayde: 'Dowghtter, I have brought the [thee] the ymage of thy sauioure'" (fol. 98r).

99   *After this the other party of my body began to dyen.* A reports, "Myne handdys felle downe on aythere syde, and also for vnpowere my heede satylde downe" [went limp] (fol. 98r).

100   *onethys.* S1 marginal gloss: *scarcely.*

            onde. S1 marginal gloss: *winde.*

106   *lever.* S1 marginal gloss: *rather.*

Chapter IV

126–27   *that He that is so reverend and dredfull will be so homley. Homeliness* is a favorite item in Julian's vocabulary. Along with *courteous*, it describes God's personal, loving attitude toward the individual soul. English mystics may also use *homely* in passages on intimate communion of the soul with the divine. The author of *The Cloud of Unknowing* writes that some aspirants do not reach "ravisching" — mystic union — "with-outyn moche & longe goostly excersise," but that others "ben so sotyl [subtle] in grace & in spirit, & so homely with God in this grace of contemplacion, that thei mowe [may] have it [i.e., God's presence] when thei wolen [wish to]" (ed. Phyllis Hodgson, EETS o.s. 218, 1944; rev. 1973 [London: Oxford University Press, 1981], p. 126). Compare *The Book of Margery Kempe*, ed. Meech and Allen,

p. 90. According to Riehle, *homeliness* translates *familiaritas*, which Gregory the Great (c. 540–604) introduced into theological language to describe the mystical union of the soul and God (pp. 97–99). S1 here glosses *homely* in the margin as *familiar*. Julian sometimes uses the word in its specialized sense, sometimes colloquially.

129   *or.* S1 marginal gloss: *before.*

139   *hir maker.* S1 *his.* S2 agrees with P's *her.*

143   *manhood.* P; S1 omits.

Chapter V

145   *for us.* P *to our helpe.*

146–47   *wrappeth us . . . tender love.* S1 is intermittently blotched by ink that has soaked through from the other side of the page. P expands the clause: *wrappeth us and wyndeth us, halseth us and all becloseth us, hangeth about us for tender love.*

151   *lesten.* S1 marginal gloss: *last.*

152   *it might suddenly have fallen to nowte for littil.* The short text continues, "In this blyssede revelacion god schewyd me thre noughtes of whilke noughttes [showed me three naughts, of which naughts] this is the fyrste that was schewyd me. Of this nedes ilke [each] man and woman to hafe knawynge that desyres to lyeve contemplatyfelye [live as a contemplative], that hym lyke to nought alle thynge that es made for to hafe the love of god that es unmade" (fol. 99v). This passage implies that Julian may have written the short text with contemplatives in mind as her primary audience. The other "naughts" are probably sin and the devil (C&W, I, 215).

161   *howe.* P *have.* S1 marginal gloss: *know.* It is tempting to follow the marginal gloss and to emend *howe* to *knowe,* so that the sense would be more parallel with the *have knoweing* in line 160. As is, *for to love and howe God that is unmade* seems to mean "in order to love and have (possess, obtain) God who is without creator."

175–76   *touchen the will.* S1 marginal gloss: *agreeing to his will.*

Chapter VI

207   *oure God.* P; S1 omits.

207–08   *that hath us all in Himselfe beclosyd.* P adds: "A man goyth vppe ryght and the soule of his body is sparyde [closed], as a purse fulle feyer. And whan it is tyme of his nescessery, it is openyde and sparyde ayen [again] fulle honestly. And that it is he that doyth this it is schewed ther wher he seyth, he comyth downe to vs to the lowest parte of oure nede" (fol. 12r). C&W offers the translation "cooked, digested food" for *soule* from OE *sufol* (II, 306). A. M. Allchin comments, "Julian is so integrated in herself, so penetrated throughout her being by this conviction of the all-encompassing goodness of God, that she can speak quite simply of the processes of the digestion and evacuation of food as ways in which God serves us. There are few spiritual writers who have spoken so directly and so naturally on this subject" (pp. 37–38).

209   *simplest office that to. to* P; S1 *do.*

212   *bouke.* S1 marginal gloss: *Bulke.*

216   *herete.* S1 marginal gloss: *heart.*

226   *blyn.* S1 marginal gloss: *cease, leave fr.*

233   *even Cristen.* S1 marginal gloss: *Xstian neighbour.*

Chapter VII

235   *the hey.* S1 *they hey.*

241–51   *In all the tyme . . . spreadeing on the forehead.* In the course of an argument that cultural representations may be constitutive of the mystic's experience, Laurie A. Finke writes that this passage hints of an intense meditation upon a visual image (for instance, in a book of hours) in which particular details "lose their relationship to the whole composition and begin to remind her of other inanimate objects. As she traces the brushstrokes, following the change in color from brownish red to bright red, finally vanishing from the canvas, other images — pellets, raindrops, herring's scales — suggest themselves to her, transforming the suffering into an artistic vision, a representation that seems self-conscious in its artifice" (*Feminist Theory, Women's Writing* [Ithaca: Cornell University Press, 1992], p. 97). Without taking anything from the absorbed intensity that Finke observes, the possibility also exists that this is simply another example of Julian's free use of everyday surroundings. Campbell has noted that fish, especially herring, may have formed a major source of wealth for Norwich as early as the eleventh century. A charter of between 1114 and 1160 records a render of at least 2,000 herring owed by a house in the city, and herring pies were among the renders which Norwich owed to the Crown in the thirteenth century (p. 7). My own sense of the passage is that this is an effort to communicate, to get the vision down exactly as remembered.

244   *semand.* S1 marginal gloss: *seeming.*

252   *mynde.* P; S1 omits.

258–59   *He shewid this opyn example.* Nuth regards this as an intimation of the lord and servant parable of chapter 51, pointing out that, like that parable, this and other passages that feature a lord or king in relation to a servant or subject appear only in the long text (p. 31).

266   *hart.* P; S1 partially illegible.

Chapter VIII

290   *that ever was, is, and ever shal bene.* This is the first of Julian's several echoes of the doxology: "Glory be to the Father, to the Son, and to the Holy Spirit who was in the beginning, is now, and ever shall be, world without end." Among many instances, see lines 815–16 and 836–37. This is the only familiar liturgical formula that Julian resorts to continually. She would have heard it at mass. J. P. H. Clark notes Julian's attribution of might, wisdom, and love to the Father, Son, and Holy Spirit respectively as the common appropriation based on Augustine and developed by the scholastics ("Fiducia," p. 225).

303   *sterid.* S1 marginal gloss: *stirr'd.*

306   *domys day.* Two doomsdays await the soul; Julian refers to the individual judgment of the soul at the individual's moment of dying; at the apocalyptic doomsday at the end of time, souls and bodies will be reunited for a final, confirming, general judgment.

310   *mervil.* S1 marginal gloss: *strange.*

314   *levyn.* S1 marginal gloss: *leave of.* The word may be glossed either *believe* or *leave.* In the first case, Julian says that since God intends the revelation not for herself alone but also for all her even Christians, they should believe it. In the second case, she urges that Christians use her report of her beholding merely as a crutch, discarding it for beholding God Himself. See also notes to lines 1585 and 2876.

Chapter IX

328–32   *And God hat made al . . . and God is in al.* In A this passages continues into Julian's apology (or apologia) for addressing fellow Christians as a teacher even though she is a woman (fols. 100v–101r), given below, Appendix A.

330–32   *For in mankynd . . . and God is in al.* This is Julian's first statement of an inclusiveness that binds God and human souls, creator, creatures, and creation, in an interpenetrating reality.

335   *But in al thing I leve as Holy Church levith, preachith, and teachith.* This is the first of Julian's affirmations of accordance with the Church's teaching.

      leve. S1 gloss: *beleeve.*

Chapter X

348   *sollowing.* A reads *sowlynge* (fol. 101v), which C&W gives as "to soil," derived from OF *suill(i)er, soill(i)er.* For Biblical background, see C&W II, 324.

351   *it vanyssched.* P; S1 omits.

355   *For I saw Him and sowte Hym.* S1: *For I saw him sowte*; marginal gloss: *sowght*. P: *And thus I saw him and sought him.*

363–65   *Than I understode . . . harme.* S1 marginal gloss: *NB*. This *nota bene* annotation is comparable to marginal hands in earlier medieval manuscripts, which call the user's attention to passages some reader favored.

364   *is with.* P; S1 illegible.

366–67   *will that.* P; S1 illegible.

370   *sprets.* S1 marginal gloss: *spirits.*

375   *the holy vernacle of Rome.* According to the legend of the vernicle, St. Veronica's kerchief became impressed with an exact image of the face of the suffering Christ when she compassionately wiped His face as He carried the cross to Calvary. Preserved at St. Peter's in Rome, the cloth became an object of pilgrimage. C&W discusses Julian's use of the vernicle, gives an account the devotion's currency in fourteenth-century England, and provides a bibliography (I, 53–55).

395   *owen to trowen.* S1 marginal gloss: *We ought to believe.*

400   *rewfull.* P; S1 *reuly.*

403   *this wrought.* P: *this is wrought.*

404   *fyndyng is.* S1 reads *fyndyng is is.*

425   *full.* S1 marginal gloss: *very.*

Chapter XI

440–41   *For He is . . . no synne.* S1 marginal gloss: *NB*.

467   *meneing.* S1 marginal gloss: *speaking.*

Chapter XII

With dazzling rapidity, Julian moves in this chapter from the specific showing of the scourging to the cosmic theaters of God's redemptive blood, earth, heaven, and hell.

The shift is also one from literal to typological to anagogical levels of allegory, as the transitions from blood to water, to generic liquid, and back to blood whip to a rhetorical peroration. But all this is guided by a specific, self-reflexive note on her associative process, "And than cam to my minde" (481).

473–74   *seming of the scorgyng.* The *seming* or furrowing is from gashes; Glasscoe's glossary gives *weals.* "Appearance" is surely one translation of *seming,* but derivation from *seam,* a furrow, groove, or gash from a long, incised wound is equally a possibility. Either makes sense. The MED cites Julian in giving "gash" for *seam.*

479   *if it had be so in kind and in substance.* Elizabeth N. Evasdaughter calls attention to the hypothetical phrasing; Julian noticed an "edge" between her visions and the ordinary perceived world and did not require that what was seen in them correspond to what would have been seen in non-visionary circumstances (p. 204).

480   *it should have made the bed al on blode and a passid over aboute.* Maria R. Lichtmann points to the "charged," "taboo" aspect of this profuse bleeding, an outpouring made even more taboo, she observes, when comparing its overflowing of boundaries to the necessity for containment of fluidity stressed in Talmudic texts (pp. 15, 18, note 11). Lichtmann's basic argument is that unlike those spiritual writers who wish to escape the prison of body, Julian regards the body as the locus of spiritual enlightenment, developing both an epistemology, the body as a vehicle for knowing God, and a theology of the body (p. 17). Elizabeth Robertson comments on this passage and compares Julian's "extraordinary and idiosyncratically female uses of blood imagery" with Richard Rolle's meditation upon Christ's blood (pp. 154–56).

483   *hys.* P; S1 *is. to wassch us.* P; S1 *illegible.*

Chapter XIII *encres.* S1 marginal gloss: *encrease.*

505–06   *all sent of salvation.* Marion Glasscoe comments that *sent* is used in a "common medieval context of divine dispensation and refers to those ordained by God to salvation" ("Visions and Revisions," 112).

510-11   *But in God may be no wreth, as to my syte.* Perhaps an implied contrast to the devil's malicious attitude, this comment can only be inferentially linked with what goes before; the theme will be taken up more fully in chapter 48.

518   *seen.* P; S1 *ben.*

522   *sothfastnes.* S1 marginal gloss: *veracity, constancy.*

524   *game.* P; S1 *same.*

Chapter XIV   *servants.* S2; S1 *servats.*

546   *that him.* S1 *that him hym.*

554   *underfongyn.* S1 marginal gloss: *received.*

561   *the lever he is to serve Him . . . his life.* Here and in similar passages, the Paris manuscript gives *she* as the pronoun for the soul to S1's *he* or *it.* Perhaps because of Latin *anima,* the medieval pronoun for the soul is frequently feminine. The phrase *the dayes of his* is lightly crossed through in S1.

Chapter XV

564   *was in al peace.* S1 reads *was was.*

567   *onethis.* S1 marginal gloss: *scarcely.*

574-76   *I migte have seid with Seynt Paul . . . I perish.* See Romans 8:35: "Who then shall separate us from the love of Christ?"; Matt. 8:25: "And they came to him and awakened him, saying: Lord, save us, we perish"; and Matt. 14:30: "he was afraid: and when he began to sink, he cried out, saying: Lord, save me." The passages from Matthew are conflated. Julian's references to the Bible are not so direct or so pervasive as those of most Middle English mystics; one gets the impression that Hilton would have no text without the Bible. Colledge and Walsh, whose appendices include a thorough one on Julian's Biblical allusions, regard her independence as a clue that she made her own translations from the Vulgate. Though she might have used a

Wycliffite translation, her wording is not close to the only ones known to have been in circulation in her time. Other possibilities are a Wycliffite Bible unknown to us or an Anglo-French translation. They conclude that her own translating is most probable. ("Editing Julian of Norwich's *Revelations*," pp. 408–11). See also Pelphrey's appendix in *Love Was His Meaning* on the influence of Scripture, pp. 331–49. The evidence is also consistent with Biblical familiarity through hearing and quotation from memory.

587   *folow.* P; S1 illegible.

Chapter XVI

594–95 *swemful.* S1 marginal gloss: *strange gastly.*

597–99 *For that same tyme . . . sigte.* S1 marginal gloss: *NB.* This is the only physical manifestion of the showings given a *nota bene.* Although cold is frequently a feature of representations of the Crucifixion in the thirteenth through the fifteenth centuries, the notice of a harsh wind is rare, if not unique, among them.

597   *same.* P; S1 *eche. Eche* makes sense, but Julian elsewhere indicates that she is aware that Christ, in fact, died but once. See A, fol. 103v.

598   *wonder.* P; S1 *wond.*

606   *and peynfully dreyden up all the lively spirits of Crists fleshe.* Vincent J. DiMarco's note to Chaucer's Knight's Tale A.2743–56 is helpful: "According to the physiology developed from Galen, there were three kinds of virtues (otherwise called spirits) that operate most of the body's vital processes: the *natural*, situated in the liver; the *vital*, localized chiefly in the heart; and the *animal*, operating through the brain" (*The Riverside Chaucer*, ed. Larry D. Benson [Boston: Houghton-Mifflin, 1987], p. 839.) For passages where Chaucer chooses *spirit* rather than *virtue*, see The Knight's Tale A.1369 and *The Book of the Duchess* 489. Among Chaucerian cases, these are the most obviously physiological, Julian's context here. DiMarco notes Bartholomaeus Anglicus as a contemporary source. See *On the Properties of Things: John Trevisa's Translation of Bartholomaeus Anglicus De Proprietatibus Rerum*, ed. M. C. Seymour and others, 3 vols. (Oxford: Clarendon

Press, 1975), 1, 103–08 (Book 3, chapters 14–16). Bartholomaeus credits Constantinus Africanus (d. 1097) as his authority; Chaucer readers will recall that as well as Galen, the second century Greek ("Galyen" A.431), "Constantyn" is among the numerous authorities known to the doctour of physik (A.433). Though her *lively spirits* seems to translate the *vertues vitales* standing in the Trevisa Bartholomaeus, it is doubtful if the work could have been known to Julian. Trevisa was a contemporary of Julian's, finishing his translation in 1398–99. But though there were numerous Latin manuscripts of Bartholomaeus available in the fourteenth century, the new English remained scarce, apparently until a printing in 1495 by Wynkyn De Worde. On the whole matter of physiological spirits, see also Walter Clyde Curry, *Chaucer and the Mediaeval Sciences*, 2nd rev. ed (New York: Barnes & Noble, 1960), pp. 140–45 and 203–06.

Chapter XVII S1 misnumbers as 18.

624   *heire.* S1 marginal gloss: *haire.*

629   *thorow.* P; S1 *thowe.*

645   *askyd.* P; S1 *asky.*

651   *thingke* P; S1 *thynyn.*

652   *for it may not be told.* The short text is more expansive here, including that Julian's mother and others were at her bedside: "Swilke paynes I sawe that alle es to litelle that y can telle or saye, for itt maye nought be tolde, botte ylke saule aftere the sayinge of saynte Pawle schulde feele in hym that in criste Jhesu. This schewynge of criste paynes fillyd me fulle of paynes, For I wate weele he suffrede nought botte anes botte as he walde schewe yt me and fylle me with mynde as I hadde desyrede before. My modere that stode emangys othere and behelde me lyftyd uppe hir hande before me face to lokke mynn eyenn for sche wenyd I had bene dede or els I hadde dyede and this encrysyd mekille my sorowe, for nought withstandynge alle my paynes, I wolde nought hafe beenn lettyd for loove that I hadde in hym" [I saw such pains that all I can tell or say is too little, for they may not be told; but each soul, after the saying of Saint Paul, should feel in him what Jesus Christ felt. This showing of the pains of Christ filled me full of pain, for I

know well He suffered but once; but He wished to show this to me and fill me with full knowledge, as I had desired before. My mother, who stood among others and beheld me, lifted up her hand before my face to close my eyes, for she thought I was dead, or else had just died. And this increased my sorrow much, for notwithstanding all my pains, I did not want to be stopped (from seeing the showing) because of the love I had in Him.] (fol. 103v).

661   *is.* P; S1 omits.

663   *sothfastly.* S1 marginal gloss: *assuredly.*

664   *so.* P; S1 illegible.

Chapter XVIII *with.* S2; S1 omits.

687   *Sain Dionyse of France.* Tradition had gathered about the mid-third century career of Saint Dionysius or Denis of France, apostle and martyr in Gaul, the lives of two other figures, the Dionysius of Acts 17 converted by St. Paul (Dionysius the Areopagite) and the late fifth- or early sixth- century author of mystical tracts, pseudo-Dionysius, who assigned his work to the apostolic contemporary. Julian gives to her figure the inscription "To the unknown God" which Paul finds at Athens and claims as a reference to Christ. *The Cloud of Unknowing* author translated writings of pseudo-Dionysius. Although not all are persuaded, it has been suggested that familiarity with pseudo-Dionysius marks Julian's thought (Reynolds, "Some Literary," pp. 23–24). Classified as possibly pseudo-Dionysian are the seeing of God in a point (427–28); the statement that all kinds flow out of God (2600–04); and the special use of *touch* (e.g., 1237, 2317, and 3346).

689–90   *kynde. auter.* S1 marginal glosses: *nature. Alter.*

Chapter XX

727–33   *And thus saw I . . . dethe.* A usual reading of this passage would regard it as a trope. Denise Levertov's "On a Theme from Julian's Chapter XX" enforces the difficult, literal reading. See *Breathing the Water* (New York: New Directions, 1984), pp. 68–69.

740   *mannys.* P; S1 *manny.*

Chapter XXI *Crosse.* S1 capitalizes *Cross* throughout this chapter.

756   *wet.* Perhaps P's *wende* is preferable.

Chapter XXII *The ninth Revelation is of the. The, of* S2; S1 *he, o.*

785   *bodyly.* S1 *dodyly.* P *bodely.*

787   *mede.* S1 marginal gloss: *reward.*

792   *beyeng.* S1 marginal gloss: *buying.*

798   *never.* S1 *neve.* P *nevyr.*

Chapter XXIII

843   *lykyng.* S1 marginal gloss: *liking.*

847   *And.* P; S1 *Ad.*

Chapter XXIV *two.* S2; S1 *tw.*

871   *that is to mene.* S1 marginal gloss: *conceive.*

878   *have.* P; S1 *hay.*

Chapter XXV

915   *conceyvyd.* P; S1 *grevid.*

Chapter XXVI

917   *Lorde.* P; S1 *Lodd. And after this.* The short version reads: "And eftyr this
    oure lorde schewyd hym to me mare gloryfyed as to my syght than I sawe

hym before, and in this was I lerede that ilke saule contemplatyfe to whilke es gyffenn to luke and seke god schalle se hire and passe vnto god by contemplacioun" [And after this our Lord showed Himself to me more glorified in my sight than I had seen Him before, and in this I was taught that to each contemplative soul to whom it is given to look and seek God shall see her and pass to God by contemplation] (fol. 106r). In the short text there is no chapter division at this point; C&W refers *hire* to Mary above, citing a belief that one's last days may be graced by a vision of Mary occurring in a prayer frequently inscribed in French books of hours (I, 243). Though the pronoun in this passage is probably not evidence of the fact, elsewhere Julian clearly advances feminine aspects of divinity.

918–19   *I was lernyd that our soule shal never have rest til it comith to Hym.* As a number of commentators have observed, the language recalls St. Augustine's *fecisti nos ad te et inquietum est cor nostrum, donec requiescat in te* [you have made us for yourself, and our hearts are restless until they rest in you (*Confessions*, 1.1)]. Reynolds places Augustine as second only to the Vulgate Bible as an influence upon Julian ("Some Literary," p. 22).

Chapter XXVII

Chapter 27 is headed as 28 in S1. This chapter begins the discussion of sin that is quoted in T. S. Eliot's "Little Gidding." According to Loretta Lucido Johnson's work in progress, Eliot became acquainted with Julian when as an undergraduate he read W. R. Inge's *Studies of English Mystics* (1906). At that time he also read Evelyn Underhill's *Mysticism* (1911) and took notes upon it (Helen Gardner, *The Composition of Four Quartets* [New York: Oxford University Press, 1978], p. 69, note 82). Eliot later met Underhill and also May Sinclair, whose *Defence of Idealism: Some Questions and Conclusions* (New York: Macmillan, 1917) refers to Julian several times. (See esp. pp. 240–89.) Eliot reviewed some of Sinclair's work, and they met socially, according to Johnson's dissertation, *T. S. Eliot's "Criterion," 1922–1939*, Columbia University, 1980, pp. 13–15. Underhill was also a contributor to *Criterion*. Julian's writing therefore reached deeply into Eliot's past when he retrieved it in the early forties for three passages in "Little Gidding" (lines 166–68, 196–99, and 255–56). The quotations from Julian are a revision; early drafts show in their place a readaptation of the familiar Eucharistic prayer "Anima Christi." When he substituted Julian's "Sin is behovely" he needed to identify the lines (and also one from *The Cloud of Unknowing*) for his correspondent, friend, and consultant, John Hayward. Gardner's book includes an excerpt from the Hayward correspondence in which Eliot says that he read "Juliana" in the Cressy edition in a reprint published "where, do you think? Why, in St. Louis, Mo." (p. 71). For details on the revision see Gardner, pp. 69–71 and pp. 201–24. Susan McCaslin reviews Eliot's choice of Julian with the further suggestion that in selecting Julian for a representation of the English mystical life, he has retrieved a writer whose experience and movements of thought between concrete and abstract parallel his own imaginative movements in their dealings with time's relation to eternity ("Vision and Revision in *Four Quartets*: T. S. Eliot and Julian of Norwich," *Mystics Quarterly* 12 [1986], 172).

936   *without reason and discretion.* A adds, ". . . of fulle grete pryde. & never-thelesse Jhesu in this visioun enfourmede me of alle that me neded. I saye nought that me nedes na mare techynge, for oure lorde with the schewynge of this hase lefte me to haly kyrke [holy church], and I am hungery and thyrstye and nedy and synfulle and freele, & wilfully submyttes me to the techynge of haly kyrke with alle myne even crystenn in to the ende of my lyfe. He aunswerde be this worde, and sayde: "Synne is behovelye . . ." (fol. 106r). Watkin glosses *behovely,* usually translated *necessary,* "has its part in the Divine economy of good" (p. 22). Sheila Upjohn translates, "Sin is behovely — it had to be —" in *In Love Enclosed: More Daily Readings with Julian of Norwich,* ed. Robert Llewelyn (London: Darton, Longman and Todd, 1985), p. 29. I owe my acquaintance with Upjohn's clear translations from Julian to Rose Ronan Halpern and Mary Daley Ronan.

950–51   *But I saw not synne, for I beleve it hath no manner of substance ne no party of being.* That evil is a privation of good, a nothingness, rather than a part of creation was a common philosophical proposition which could have come to Julian from several sources, among them St. Augustine (see *Confessions* 3.7 and 7.12–16) or Boethius (*Consolation* 4.2); Colledge and Walsh have proposed that Julian just may have read Chaucer's translation of Boethius ("Editing Julian of Norwich's *Revelations,*" p. 422).

Substance is technical and philosophical here, referring to the core reality of any manifestation, material or spiritual. Substance is the inner actuality independent of external changes. Later, Julian will assert that our natural substance is always kept safe in God (1565–66 and 1597–98), and even that there is no difference between God and our substance (2221), quickly re-stating: "God is God, and our substance is a creture in God" (2222–23). The "fullest substance" is the "blissid soule of Criste" (2203). Earlier uses of the word informed by this meaning occur at lines 157–58, "substantially onyd," and line 668, "a substance of kynd love."

960   *sythen*. P; S1 *seith*.

Chapter XXVIII

974   *lakid*. S1 marginal gloss: *not liked of, from the dutch word lackon, to dispraise, to blame, being the opposit to the D. word* prijsen, *to praise*.

Chapter XXIX

994   *menyng*. S1 marginal gloss: *thought*.

1000   *asyeth*. S1 marginal gloss: *satisfaction*.

Chapter XXX

1008   *mankynde*. P; S1 *mankyd*.

1009   *councellid*. S1 *counellid*. P *counceylyd*.

1015   *privy councell*. The OED gives Barbour's *Bruce*, 1375, as its first instance of *privy council* to designate a group of private counsellors to the sovereign. Julian's quick troping of a political term new in the vernacular indicates an absorbing mind, or it may merely signal that she knew Latin. James F. Baldwin's *The King's Council in England during the Middle Ages* (1913; rpt. Gloucester, Mass.: Peter Smith, 1965) notes that the terms *secretum consilium* and *privatum consilium* appear in official records from the first quarter of the century; French equivalents such as *le privé counseil* also became current at this time. The term did not refer to the more powerful ancestor of the present British institution, but simply to a royal council secretly summoned (p. 105). Julian's diction is politically allusive. In this passage, it is an added force that "ryal lordship" referred to real and great, not titular, power in the daily world. The positioning of lord and servant in chapter 51 speaks to daily power relations with which Julian would expect any conceivable audience to identify. Even a term like *courtesy*, so frequent in her *Shewings*, was tinged by the existence of courts which functioned as real centers of power, sources of support, and cultural models.

Chapter XXXI

1033   *shalle.* P; S1 *sha.*

1040   *fully.* P; S1 *filly.*

1042   *amenst.* Probably for *anemst*, "concerning," as in line 1047 and after. S1 reads *amenst the God the godhede.* S1 marginal gloss: *as concerning, or w[i]th respect unto.*

Chapter XXXII

1077   *dedes.* S1 *dedse.* P *dedys.*

1078   *harmes.* P; S1 *harmy.*

1094–96   *This is the grete dede . . . wele.* S1 marginal gloss: *NB.* Several commentators have speculated that the great deed planned from time's beginning to be known only at time's end is universal salvation. Although she concludes that "Julian does not, strictly speaking, teach a doctrine of universal salvation," Joan Nuth assembles anew the evidence for such a possibility (pp. 162–69).

1099   *growndid.* S1 *gowndid.* P *groundyd.*

Chapter XXXIII

1118   *prefe.* P; S1 *privy.*

        that. S1 reads *that that,* reiterating the word at the end of the MS line with an abbreviation at the head of the next line. The scribe does the same thing with the *that* in line 1123.

1123   *that.* S1 reads *that that.*

1133   *But I saw not so propirly specyfyed the Jewes.* Julian discriminates between what her visions tell her and what she understands to be the church's teaching. She does not contradict the second, but her showings simply do not include cursed Jews; and she says they do not. The devil is within her imaging of the spiritual world, but damned souls are not. She gives no evidence that she participated in the anti-Semitism of her time and place. The first legend of Jewish ritual child murder comes from Norwich, that of St. William, d. 1144. "The mutilated body of this twelve-year-old boy was found in a wood outside Norwich; five years later it was alleged that he was a victim of ritual murder by Jews. The authorities seem not to have credited the story; but the common people did, and William was venerated locally as a martyr" (Donald Attwater, *The Penguin Dictionary of Saints* [Harmondsworth, Eng.: Penguin Books, 1965], p. 342). Chaucer readers will recall "yonge Hugh of Lyncoln" (d. 1255) "slayn also / With cursed Jewes," whom the Prioress apostrophizes as she closes a similar, later story (VII.684–85). England had expelled its Jews in 1290. There had been a Jewish community in Norwich from about 1144; Jews gave the city its "only early physicians" (Walter Rye, *Some Historical Essays Chiefly Relating to Norfolk,* Part II [Norwich: H.W. Hunt, 1926], p. 136). They did not have an easy time there. See V.D. Lipman, *The Jews of Medieval Norwich* (London: Jewish Historical Society, 1967) for an account of the community. The story of William and accounts of other episodes of Christian conflicts with the Jewish community during the some hundred and fifty years of its existence are given on pp. 49–64.

1135   *dampnyd.* P; S1 *dampny.*

Chapter XXXIV

1153   *we may.* P; S1 *me way.*

1158–59   *He is the techyng, He is the techer, He is the leryd.* For a survey of Christ as teacher in Julian and a compressed account of the background tradition see Sister Ritamary Bradley, "Christ, the Teacher."

1161   *seke.* P; S1 *seky.*

Notes

Chapter XXXV

1166   *Hys*. P; S1 *hss*.

1167   *a certeyn creature that I lovid*. The short text does not give the information that the person in whom Julian takes an interest had begun in "good lyvyng," but does indicate that this beloved soul was a woman: "And when God alle myghttye hadde schewed me plentyuouslye and fully of his goodnesse, I desyred of a certayne persoun that I lovyd howe it schulde be with hire. And in this desyre I lettyd [hampered] myselfe, for I was noght taught in this tyme" (fol. 108r). It has been proposed that the person may have been a child, Emma, the daughter of Sir Miles Stapleton, whose house was visible from the cell window of Saint Julian's church, according to Robert Flood. Lady Emma Stapleton later was a recluse at White Friars Priory (1421–42). Flood imagines the circumstances of Julian's concern for this neighbor child, who would have traveled the road past the cell on her way to another of the Stapleton residences: "Doubtless she had many conversations with the lady through her window . . ." (p. 39). Of course any such identification is speculative. Flood's small book (see Introduction, p. 9, note 12), is an attractive, affectionate effort to propose for Julian's words literal details of the precise local world of their utterance as well as a report of the church structure, which Flood studied before the bombing of 1942.

1178   *Hymselfe*. S1 *hymsef*.

1188   *by*. P; S1 omits.

1189   *onto*. S1 reads *onto to*.

1191   *Hymselfe*. S1 *hymsef*.

            werks. S1 *weks*. P *workes*.

1192   *soule that seith*. *that*. P; S1 *the*.

1198–1200   *And by His sufferaunce we fallyn. . . . And be mercy and grace we arn reysid*. Pelphrey writes that Julian uses neither of the chief versions of progress in spiritual life offered in medieval mystical theology, ascent (as in the image of Hilton's scale) or the triadic stages of purgation, illumination, and union with God. She does not speak about ascent or about distinctions in spirituality, but offers the image of falling and rising with the falls also benefitting the soul. A theology of falling and rising is developed through chapters 47–49 and 61–85 (*Love Was His Meaning*, pp. 199–204). For summing statements, see lines 2080–81, 3138–42, and 3333–35.

1199   *sufferaunce*. P; S1 *suffranc*.

Chapter XXXVI *known*. S2. S1 *kowen*.

1204   *Hymselfe*. S1 *hymsef*.

1209   *shalle*. P; S1 *sha*.

1216   *He*. P; S1 omits.

1229   shalle. P; S1 *sha*.

1233–34   *matter of mekenes . . . matter to enjoyen in me*. In their translation of the long text, Colledge and Walsh indicate that Julian uses *matter* in its philosophical sense as the primary stuff of creation "to which form is to be given" (*Julian of Norwich: Showings*, p. 239, note 163). Panichelli refers *matter* in this passage to the antecedent *sin*, and sets this dialectically against the view that sin has no "manner substance ne no party of being" which Julian has advanced in chapter 27 (pp. 304–05; p. 310).

1238–39   *Lete be al thi love . . . thi salvation*. Margaret Gascoigne, member of the seventeenth-century Benedictine community which almost certainly is responsible for the writing of S1 and P, quotes these lines and identifies them as being by "a deere childe of thine . . . Julian the Ankress" (see Introduction above, pp. 15–16). She follows the P reading, "Lett me aloone, my derwurdy chylde" (fol. 65v). C&W suggest that the P reading can be understood as "Do not seek to hinder me," with precedent for the phrase in Exodus 32:9–10 (II, 439). The S1 reading may be understood as "Allow all your love to come into its full existence," or as "Let alone — have done with — lesser attachments and loves." The second possibility would reinforce the folly of "beholdying of the reprovyd," which is the immediate context of this divine locution.

1240   *Lordys*. P; S1 *Lods*.

1245   *we.* P; S1 omits.

1259   *for sorrow. for.* P; S1 omits.

Chapter XXXVII

1264   *that.* S1 *tha.*

1273-74 *For in every soule that shal be savid is a godly wil that never assentid to synne ne never shal.* The statement has been called heretical (e.g., Hudleston, pp. xxiii–iv, and Wolters, pp. 37–38). See Hanshell's essay for a review of the question, and Clark, "Fiducia," for precedents in Cassian and William of St. Thierry (p. 218). See also Judith Lang, "'The Godly Wylle' in Julian of Norwich," *The Downside Review*, 102 (1984), 163–74; del Mastro (1988), pp. 84–93; Gilchrist, pp. 77–88; and C&W I, 254, note 9, and II, 443, note 15.

1278-79 *as wele. as.* P; S1 *a.*

Chapter XXXVIII

1287-88 *the goodnes of God suffrith never that soul to synne that shal come there.* P reads: *that soule to synne fynally that shalle come ther.* Without *fynally,* Julian appears to be stating that God does not permit a Christian to sin at all. Pelphrey, opposing a suggestion that *fynally* may have been a scribal insertion, observes that without this, the sentence contradicts what Julian says elsewhere, that she has been given to understand that she and her even-Christians will sin (*Love Was His Meaning,* pp. 275–76).

1288   *but which synne shal be rewardid . . . made knowen.* Charles Cummings comments upon Julian's insights as analogous to Christ's appearance to Thomas, with wounds in hands and side, the risen Christ standing in continuity with the historical Jesus. Julian's insight amounts to a "safeguard of individual identity. The continuity of the individual person is preserved, with his or her unique identity shaped through life by failures as well as triumphs. . . . The total reality of sinful as well as virtuous deeds remains a fact of personal history and world history. It is the same, historical, sinful, forgiven person who is predestined, called, justified and glorified" ("Wounded in Glory," *Mystics Quarterly* 10 [1984], 74–75).

1293   *Thomas of Inde.* S2. A agrees. Variations in S1 and in P offer different examples of how manuscript variations may occur. S1 reads *those of Inde,* a contraction of *Thomas* in the copy text evidently responsible for this Mandevillian aura. The Paris manuscript gives *Thomas and Jude.* Here the scribe evidently transcribes the i/j and the minims of u/n from copy, perhaps accurately, but less probably, as *j* and *n.* So far as we know, Jude's life was blameless; the doubter's journey to India long formed a part of his tradition. Saint John of Beverley's story is told in Bede. Julian clearly relishes the heavenly fame of her neighbor and the immortal survival of his local identity. There are fewer local persons in the longer text — her mother and the child accompanying her curate disappear. The designation of the beloved of chapter 35 has been changed from "person" to "creature." But although Saint Cecilia is excised, the long text includes more anecdotal material drawn from church or Biblical legend, the stories of "Sain Dionyse of France," Pilate, the vernicle, and this neighboring saint.

1296   *party.* P; S1 illegible.

Chapter XXXIX

1311   *and noyith him in his owne syte.* The temperate *noyith* may indicate, as suggested in C&W, that the S1 scribe mistook a *noght* in the exemplar; the A reading in the corresponding passage is *noghtes* (I, 256 and II, 449). The P reading is *purgyth.* There is, however, something psychologically appropriate about *noyith.* Further, the Middle English shades into stronger meanings than does our *annoy,* including *impair, damage,* and *distress.*

1315   *tunyd.* P has a more probable *turned,* but a musical metaphor is not impossible.

1318   *undertakyth.* P; S1 *underforgyth.* S1 marginal gloss: *undergoeth.*

1322   *wil be cast in.* P reads *we be cast in,* which may be preferable. The *wil* of S1, however, is a more powerful corrective to the popular impression that Julian is unrealistically optimistic.

Notes

Chapter XL *we.* S2; S1 omits.

1355   *He.* P offers *it*, making the soul the one who has been in pain and prison.

1358   *onyd.* P; S1 *onye.*

1379–80   *For a kynde soule hath non helle but synne.* P adds, "For alle is good but syn and nought is yvell but synne." The short text includes this statement and continues, "Synne es nowthere deed no lykynge, botte when a saule cheses wilfully synne, that is payne, as fore his god, atte the ende he hase ryght nought" [Sin is neither deed nor inclination, but when a soul chooses sin wilfully, that is payne, and as to his good (or, before his God), at the end he has absolutely nothing] (fol. 109r).

1382   *wyllyng.* P; S1 *willy.*

1387   *evyn.* P; S1 *evn.*

1388   *hate.* P; S1 *hatenly.*

1390   *God.* P; S1 omits.

Chapter XLI

1391   *After this, our Lord shewid for prayers.* The short text differs in many details in the discussion of prayer, including reference to the common daily prayers said by lay people: "and in this we say Pater noster, Ave, and Crede with devocioun as god wille gyffe it" (fol. 109v). With the bidding of beads mentioned in the long text's account of the apparition of the fiend (chapter 69) and a reserved attitude toward "menes" (chapter 6), these constitute Julian's reflections on ordinary prayer. Molinari discusses Julian's teachings on contemplative prayer (pp. 73–139). Pelphrey's discussion of Julian's theology of prayer (*Love Was His Meaning,* pp. 214–54) supplements Molinari.

1397   *shewed.* P; S1 *swewid.*

1404   *And in the sixth reason.* The seeming skip from one to six may be partly explained as follows: The first reason, stated comprehensively, is that the

Lord is "ground of thi besekyng," which also serves as a heading for a sub-set, the four clauses that follow, which are reasons 2, 3, 4, and 5, respectively. The interrogative, *"How shuld it than be?"* with its implied answer, is the sixth reason and the conclusion of the reasoning process. Julian's designation of the first reason as *"And thou besekyst it"* remains a problem.

1413   *onyd.* P; S1 *ony.*

1425   *febelnes.* P; S1 *febihede.* Perhaps *febilhede* would be preferable.

1431   *discrecion.* P; S1 illegible.

1432   *fifteenth Revelation.* P; S1 *fifth.*

1433   *aforn.* S1 *for aforn.*

1434   *Thankyng is a new, inward knowing. Thankyng.* P; S1 *thakyng.* See Father John-Julian, OJN, *"Thankyng* in Julian," *Mystics Quarterly,* 15 (1989), 70–74, for the view that the etymological link that *thank* shares with *think* (OE *thencan*) informs this passage and others (e.g., line 1012) where Julian speaks of thanking. Using P's *true* for *new,* and amending *lovely* to *lowley,* he translates *thankyng* in this passage as "a steadfast, inner awareness with great veneration and humble awe, which turns us with all our strength towards the deeds to which our good Lord guides us" (72). The link with *think* seems especially valuable as an example of Julian's way with words, although the P reading and the emendation conventionalize the more spiky, difficult, and rewarding, S1 reading *thakyng* (throbbing, beating).

Chapter XLII

1475   *to.* P; S1 omits.

1477   *the dede that is now in doyng.* This on-going deed is not the eschatological deed that is to make all things well ultimately (chapter 30). See Hanshell, pp. 80–81, and Pelphrey, *Love Was His Meaning,* pp. 295–305.

1486   *other.* S1 has a squiggle over the *o* which might suggest *owther* or *nother.* S2 reads *either.*

Chapter XLIII

1513–16   *But whan . . . .syte.* S1 marginal gloss: *NB.*

1513   *Hymselfe.* P; S1 *hymsefe. eur.* P gives *oure,* S2 *our.* The scribe of S has written *eur* above a canceled but still legible *the. Eur,* an infrequent form of *eower,* is the indefinite *your,* equivalent to *one's.* Pronoun shifts are common in Middle English. Compare the movement from first to third to a second person *thyselfe* in lines 408–11 above, and, more jarringly, the *my* of line 3110 below.

1516   *unperceyvable.* P; S1 *onperciable.*

1541   *fulsomly.* P; S1 *fusumly.*

1545   *strengthyth.* P; S1 *stengtneth.*

Chapter XLV

1565   *kynde substance.* See note 950–51.

1569   *is herd. is.* P; S1 omits.

1583   *Hymselfe.* S1 hymseff.

1585   *I myte in no way levyn the lower dome. Levyn* could mean either "believe" or "leave" and make satisfactory sense, but to translate "leave" sharpens Julian's sense of dilemma, evident also in her acceptance of damnation as a doctrine and her vision's resistance to offering "sight" of this idea. "Believe" is attractive in that it would confirm Julian's loyalty, after a single backsliding (see chapter 66) to her vision's authority, but such a translation would tendentiously contradict other affirmations, such as those in lines 334–38 and 1611–17, of adherence to church teaching. On the two "domes" of God and of the church, see Pelphrey, *Love Was His Meaning,* pp. 295–99. For a succinct outline of Julian's apparent divergences from "popular understanding" of church teaching, see M. L. del Mastro (1988).

1596   *kyndly.* P; S1 *kyndy.*

1597   *kindly substance.* See note 950–51.

Chapter XLVI

1599–1600 *But our passand life . . . what ourself is.* The place of the concept of *self* in the *Shewings* is discussed by Ritamary Bradley, "Perception of Self in Julian of Norwich's *Showings*," *The Downside Review* 104 (1986), 227–39.

1604   *forthing.* S1 *foething.* P *fortheryng.*

1615   *liken.* S1 marginal gloss: *loven.*

1616   *encrese.* P; S1 *encrecy.*

1621   *I saw sothfastly that our Lord was never wroth.* Robert Llewelyn discusses as basic to Julian's theology the passages in which she says she sees no wrath in God ("Woman of Consolation and Strength," *Julian: Woman of Our Day,* ed. Llewelyn, pp. 121–39).

1625–26   *God is the goodnes . . . goodnes.* S1 marginal gloss: *NB.*

Chapter XLVII

1649–50   *But how I understode . . . grace.* S1 marginal gloss: *NB.*

1676   *is.* P; S1 omits.

Chapter XLVIII

1681–82   *For I sow no wrath . . . love.* S1 marginal gloss: *NB.*

1681   *wrath.* P; S1 illegible.

1692–94   *Mercy . . . lif.* S1 marginal gloss: *NB.*

1699   *moderhode.* P; S1 *moderid.*

1714–15   *And whan I saw all this . . . wasten our wreth.* S1 marginal gloss: *NB.*

Chapter XLIX

1734–35   *For I saw . . . God.* S1 marginal gloss: *NB.*

1737   *agaynst.* P; S1 *ageys.*

1749   *oureselfe.* P; S1 *ourseffe.*

1757   *cum.* S1 *cun;* P *come.*

Chapter L

1767   *knowyng.* P; S1 *kowyng.*

1779   *awer.* The definitions given here, *trouble,* and at 2163, *concern,* are contextual. *Awer* may come from *awerden* (OE) which means to harm or destroy. The MED yields *awer-mod,* "a disposition to do harm, ill-will," citing *Ormulum,* line 4720 (c. 1200). Perhaps in the late fourteenth century, a local variant meant being troubled oneself rather than troubling others. S2, which modernizes words from S1 a number of times, lets *awer* stand in both passages. P gives *feer.*

Chapter LI

This chapter is the longest and most significant addition to the long text, its parable of the lord and the servant Julian's most searching consideration of sin and evil. With its explication, the parable adds one-seventh to the length of the text. Most writers on Julian conclude that the reason for its omission from the shorter text resides in her need to ponder the "mysty" example. The unfolding of the vision in her understanding took "nere twenty yeres." Readers may see in the "example" and in Julian's analysis a compact, striking fable of theodicy, but Julian refers it only to sin. Julian gives her own vision a full four-level allegoresis with typological, tropological, and anagogical levels as well as the literal one. See Patricia Mary Vinje on Julian as an allegorical writer. For a discussion of the status of the parable as a showing and its links to Julian's themes, see

Glasscoe, "Means of Showing," pp. 167–75. Sister Anna Maria Reynolds (1984), pp. 118–25, discusses the chapter as a "concise and accurate" summary of salvation history.

1794   *full mystily.* Late Middle English blends OE *mist* and ME *mystike* to give *mystily,* "conveyed darkly and symbolically, after the manner of Scriptural parables" (C&W II, 513).

1796   *syght.* P; S1 *sgte.*

1810   *that.* P; S1 *the.*

1829–30   *a ledying . . . enjoyen.* P's reading is easier to follow: "a ledyng of my understandyng in to the lorde, in restoryng whych I saw hym hyely enjoy. . . ."

1835   *reward.* P; S1 illegible.

        mayme. P; S1 *maine.*

1866ff.   *It longyth to the. . . .* Julian outlines a method and proceeds to analyze the showing in accordance with it, much as a Jungian-trained psychologist would lead a client to "work" a dream. R. H. Thouless in *The Lady Julian: A Psychological Study* (London: Society for Promoting Christian Knowledge, and New York: Macmillan, 1924), pp. 81–84, was, so far as I know, the first to notice the resemblance to clinical dream analysis. Nuth finds a basis for Julian's method in the monastic practice of *lectio divina,* meditating upon details of a reading (p. 36).

1868–69   *seeing.* P; S1 omits.

1884   *blyndyd.* P; S1 *blindhed.*

1890   *knowyng.* P; S1 *kowyng.*

1893   *bryngen.* S1 *brynen.* P *bryng.*

1896   *The color of his cloth was blew as asure.* In the ante-reliquary chapel of Norwich Cathedral, the vaulting has at its crown a small medallion with a figure of Christ in a blue mantle. The painting scheme is put at 1325 by E. W. Tristram in *English Wall Painting of the Fourteenth Century* (London:

Routledge & Kegan Paul, 1955), p. 230. Blues were, of course, particularly clear and brilliant in the illuminated manuscripts of the period. Later, Julian sees Christ himself in a medley of colors, and notes that they are more glorious than the robe of the lord as God the Father (2054–57). Pelphrey finds the image of Christ's new, multi-colored garment reminiscent of the emerald rainbow surrounding the throne of Christ in Revelations 4:3 and the garment of the Son of Man in Revelations 1:13 (p. 197).

1905   *the Fadir. the* P; S1 omits.

1913   *Notwithstonding I saw.* S1 here has *ne saw.* P, more comprehensibly, omits *ne.*

1925   *al.* S1 *a;* P *all.*

1937   *lord.* P; S1 *Lodd.*

1938–39   *And inward . . . to hym.* S1 marginal gloss: *NB.*

1946   *that is to sey. that.* P; S1 *tha.*

1950   *a man.* S1 reads *a a man.*

1965   *groundyd.* P; S1 *grounld.*

1984   *understode.* S1 *undestode;* P *understonde.*

1985   *that.* P; S1 *tha.*

1986   *Lord.* S1 *Lod.* P *Lorde.*

1999   *The which kirtle.* P reads *wyth,* white. *now.* P reads *noght,* possibly correct. However, the *now* compresses the human and divine identities of God's Son, looking forward to His ascension, and anticipating the *nows* of lines 2058–59.

2003   *I stond before The in Adams kirtle.* For background on this figure, see Grayson.

2012   *shall.* P; S1 *sha.*

2021   *Lordis.* S1 *Lodis.* P *Lordys.*

2029   *wombe.* P; S1 *wonbe.*

2032   *even.* S1 *eve.* P *evyn.*

2041   *pecys.* P; S1 *pets.*

2045   *mankynd.* S1 *mankyd.* P *mankynde.*

2052   *streyte.* P; S1 *steyte.*

Chapter LII   *mother.* S2; S1 *bother.* *perfectly as in heaven.* S2; S1 omits.

2074–75   *God enjoyeth that He is our moder.* This theme, anticipated in line 1699, is here introduced almost casually, embedded in other relationships of the soul to God which are traditional analogies of varying currency which in Julian seem to stand half-way between figurative and literal. The theme will close in chapter 83 when in a Trinitarian sentence Julian refers to the light, "our Moder, Criste" (3355–56). Intensive treatment of the motherhood of Christ comes in chapters 57–63. For discussion of doctrinal, devotional, and rhetorical aspects of the motherhood of Christ in the tradition that preceded her and in *The Shewings*, see Heimmel, Børresen, Bynum, Cabassut, McLaughlin, McNamer, Molinari (esp. pp. 169–86), Pelphrey (esp. pp. 84–89), and Bradley, "The Motherhood Theme."

2080–81   *We have in us . . . deyand.* See note 1198–1200.

2122–24   *But we may wele be grace kepe us from the synnes which will ledyn us to endles paynes . . . and eschewen venial.* The distinction is between mortal and venial sin, mortal sins being so grave in nature and undertaken so deliberately and whole-heartedly, that one suffices to damn an uncontrite soul. Venial sins are less critical deviations, almost inescapable ones, from love of God and neighbor.

2123   *paynes.* S1 *payes.* P *payne.*

2139   *never.* S1 *neve.*

2145   *two.* P; S1 *tw.*

2146   *asseth.* S1 marginal gloss: *propitiation.*

Chapter LIII *ruthfulhede.* In view of lines 2170 and 2173 the word should perhaps be *rythfulhede.* S2 reads *ruthfulnes,* however.

2162–67   *And in this that I have now seyd . . . in the syte of God.* S1 marginal gloss: *NB.*

2163   *grete.* P; S1 *gre.*

2166   *evermore.* S1 *evemore.* P *evyr more.*

2169   *Lord.* S1 *Lod.* P *Lorde.*

2177–88   *For I saw . . . knitt to God.* For the biblical basis, see especially Eph. 1:3–10 and Col. 1:12–20.

2181–84   *The Mid-Person . . . without begynnyng.* S1 marginal gloss: *NB.*

2187   *the myte of.* Repeated in S1.

2202   *ever.* S1 *eve;* P *evyr. mankynd.* S1 *makynd.* P *mankynde.*

2205   *which knott is sotil.* It is possible, if no more than that, that Julian contributed to Donne's "the subtle knot which makes us man" ("The Ecstasy"). Julian's work was saved and copied in circles which would have been congenial to his recusant ancestors.

2207–08   *that al the soules . . . in this holyhede.* S1 marginal gloss: *NB.*

2205   *that it is onyd.* P; S1 *that is onyd.*

Chapter LIV For the use of *substance* in this chapter, see note 950–51.

2210   *departing.* S1 marginal gloss: *difference.*

189

2211–14   *For it is full hesy. . . savid be Crist.* S1 marginal gloss: *NB.*

2217–18   *And hey understonding . . . our soule.* S1 marginal gloss: *NB.*

2221–23   *And I saw no difference . . . creture in God.* S1 marginal gloss: *NB.*

2225–26   *The hey goodnes. . . and He in us.* S1 marginal gloss: *NB.*

2230–31   *our sensual soule.* See note 2250–51.

2232–34   *For it is not ell . . . which we se not.* S1 marginal gloss: *NB Fides quid.*

Chapter LV

2241   *His Fader.* his. P; S1 *ha.*

2247–48   *And notwithstanding . . . than in erth.* S1 marginal gloss: *NB.*

2250–51   *And what tyme that our soule is inspirid into our body.* "Julian distinguishes between 'the substance' of the soul grounded and dwelling in God and 'the sensuality' of the soul in which God dwells. The sensuality is the soul as informing the body, its life principle and the subject of our psycho-physical experience. It begins to exist 'what time our soul is inspired in our body'" (Watkin, p. 17). For a recent comment on "sensualyte" in Julian, see Lichtmann. S1 marginal gloss: *NB.*

2251   *as.* P; S1 *aso.*

2260   *in which se.* Julian is referring to the center of authority in a bishop's jurisdiction. She uses various figures of location — home, city, seat, see — to denote God's abiding presence in the human soul.

2276   never. S1 *neve.* P *nevyr.*

2284   *I myte not, for the mene profir.* A friendly voice had proposed to Julian who is gazing upon the image of Christ crucified that she look up to "His Fader," a suggestion which she declines (lines 696–706).

Chapter LVI

2287–90   *And thuss I saw . . . to whom it is onyd.* S1 marginal gloss: *NB.*

2294–97   *God is nerer . . . shall never departyn.* S1 marginal gloss: *NB.*

2298–99   *For our soule sittith in God in very rest . . . endles love.* S1 marginal gloss: *NB.* The seated soul is at rest, as Julian says not only of the human soul seated in Christ but also of the soul of Christ reciprocally seated in the human soul (lines 2298–2306). The theme of the soul as Christ's seat reappears: "And this was a singlar joy and bliss to me, that I saw Him sitten" (lines 2825–26). See also lines 2375–77 and 2791–97. Riehle discusses the popularity of the image of God sitting in the soul in medieval mysticism and most particularly among English writers, where allegorical interpretations of the Song of Songs 2:3 informed the theme as did emphasis on the help a seated position gives for full meditative concentration (pp. 132–36). James Walsh in "God's Homely Loving: St. John and Julian of Norwich on the Divine Indwelling," *The Month*, n.s. 19 (1958), 164–72, discusses the Johannine basis of Julian's passage. See also J. P. H. Clark, "Nature, Grace and the Trinity in Julian of Norwich," *The Downside Review*, 100 (1982), 203–20. The key Biblical passage is John 15:4. Julian, of course, is aware that souls are not literally seated, and takes care to make that unmistakable when she says of the Father as lord and the Son as servant, "But it is not ment that the Son syttith on the ryte hond, syde be syde, as on man sittith be another in this lif, for ther is no such syttyng, as to my syte, in the Trinite" (lines 2066–68).

2302–04   *And anempts our substaunce and sensualite . . . God.* S1 marginal gloss: *NB.*

2303   *substaunce.* P; S1 *substane.*

2307–09   *And I saw . . . our own soule.* S1 marginal gloss: *NB.*

2315   *substance.* P; S1 *substane.*

2316–17   *I had in partie touching.* C&W: "The word is technical, belonging to the vocabulary of the spiritual senses, and frequently employed by Julian to convey that she is being directly affected and moved by the Holy Spirit to experience the reality of God, in a way which is above intellectual comprehension, but which accompanies and supports some form of inner seeing"

(II, 573–74, note to 38). For other examples see lines 1237 and, especially, 3346. See note 687 above for the possible influence of pseudo-Dionysius.

2318   *heyhede.* Thus S1, with the marginal gloss: *kindhede.* P reads *kyndnesse* which seems more likely in view of the reliance upon the idea of "kindhede" in this passage. S2 confirms S1's *heyhede,* and the gloss *kindhede.* "Substantial heyhede" and "substantial kindhede" are informed here by the philosophical sense of *substance.* See note 950–51.

2320–22   *For in kind . . . fulfilling.* S1 marginal gloss: *NB.*

2330   *werkynges.* P; S1 *wekyng.*

Chapter LVII *substance.* S2; S1 *subsance.* In chapters LVII–LXIII the scribe of S1 frequently (but not always) capitalizes the words *Moder* and *Moderhede.* The visual effect in reading the manuscript is quite striking in that the masculine pronouns for God are not capitalized. Some of the effect is muted in the present edition in that I have followed the policy of the Middle English Texts Series and thus capitalized personal pronouns and titles for God. But I have followed the manuscript's capitalization of *Moder* and *Moderhede* in these chapters, given the possibility that the practice might reflect scribal intention or, perhaps, even Julian's authority.

2334–35   *And anempts our substance . . . worship.* S1 marginal gloss: *NB.*

2335   *I.* P; S1 omits.

2341   *godhede.* S1 marginal gloss: *goodnes.*

2347   *in.* P; S1 *is.*

2374   *never.* S1 *neve.* P *nevyr.*

2380   *kepyng.* P; S1 *kepid.*

2381   *substance.* S1 *substane.* P *substaunce.*

Notes

Chapter LVIII

2387   *Hymself.* S1 *hymseffe.*

2400   *kyndly.* S1 *kindy.* P *kyndely.*

2404   *yeldyng.* P; S1 *reldyng.*

2424   *thred.* S1 *tred.* P *thurde.*

2430   *gevyng.* P; S1 *vefyng.*

2430–32   *And our substance . . . al goodnes.* S1 marginal gloss: *NB.*

2433   *is hole.* S reads *is is hole.*

2436   *wretchidnes.* S1 *wretchidns.* P *wrechydnesse.*

Chapter LIX

2439–41   *which manner of bliss we myte never had ne known . . . wherby we have this bliss.* This is Julian's version of the fortunate fall.

2462   *wyllyth.* P; S1 omits.

2475   *taken.* P *takyng.* The reference is to the Incarnation. See lines 2470–71.

Chapter LX

2488   *rayhid.* For *arrayed*, the S2 reading; P has *arayed.*

2491   *but.* P; S1 omits.

2497   *aseth.* S1 marginal gloss: *satisfaction.*

2511   *tenth.* S1, S2, and P read *ninth.* However, the quotation following is from the tenth showing. See chapter 24.

2522–23   *she suffrid that it be bristinid in brekyng downe of vices.* This is as close as Julian comes to using motherhood to figure a God who judges and disciplines as well as creates and loves. Others had occasionally developed the image severely. The thirteenth-century mystic Gertrude of Helfta sees God as a mother who loves but also tests, to the point of frightening the strayed child back into her arms by wearing terrifying masks (Bynum, pp. 189–90). In fact the word *bristinid* is very strong, appearing chiefly in violent contexts. See MED *s.v.*

2527–28   *our dett that we owen, be Gods biddyng.* The transfer of the fourth commandment's obligation from human to divine parent accords with the longer version's deletion of reference to Julian's own mother.

Chapter LXI

2533   *kyndelyth.* P; S1 *kydelyth.*

2538   *to bend payd with Him.* Thus S1; P has a less resonant *be* for *bend.*

2539   *And we fallen, hastily He reysith us.* See note 1198–1200.

2540   *strenthyd.* P; S1 *stengtid.*

2544–47   *And than wene we . . . ourselfe.* S1 marginal gloss: *NB.*

2555–57   *For therby . . . not profitt us.* S1 marginal gloss: *NB.*

2558   *syth.* S1 marginal gloss: *afterwards.*

2560   *never.* S1 *neve.* P *nevyr.*

2570   *myselfe.* S1 reads *myselfe my.*

2572   *al swithe.* S1 marginal gloss*: immediately or all on a sudden.*

2573–74   *For if He sen . . . for love.* S1 marginal gloss: *NB.*

2583   *foode of mercy.* P offers *flode* for *foode.*

2588   *to don it. it.* P; S1 *us.*

Chapter LXII

2593   *myght.* P; S1 *my.*

2600   *that is to sey.* S1 *that it is to sey.*

2605–07   *For of all kyndes . . . worshipp.* S1 marginal gloss: *NB.*

2616   *begynnyng.* S1 *begynnig;* P *begynyng.*

Chapter LXIII

2619   *bryngen.* S1 *byngen.* P *bryng.*

2629   *sothly.* S1 *sothy;* P *trewly.*

2631   *techyth.* P; S1 *tehith.*

2635   *never.* S1 *neve.* P *nevyr.*

2643   *fordreth.* P; S1 *foethes.*

2649   *other.* P; S1 *othe.*

2658–60   *Thus I understode . . . be grace.* S1 marginal gloss: *NB.*

Chapter LXIV *God wil we take. we take* S2; S1 omits *we.*

2682   *a bolned quave of styngand myre.* The S1 marginal gloss gives "puffed up" for *bolned* and "a quaggmire," for *quave.* P's "a swylge stynkyng myrre" helps with "styngand."

2684   *swyft.* P; S1 *swifie.*

2687   *I.* P; S1 omits.

2691   *yf.* S1's reading. S2 joins P in reading *that. That* does accord with a security which Julian seems to feel throughout.

2703   *over.* P reads *evyr.*

Chapter LXV

2710–12   *And thus I understode . . . that grace.* S1 marginal gloss: *NB.*

2716–17   *This reverens . . . is knitt.* S1 marginal gloss: *Timor domini quid.*

2725   *himselfe.* S1 *himseffe.* P *them selfe.*

2728–30   *For it is His will . . . lovith.* S1 marginal gloss: *NB.*

2729–30   *he shall not dredyn but Him that he lovith.* P gives the reading *she* here. See note 561 above.

2734   *if we knowen.* S1 omits *we*; P includes it.

2735   *great.* P; S1 *gre.*

2740   *the morne.* S1 reads *the the morne.*

2742   *none of the day overpassid.* Since *none* could here mean noon or nones, the hour of the office nones (from L *nona*, nine, the ninth hour of the day reckoned from sunrise), that is, about 3 p.m., it is difficult to fix the time exactly. P reads *or paste* for *overpassid.* Julian uses both clock time and canonical hours in fixing times. (See lines 2865–66.) The hour of mid-day appears as an ordinary sense of the word by the fourteenth century. Marion Glasscoe in "Time of Passion: Latent Relationships between Liturgy and Meditation in Two Middle English Mystics" (*Langland, the Mystics and the Medieval English Religious Tradition: Essays in Honour of S. S. Hussey,* ed. Helen Phillips [Cambridge: D. S. Brewer/Boydell & Brewer, 1990]), pp. 154–58, argues that the showings assume sharper definition when related to the liturgy of the hours. The showings began, as Julian writes at the close of chapter 65, at about 4 a.m., the hour of Lauds.

Notes

Chapter LXVI

2750   *fulfillid.* S1 *fufillid.* P *fulfyllyd.*

2753   *peynes.* S1 *peyes.* P *paynes.*

2759   *that sawe.* P; S1 *than saw I.*

2767   *I lay still. I* P; S1 omits.

2772   *blak spots therin like blak steknes.* P: *blacke spottes . . . lyke frakylles.* S 2: *frecknes. Steknes* is difficult; Glasscoe's glossary gives "speckles." The word may be from *sticchen,* "to stitch," or "to stick" (i.e., to fasten). ME *stiche* "stitch" is from OE *stice,* equivalent to Old Frisian *steke.* The OED gives *steke* as a Scottish or Northern form for *stitch,* but with examples from 1520. Contemporary personifications of pestilence sometimes were pictured with spots like small, vertical stitches or gashes; more rarely a fiend would be thus dappled, or even a suffering Christ. Judging from accounts of symptoms, the plague itself could be the source of the detail in this, Julian's only non-waking vision. For bubonic plague, the initial symptom was a blackish postule, followed by a subcutaneous hemorrhaging making the blotches purple. With fatal septiacaemic plague, a rash came within hours, and the larger "buboes" that Boccaccio describes in *The Decameron,* perhaps the best-known of medieval descriptions of plague symptoms, did not have time to form. Julian would have been six or seven when the Plague arrived in Norwich in January of 1349. It lasted till spring of 1350. Morbidity was extraordinary. Half of the beneficed clergy and variously one-third to fifty per cent of the secular population are estimated to have perished. See Robert S. Gottfried, *The Black Death: Natural and Human Disaster in Medieval Europe* (New York: Free Press/Macmillan, 1983) p. 8, pp. 65–66.

2784   *I askid hem that wer with me if thei felt ony stynke.* James T. McIlwain conjectures that the foul smell, not perceptible to others, may have come from infected mucus membranes. He discusses the physical symptoms that Julian reports and offers possible diagnoses. For the period, Julian's account of symptoms is unusally rich, he says ("The 'Bodelye syeknes' of Julian of Norwich," *Journal of Medieval History* 10 [1984], 171).

Chapter LXVII

2791–92   *And than our Lord . . . herte.* S1 marginal gloss: *NB.*

2816   *than.* P; S1 *that.*

2819   *than.* P; S1 *that.*

Chapter LXIX   S1 omits numbering this chapter. S2 gives the number.

2851   *soft.* S1 *foft.* P is onomatopoeic: "softe whystryn."

2856   *that had.* S1 reads *that had that had.*

2866   *prime day.* Soon after sunrise, indicated by the liturgical hour. Matins and lauds, prime, tierce, sext, nones, vespers, and compline were scheduled times for common daily prayer in monastic houses. Most religious and, in the fourteenth century and usually in abbreviated forms, some devout lay people, said the hours.

2869   *For therwith is the fend overcome, as our Lord Jesus Criste seid aforn.* In the short version an apostrophe to sin follows, "A, wriched synne, whate ert thou?" (fol. 113r). See Appendix A. For a cogent explanation of why Julian would omit this passage, stylistically a tour de force, see C&W, I, 271.

Chapter LXX

2876   *and therefore I leve it. Leve* is neatly ambiguous, both "believe" and "leave" making sense. Piquantly ambiguous *leaves* occur also at lines 314 and 1585.

2878–80   *Thus I am bounden . . . I had ravid.* S1 marginal gloss: *NB.*

2886   *thereupon.* P; S1 *therupo.*

2893   *blindhede.* S1 *blinhede.* P *blyndnesse.*

Notes

Chapter LXXI   *glad.* S2; S1 *gad.*

2904–05   *For He havith us . . . His mede.* S1 marginal gloss: *NB. He* P; S1 *be.*

2912   *nede.* P; S1 omits.

2915   *beer.* P; S1 *barer.*

2917   *agaynst.* P; S1 *ageys.*

2922   *alle manner.* P; S1 *alivaner.*

Chapter LXXII

2925   *withouten end.* S1 *withoutend end.*

2926   *never.* S1 *neve.*

2931   *medled.* S1 blotched, perhaps *medlid.* P *meddlyd.*

2936–38   *And thus we arn ded . . . never fro us.* S1 marginal gloss: *NB.*

2949   *And in this I saw matter of myrth . . . monyng.* S1 marginal gloss: *NB.*

2950   *sekirness.* S1 *sekirne.* P *feythfulnes.*

2957–58   *This weping meneth not al . . . understondyng.* S1 marginal gloss: *NB.*

2961   *stynten of.* S1 *stynt n of.* Perhaps the reading should be *stynt ne of*, thus creating a neither-nor syntax.

2963   *thynke.* S1 *thyke.* P *thyngk.*

2964   *in.* S1 *in in.*

2967–68   *I it am . . . that is all.* S1 marginal gloss: *NB.*

Chapter LXXIII *sekenes.* S2; S1 *sekernes.*

2976–78   *For the bodily sygte, I have seid . . . sumdele.* Of the nearly identical passage in the short text, Lynn Staley Johnson argues that Julian here conjures up a scribe whose activity verifies Julian's account of her visions (p. 830). Johnson believes, however, that the force of the scribal scene is mitigated in the long text because Julian has assumed a more authoritative persona in no need of an exterior scribal validation and because in the long text the position of the passage is further from the conclusion.

2978   *never.* S1 *neve.* P *nevyr.*

2980–87   *That on is onpatience or slaith . . . most enclinand to these.* As Julian will state again (lines 3127–32), she regards sloth as a particular obstacle in a religious vocation. By Julian's time, analysis of this capital sin had a long history. What she calls "onpatience," a restlessness exacerbated by enclosure, as much as laziness or bearing "trevell . . . hevily," remained in the continuum commentators discuss. Sloth (*acedia*) as a deterrent in the life of anchoritic withdrawal is discussed in the milieu of the Lower Egyptian hermits of the fourth century. On the somnolence side, Clay (*Hermits and Anchorites,* p. 101) calls attention to the *Hortus Deliciarum* of Herrad, twelfth-century abbess of Landsberg, where in one illumination various climbers lose their footing from a ladder of virtues, beguiled by characteristic distractions, the knight by a horse, the anchorite ("inclusus") by a bed. The illumination is reproduced in the edition of Aristide D. Caratzas with notes and commentary by A. Straub and G. Keller (New York: Caratzas Bros., 1977), Plate LVI, p. 197. For other references in Julian see lines 418–20 and the self-criticism of lines 2665–67. The early appearance of the sin in hermitic texts is set forth by Siegfried Wenzel, *The Sin of Sloth: Acedia in Medieval Thought and Literature* (Chapel Hill: University of North Carolina Press, 1960), pp. 2–18; see also p. 211, note 87.

     S1 marginal gloss: *NB.*

2981   *peynes.* S1 *peyes;* P *payne.*

2989   *Lord.* S1 *Lod.* P *Lorde.*

2992   *peynes.* S1 *peyes;* P *paynes.*

2992–93   *And the cause . . . onknoweing of love.* S1 marginal gloss: *NB.*

2997–99   *For som of us leven . . . we astynten.* S1 marginal gloss: *NB.* S1 reads *we s astynten.*

3006–07   *And this drede . . . waykenes.* S1 marginal gloss: *NB.*

3008   *another.* P; S1 *anothe.*

Chapter LXXIV

3027–28   *For it may never . . . goodnes.* S1 marginal gloss: *NB.*

3043   *asunder.* S1 *asuder.* P *onsonder.* The discussion of dread closes the short text: "Therefore it is goddes wille and oure spede that we knawe thamm thus ysundure; for god wille ever that we be sekere in luffe, & peessabille & ristefulle as he is to us, and ryght so of the same condicioun as he is to us, so wille he that we be to oure selfe and to oure even christenn. Amen. Explicit Juliane de Norwych" (fol. 115r).

3044–49   *That drede . . . good, and true.* S1 marginal gloss: *NB.*

3055–56   *Desir we . . mytyly.* S1 marginal gloss: *NB.*

Chapter LXXV   *and littlenes.* S2; S1 *lulshed; and* omitted.

3064–65   *I shall seyen, neden.* P *I shall say nede.* C&W emend to *I shall say (vs) nede,* noting that the opening sentences of this chapter are much corrupted (p. 678).

3066–69   *For the threist of God . . . longith.* S1 marginal gloss: *NB.*

3067   *drawyn.* P; S1 *anwin.*

3083–84   *And evermore . . . suffrid.* S1 marginal gloss: *NB.*

3096   *in.* P; S1 omits.

Chapter LXXVI S1 gives only the number, not its customary abbreviation for *chapter*.

3106–08   *And therefore it is Goddis will . . . risen redily.* S1 marginal gloss: *NB.*

3110–12   *The soule . . . agayne it.* S1 marginal gloss: *NB.*

3110–11   *to my mynde.* P reads *to mynde.*

3112   *agayne.* P; S1 *ageys.*

3116   *I.* P; S1 omits.

3121   *This blissid freind is Jhesus.* S1 marginal gloss: *NB.*

3130–32   *namely in slauth . . . goodness.* See note 2980–87. S1 marginal gloss: *NB.*

Chapter LXXVII *specially.* S2; S1 *speially.*

3137–38   *Our good Lord shewid the enmite . . . of his parte.* S1 marginal gloss: *NB.*

3143   *he hath.* P; S1 omits *he.*

3148–50   *I know wele . . . tendirly.* S1 marginal gloss: *NB.*

3159–61   *For whan we have mend . . . that seen it.* S1 marginal gloss: *NB.*

3161   *this.* P; S1 omits.

3164–65   *tho thou do. thou* P; S1 omits *thou.*

3170–72   *Our wey and our Hevyn . . . Hevyn.* S1 marginal gloss: *NB.*

3171   *He gaf understonding.* S1 reads *he he.*

3175–76   *For our curtes Lord . . . desiren.* S1 marginal gloss: *NB.*

3180–81   *And to be like our Lord . . . bliss.* S1 marginal gloss: *NB.*

3182   *is.* P; S1 omits.

Chapter LXXVIII

3184   *of His.* P; S1 *is of His.*

3190   hem. S1 *him;* P *them.*

3200–03   *And be this meke knowing . . . one us to Him.* S1 marginal gloss: *NB.*

Chapter LXXIX

3245   *kepith.* S1 *repith* (?), though, if so, the *e* is oddly formed.

            P *kepyth.* S2 has *clepyth,* which could be the preferred reading.

3247   *not that we beseyn.* S1 is partially illegible. P reads *nott that we besy,* which makes better sense.

3249   *alufe.* P reads *aloone.*

3253   *shewyng.* P; S1 *sweing.*

Chapter LXXX

3266   *in the last end.* This, the only apocalyptic touch in *The Shewings,* may indicate that Julian considers her own time the final stage of secular history before the general judgment. Belief that the last end was imminent was common in the fourteenth century.

            in. P; S1 omits.

3267   *wonnyth.* S1 *wonnyh;* P *dwellyth.*

3270   *it.* P; S1 omits.

3271–72   *I leve and understonde . . . not shewid me.* S1 marginal gloss: *NB.*

3276–77   *And all swich . . . it is Christ in us.* S1 marginal gloss: *NB.*

3286–89   *But thow . . . in His syte.* S1 marginal gloss: *NB.*

Chapter LXXXI

3298–3301   *Mervelous and solemne . . . fallings.* S1 marginal gloss: *NB.*

3302–03   *For it is the most . . . penance.* S1 marginal gloss: *NB.*

3302   *is.* P; S1 omits.

3306–09   *For His love . . . as to my syte.* S1 marginal gloss: *NB.*

Chapter LXXXII   *blame.* S2; S1 *blom. And so we.* S1 reads *we we.*

3324   *the.* S1 reads *the the.*

3334   *in falling and in ryseing.* See note to lines 1198–1200.

3335   *ever.* S1 *eve.* P *evyr.*

3344   *be.* P; S1 omits.

3345   *ende.* P; S1 illegible.

Chapter LXXXIII   *clarity.* S2; S1 illegible.

3348   *I it am.* P; S1 omits.

3349   *propertees.* P; S1 illegible.

Notes

Chapter LXXXIV *nedefull.* S2 gives *medefull,* an attractive reading.

3368 *with.* P; S1 *wth.*

3369 *the of. of* P; S1 *soft.*

Chapter LXXXV *He never.* S2; S1 *he neve.*

3388 P's reading also has appeal: *with one voyce.*

3402–03 *And fifteen yer after and more I was answerid in gostly understonding.*
   Colledge and Walsh believe this indicates that Julian began working on the
   long account about 1388. They further posit two editions by Julian of the
   long text because Chapter l's summary of the fourteenth showing does not
   mention the lord and servant allegory of chapter 51, and this is the only
   summary without reference to the revelation's visions or locutions (I, 25).
   Full understanding of the lord and servant showing comes in the five years
   between the fifteen years mentioned here and the twenty years, short of
   three months, mentioned in chapter 51. Perhaps discovery of another manuscript of Julian will confirm this, as the appearance of the short version
   corroborated Blomefield.

Chapter LXXXVI This heading has been taken as evidence that the short text is the
earlier version of the *Shewings.* It is possible that the statement is an
editor's summary of the chapter's first sentence, which could point to the
future rather than to the work itself in any form.

3413 The Paris manuscript closes here with the rubric: *Deo gracias. Explicit liber
   revelacionum Julyane anatorite Norwyche cuius anime propicietur deus.*
   [Thanks be to God. This ends the book of revelations to Julian, anchorite of
   Norwich, for whose soul God be prayed.]

3417 S2 inserts: "Here end the sublime and wonderful revelations of the unutter-
   able love of God in Jesus Christ, vouchsafed to a dear lover of his and in
   her to all his dear friends and lovers, whose hearts, like hers, do flame in
   the love of our dearest Jesu." P and the short version lack the warning following, one that is probably not authorial. Although in part conventional,

such caveats can be intimidating and sometimes were meant to be. *The Cloud of Unknowing* opens with a very strong prohibition: "I charge thee & I beseche thee, with as moche power & vertewe as the bonde of charite is sufficient to suffre, what-so-ever thou be that this book schalt have in possession, outher [either] bi propirte outher by keping, by bering as messenger or elles bi borowing, that in as moche as in thee is by wille & avisement, neither thou rede it, ne write it, ne speke it, ne yit suffre it be red, wretyn, or spokyn, of any or to any, bot yif it be of soche one or to soche one that hath (bi thi supposing) in a trewe wille & by an hole entent, purposed him to be a parfite folower of Criste, not only in actyve levyng, bot in the sovereinnest pointe of contemplatife leving . . ." The author goes on to insist that the book must be read "al over." As for "Fleschely janglers, opyn preisers & blamers of hem-self or of any other, tithing tellers, rouners & tutilers of tales, & alle maner of pinchers" (tellers of tidings, whisperers and tale bearers, and all kinds of fault finders), he does not care if they never see the book. "For myn entent was never to write soche thing unto hem [them]. & therfore I wolde that thei medel not ther-with, neither thei ne any of thees corious lettred or lewed [learned or unlearned] men. Ye, though al that thei be ful good men of active levyng yit this mater acordeth nothing to hem" (ed. Hodgson, pp. 1–3).

3418   *them.* S2; S1 *then.*

Appendix A

Two Passages from the Short Text

I. From MS Additional 37790, fols. 100v–101r.

"For I am a womann — "

For god is alle that ys goode and god has made alle that ys made & god loves alle that he has made and yyf anye man or womann departe his love fra any of his evynn crysten, he loves ryght nought, for he loves nought alle. And so that tyme he ys nought safe, for he es nought in pees; and he that generaly looves his evynn crystynn, he loves alle that es. For in mankynde that schalle be saffe is comprehende alle that ys, alle that ys made and the makere of alle; for in manne ys god & so in man ys alle. And he that thus generalye loves alle his evyn crystene, he loves alle, and he that loves thus, he is safe. And thus wille I love, & thus I love, and thus I am safe. For y mene in the personn of myne evyn crystene. And the more I love of this lovynge whiles I am here, the mare I am lyke to the blysse that I schalle have in hevene withowten ende, that is god, that of his endeles love wolde become owre brothere & suffer for us. And I am sekere that he that behaldes it thus, he schalle be trewly taught & myghttelye comforthtede, if hym nede comforthe.

Botte god for bede that ye schulde saye or take it so that I am a techere for I meene nought soo, no I mente nevere so. For I am a womann, leued, febille & freyll. Botte I wate wele this that I saye; I hafe it of the schewynge of hym thas es soverayne techare. Botte sothelye charyte styrres me to telle yowe it. For I wolde god ware knawenn, & mynn evynn crystene spede, as I wolde be my selfe to the mare hatynge of synne & lovynge of god. Botte for I am a womann, schulde I therfore leve that I schulde nought telle yowe the goodenes of god, syne that I sawe in that same tyme that is his wille that it be knawenn, and that schalle ye welle see in the same matere that folowes aftyr, if itte be welle and trewlye takynn. Thane schalle ye sone forgette me that am a wrecche, and dose so that I lette yowe nought, & behalde Jhesu that ys techare of alle.

[For God is all that is good, and God has made all that is made, and God loves everything that He has made; and if any man or woman keeps his love from any of his fellow Christians, he does not love rightly, for he does not love all. And so, for that time, he is not safe, for he is not in peace; and he that loves his fellow Christians in general, he loves all that is. For in mankind that is to be saved is comprehended all, that is, all that is made and the maker of all; for God is in man, and so in man is all. And he that thus generally loves all his fellow Christians, he loves all; and he that so loves, he is saved. And thus I will love, and thus I do love, and thus I am safe. For I consider myself as in the person of my fellow Christians. And the more I love of this loving while I am here, the more I am akin to the bliss that I shall have in heaven without end — that is God, who of His endless love willed to become our brother and suffer for us. And I am sure that he that sees it thus, he shall be truly taught and mightily comforted, if he needs comfort.

But God forbid that you should say or take it that I am a teacher, for I do not mean that, no I never meant so. For I am a woman, ignorant, feeble, and frail. But know well, this that I saye; I have it of the showing of Him who is the sovereign teacher. But truly charity stirs me to tell you of it. For I would that God were known and my fellow Christians sped, as I would be myself, to hate sin more and love God more. Because I am a woman, should I therefore believe that I should not tell you the goodness of God, since I saw in that same time that it is His will that it be known? And that you shall see well in what follows, if it is well and truly understood. Then you shall soon forget me, a wretch; and do this so that I do not hamper you — and behold Jesus, who is the teacher of all.]

II. From MS Additional 37790, fol. 113r–113v.

"A wriched synne — "

A wriched synne, whate ert thou? Thowe er nought. For I sawe that god is alle thynge; I sawe nought the. And when I sawe that god hase made alle thynge, I sawe the nought. And whenn I sawe that god is in alle thynge, I sawe the nought. And whenn I sawe that god does alle thynge that is done, lesse and mare, I sawe the nought. And when I sawe oure lorde Jhesu sitt in oure saule so wyrschipfully, & luff and lyke and rewle and yeme alle that he has made, I sawe nought the. And thus I am sekyr that thou erte nought, and alle tha that luffes the and lykes the and folowes the and wilfully endes in the, I am sekyr thay schalle be brought to nought with the and endleslye confownded. God schelde us alle fra the. Amenn pour charyte.

And whate wrecchednesse is I wille saye, as I am lernede be the schewynge of god. Wrecchydnesse es alle thynge that is nought goode, the gastelye blyndehede that we falle in to in the fyrste synne, and alle that folowes of that wrecchydnesse, passions & paynes gastelye or bodely, and alle that es in erth or in othere place whilke es nought goode.

And than may be asked of this: whate er we? And I answere to this: Yif alle ware departed fra us that is nought goode, we schulde be goode. Whenn wrechidnesse is departed fra us, god and the saule is alle ane, and god and man alle ane. Whate is alle in erthe that twynnes us? I answere and saye, in that, that it serves us, it is goode, and in that, that it schalle perisch, it [is] wricchednes, and in that, that a mann settys his herte theroponn othere wyse than thus, it is synne. And for that tyme that mann or womann loves synne, yif any be swilke, he is in payne that passes alle paynes. And whenn he loves nought synne, botte hates it and luffes god, alle is wele. And he that trewlye does thus, thowgh he synn sum tyme be frelty or unkunnynge, in his wille he falles nought, for he will myghtely ryse agayne & behalde god, whamm he loves in alle his wille. God has made thamm to be loved of hym or hire that has bene a synnere, bot ever he loves and ever he langes to hafe oure luffe. And when we mighttely and wisely luffe Jhesu, wee er in pees.

[Ah, wretched sin, what are you? You are nothing. For I saw that God is all things; I did not see you. And when I saw that God has made all things, I saw you not. And when I saw that God is in all things, I saw you not. And when I saw that God does all things that are done, less and more, I saw you not. And when I saw our Lord Jesus sit in our soul so honorably, and love and take pleasure in, and rule and guide all that He has made, I did not see you. And thus I am sure that you are nothing, and all they who love you and take pleasure in you and follow you and wilfully end in you, I am sure they shall be brought to nothing with you and be endlessly confounded. God shield us all from you. Amen. For charity.

And what wretchedness is, I will say, as I am taught by the showing of God. Wretchedness is everything that is not good, the spiritual blindness that we fall into in the first sin, and all that follows of that wretchedness — passions and pains, spiritual or bodily, and all that is in the earth or in any other place which is not good.

And then this may be asked: What are we? And I answer to this: If all were taken from us that is not good, we should be good. When wretchedness is taken from us, God and the soul are entirely one, and God and man all one. What is all on the earth that separates us? I answer and say, in this, that it serves us, it is good; and in this, that it shall perish, it is wretchedness, and in this, that a man sets his heart thereupon [valuing it] otherwise than in this way, it is sin. And for that time that a man or woman loves sin, if there be any who do, he is in payne that passes all pains. And when he does not love sin, but hates it, and loves God, all is well. And he that truly does thus, though he may sin sometime by frailty or ignorance, in his will he does not fall, for he will mightily rise again and behold God, whom he loves in his entire will. God has made them [earthly things] to be loved of him or her who has been a sinner, but ever He loves and ever He longs to have our love. And when we mightily and wisely love Jesus, we are in peace.]

Appendix B

Margery Kempe's Visit to Julian of Norwich

From *The Book of Margery Kempe*, ed. Sanford Brown Meech and Hope Emily Allen. EETS o.s. 212 (London: Oxford University Press, 1940), pp. 42–43. [Characters normalized.]

And than sche was bodyn by owyr Lord for to gon to an ankres in the same cyte whych hyte Dame Jelyan. And so sche dede and schewyd hir the grace that God put in hir sowle of compunccyon, contricyon, swetnesse and devocyon, compassyon wyth holy meditacyon and hy contemplacyon, and ful many holy spechys and dalyawns that owyr Lord spak to hir sowle, and many wondirful revelacyons whech sche schewyd to the ankres to wetyn yf ther wer any deceyte in hem, for the ankres was expert in swech thyngys and good cownsel cowd yeven. The ankres, heryng the mervelyows goodnes of owyr Lord, hyly thankyd God wyth al hir hert for hys visitacyon, cownselyng this creatur to be obedyent to the wyl of owyr Lord God and fulfyllyn wyth al hir mygthys what-evyr he put in hir sowle yf it wer not a-geyn the worschep of God and profyte of hir evyn-cristen, for, yf it wer, than it wer nowt the mevyng of a good spyryte but rathar of an evyl spirit. The Holy Gost mevyth nevyr a thing a-geyn charite, and, yf he dede, he wer contraryows to hys owyn self, for he is al charite. Also he mevyth a sowle to al chastnesse, for chast levars be clepyd the temple of the Holy Gost, and the Holy Gost makyth a sowle stabyl and stedfast in the rygth feyth and the rygth beleve. And a dubbyl man in sowle is evyr unstabyl and unstedfast in al hys weys. He that is evyr-mor dowtyng is lyke to the flood of the see, the whech is mevyd and born a-bowte wyth the wynd, and that man is not lyche to receyven the yyftys of God. What creatur that hath thes tokenys he m[uste] stefastlych belevyn that the Holy Gost dwellyth in hys sowle. And mech mor, whan God visyteth a creatur wyth terys of contrisyon, devosyon, er compassyon, he may and owyth to levyn that the Holy Gost is in hys sowle. Seynt Powyl seyth that the Holy Gost askyth for us wyth mornynggys and wepyngys unspekable, that is to seyn, he makyth us to askyn and preyn wyth mornynggys and wepyngys so plentyuowsly that the terys may not be nowmeryd. Ther may non evyl spyrit yevyn thes tokenys, for Jerom seyth that terys turmentyn mor the Devylle than don the peynes of Helle. God and the Devyl ben evyr-mor contraryows, and thei shal nevyr dwellyn to-gedyr in on place, and the Devyl hath no powyr in a mannys sowle. Holy Wryt seyth that the sowle of a rytful man is the sete of God, and so I trust, syster, that ye ben. I prey God grawnt yow perseverawns. Settyth al yowr trust in God and feryth not the langage of the world, for the mor despyte, schame,

210

and repref that ye have in the world the mor is yowr meryte in the sygth of God. Pacyens is necessary un-to yow, for in that schal ye kepyn yowr sowle." Mych was the holy dalyawns that the ankres and this creatur haddyn be comownyng in the lofe of owyr Lord Jhesu Crist many days that thei were to-gedyr.

[And then she was bade by our Lord to go in the same city to an anchoress who is called Lady Julian. And so she did, and showed her the grace of compunction, contrition, sweetness and devotion, compassion with holy meditation and high contemplation that God had instilled in her soul, and many holy speeches and conversations that our Lord spoke to her soul; and she showed the anchoress many wonderful revelations in order to know if there were any deceit in them, for the anchoress was expert in such things and could give good counsel. The anchoress, hearing this marvelous goodness of our Lord, thanked God highly with all her heart for his visitation, counseling this creature to be obedient to the will of our Lord God and with all her might fulfill whatever he put in her soul, if it were not against the worship of God and welfare of her fellow Christians; for, if it were, then it would not be the moving of a good spirit but rather of an evil spirit. The Holy Ghost never moves anything against charity, and if he did, he would be contrary to his very being, for he is all charity. Also, he moves the soul to perfect chastity, for those living chastely are called the temple of the Holy Ghost. And the Holy Ghost makes a soul stable and steadfast in true faith and right belief. And a man double in soul is always unstable and unsteadfast in all his ways; he that is continually doubting is like the flood of the sea, which is moved and borne about by the wind, and that man is not likely to receive the gifts of God. That creature that has these tokens must steadfastly believe that the Holy Ghost dwells in his soul. And much more, when God visits a creature with tears of contrition, devotion, or compassion, he may and ought to believe that the Holy Ghost is in his soul. Saint Paul says that the Holy Ghost asks for us with mourning and weepings unspeakable, that is to say, he makes us to ask and pray with mournings and weepings so plenteously that the tears cannot be numbered. No evil spirit may give these tokens, for Jerome says that tears torment the devil more than do the pains of hell. God and the devil are forever contraries, and they shall never dwell together in one place. And the devil has no power in a man's soul. Holy Writ says that the soul of a righteous man is the seat of God. And so, I trust, sister, that you are. I pray that God grant you perseverance. Put all your trust in God and do not fear the language of the world, for the more spite, shame, and reproof that you have in the world, the more is your merit in the sight of God. Patience is necessary to you, for in that you shall keep your soul. Much was the holy talk that the anchoress and this creature had in the mutuality of their love of our Lord Jesus Christ the many days that they were together.]

Glossary

a *a; ah;* (v.) *have*

adyte(n) *assign; prepare; arrange or equip*

afor(e), aforn(e) *before*

afornseid, afor(n)seyd *foresaid*

agen(s), ageyn(e), ageyns *again; against*

al *all*

allthing, althing(e), althyng *everything*

althow(e), thow(e) *although*

alway *always*

and *and; if*

anem(p)st, anempt, anemptys, anemts *concerning; close to, toward*

ar(n) *are*

as(s)eth, asyeth *atonement, satisfaction, compensation, amends*

bare(n) *bear, endure; give birth to; carry*

be *be; by*

beclosid, beclosyd *enclosed*

be(e)n(e) *be, are*

behovith, behovyth, behovid, behovyd *behooves; is necessary, appropriate, incumbent; behooved; was appropriate or incumbent*

besekyn *to petition, beseech, ask, pray for*

besekyng *beseeching, prayer, petition*

besy *busy*

beyng *being*

bled(e)ing *bleeding*

blindhed(e), blyndhed(e) *blindness, stupidity*

blissed *blessed*

blode *blood*

blyndhed(e) see **blindhed(e)**

bowte *bought, purchased, redeemed*

browne *brown; deep, shining; dull, wan*

browte *brought*

bysynes, bysynis *affairs, business, occupation*

cam *came*

cher, che(e)re *face; expression; attitude*

chongyng *changing*

cler(e)ly *clearly*

com, com(m)en, cum(e), cummith, cum(m)yth *come; comes*

com(m)en, comon *common, general;* (v.) *come*

continu(a)ly, continua(n)t(e) *continually, continual*

contrarious *opposite, in opposition to*

contrario(u)st(e) *contrariety, perversity*

corone *crown*

coude, couthe, cowd(e), cowthe(e) *could; knew, know, could learn*

cum, cummith, cum(m)yth see **com**

curtes(ly), curtis *courteous; courteously*

curtesye *courteous, loving attitude and behavior*

Cristen(e) *Christian, Christians*

213

dearworthy, der(e)worthy *precious, valued*

dede(n) *deed;* (adj.) *mortal, death-like, dead*

dedely *deadly, death-like; mortal*

deming, demyng *judging, deciding; judgment, opinion*

departid *separated, severed*

depart(yn) *separate, divide*

deth(e) *death*

dett(e) *debt*

dey, dyen *die*

deyand, deyeng, deyng *dying*

diligens *diligence*

disese *anxiety, uneasiness, discomfort*

dispeir *despair*

divers, dyvers *several*

doith *does*

dome, domys *judgment, judgments*

domysday *doomsday, judgment day*

don(e) *do; done; to cause something to be done; finished*

dredful(l) *awe-inspiring; reverent; fearful*

dredfully *reverently*

dyen see **dey**

dyte *prepared;* **dyte him** *dressed himself*

ell *else*

enow *enough*

er, or *ere, before*

erth *earth*

ese *ease*

esyd *eased*

even, evin, evyn *fellow, equal*

eyen *eyes*

fader, fadir *father*

faire *beautiful, excellent*

fairehede *beauty, perfection*

faylyng *failing*

feith *faith, belief; religious affiliation*

fele(n) *many;* (v.) *feel*

feling, felyng *feeling*

fend fiend

festined *fastened*

fle(en) *fly from or toward, avoid or seek*

foly *folly*

for(e)seing, forseyng *foreseeing, providential*

fre(i)nd *friend*

frel(e)te, frelty *frailty, fragility, weakness*

frely *freely, generously*

ful *very, completely*

ful(l)hede *fullness, abundance*

fulsom(e)ly *fully; to completion*

geft *gift*

geve(n), gevyn, goven *give, given*

gevith, gevyth *gives*

gevyng *giving*

g(h)ostly *spiritual(ly), supernatural(ly)*

god(e) *good*

Goddys *God's*

goven see **geve**

gret(e) *great*

gret(e)nes(s) *greatness*

hat, hath *has*

haten *hate*

hatith *hates*

hede *head; heed* (v.); *as suffix, ness, as in* **plentioushede**

hem *them, those*

her *here; their*

herd(e) *hard*

herete, hert(e), herrte *heart*

214

hey, heygh *high*
heyest *highest*
heyly *highly*
hir(e), hirr, hyr *her, their*
hole *whole; wholeness; health*
homel(e)y, homley *familiar(ly),*
   intimate(ly); comfortably; personally
homl(e)yhede *intimacy, intimate*
   communion; familiarity
hote *hot*

ilk(e) *same*

joyand *enjoying*

ke(e)p(e)and, keping, kepyng *keeping*
kepe(n), kepith, kepyth *keep, keeps*
keper *keeper*
keping, kepyng see **ke(e)p(e)and**
kinde, kind *kind; natural;* (n.) *nature*
kirtle *coat, tunic*
knowen *know*

lauhen, lauhyn, lawhyn *laugh; laughed*
ledand, ledyng *leading*
leden *lead*
leking, lekyng, likeing, likyng, lykyng
   something pleasant; pleasure, delight,
   joy, happiness; pleasurable; taking
   pleasure in
lekyth, liketh, likith, likyth, lyket,
   lykyt(h) *likes, is pleasing to, enjoys*
lern(e) *teach, learn*
ler(n)id, ler(n)yd *learn; teach; to be*
   or *have been taught*
lernyng, lerning *learning, instruction,*
   teaching
leste *least*

lesten, lesteth, lestin, lestyn, *last,*
   continue
lesti(ni)d *lasted*
lestingly *lastingly*
lett(yn) *stop, hamper, prevent*
lettith *hinders, prevents, lessens*
leve *believe; leave, leave aside; live;* (n.)
   permission
leven, le(y)vyn *live; believe, believe in;*
   leave
lif *life*
liken, lyken *to enjoy, like or love, give*
   pleasure to, feel affection for; to
   compare
likeing see **leking**
liketh, likith, likyth, lyket, lykyt(h) see
   lekyth
likyng see **leking**
lively *living, alive, vibrant*
loke *look*
loked, lokid, lokyd *looked*
longith, longyth *longs, yearns; belongs*
   to, is a constituent part of
longyng *belongs to; yearning*
lov(e)and *loving*
lyken see **liken**
lykyng see **leking**
lyt(e) *light*

mad *made*
man *man, human being; human being's*
man(n)ys *man's, human being's*
mayden *maiden, virgin; maiden's*
mech *much*
mede *reward, gift, compensation*
medlur *mixture*
meke *meek*
mekely *meekly, humbly*

mekenes(s) *meekness, humility*

mekil, mekyl *much*

menand, men(e)ing, men(e)yng *meaning, intention*

mend, mende, mynd(e) *mental attention to, active understanding of; mind, memory, thoughts*

mene, me(a)nys *mediator, intermediary; means, ways, methods;* (v.) *mean, intend; say*

menin, menyn *mean, intend*

mening, menyng see **menand**

menith, menyth *means, intends*

mervel(l)id, mervel(l)yd *marveled, felt awe, wondered at or about*

mervelyng *wondering, maveling at*

methought, methowte *it seemed to me*

migt(e), myht, myte, myte(n) *might, power, capabilities;* (v.) *might*

mischevous *ill, bad*

moder *mother; mother's*

mon(e)ing, monyng *moaning, mourning*

mor *more*

morn(e)ing, mornyng *mourning*

myn(e) *mine*

myte see **migt(e)**

nan *none*

ne, ner *nor*

nede, ned(e)s, nedis, nedys *need, needs;* (v.) *need, require;* with forms of **behoove,** *must, necessarily*

neybor *neighbor*

nobleth, noblyth *nobility, splendor and worthiness*

nowte *naught, a cipher; nothing; not;* (v.) *cancel, strip; reduce to nothingness; despise*

nowted, nowtid, nowtyd *made nothing, deprived*

nowting *humiliation; annihilation*

of *of; off; by; from*

off *of; off*

on *one; over* (**al on blood** *blood all over*)*; to* (**bringith it on life**)*; privative prefix* (**onskilful**)*; in* (**on this wise,** in this way)

one *one;* (v.) *join*

onethis, onethys *scarcely*

onknowing, onknowyng *unknowing, ignorant*

ony *any*

onyd, unyd *joined, united, merged with, made one in union*

onys *once*

opteyned *obtained*

or *or; ere, before*

overpassing, overpassyng *surpassing, transcendently*

owe(n) *ought, owes*

paid, payd(e) *pleased, satisfied; liking*

parte, partie, party *part; openly, in public*

passand, passend *passing*

payeyng *pleasing, satisfying;* (n.) *pleasure, satisfaction, enjoyment*

payne, paynys, peyne, peynis *pain, pains; torture*

peas, pece, pese *peace*

pety, pit(t)e *pity*

peynt(e), poynt(e) *point, center; something to be noted or understood; goal*

plesith, plesyth *pleases*

Glossary

poynt(e) see **peynt(e)**
prayor *prayer*
pretious *precious*
prive, privy(e) *in secret, inward, hidden*
privities, privityes *mysteries, secrets*
properte, propertye *property, characteristic, distinctive attribute*

reys(e)ing, reysyng, ryseing *rising*
rysen, reysid *rise, risen, raised*
ryth(e), rythful(l) *very; right, correct*
ryt(h)fulhed(e) *righteousness, fullness of justice*
rythfully *fairly, rightly*

sad(de) *calm, dignified, serious, grave; sad*
saf(e), save *safe; saved, assured of salvation; except; (v.) keep*
saven *save*
se, se(e)n, seeth, seith, seien, sey(e)n *see, sees; saw; say, says*
seid, seyd *said*
seken, sekyn; sekyng *seek; seeking*
sekeness(e) *sickness, illness*
sekir *sure*
sekirly *securely, with certainty*
sekirnes(se) *sureness, security, certainty*
semand *seeming*
sem(e)ly *apppropriate, attractive*
semith, semyt(h) *seems*
se(y)and *saying*
sey(en) *say, saw*
shew(e)ing, shew(e)yng *vision, revelation*
shewin, shewyn, shewid, shewyd *show, shown, showed*
shold, shu(l)d *should*

sigt(e), sygte, sy(h)t(e) *sight, point of view*
sily *innocent, simple*
sith(en), syth(e), sythen *since*
slauth, slawth *sloth*
soden(ly) *sudden; suddenly*
solemn(e); solemnly *festive, dignified and splendid; (adv.) splendidly*
sone *soon*
sot(h)ly *truly*
sovereyn *sovereign*
spede *profit; a help; (v.) aid, help along*
spedeful(l) *profitable*
stede *place; a position occupied by custom or right, an appointed place*
stered, ster(r)id, steryd *stirred up, prompted, inspired or agitated*
stering, steryng *inspiration, instigation, idea, provocation*
stond(e), stonden, stondyn *stand*
stondith, stondyth *stands*
stonding, stondyng *understanding that; it being the case that; standing*
suffren, suffryn *suffer*
suich, swich *such*
sum(e) *some*
sumdel(e) *somewhat*
sumtime, sumtyme *sometime*
swete *sweet; sweat*
swetely *sweetly*
swetenes(s) *sweetness*
swich see **suich**
swith(e) *swift, swiftly*
syd(e) *side; long, ample*
sygte, sy(h)t(e) see **sigt(e)**
synne *sin*
syth(e), sythen see **sith(en)**

217

taken *take*

teching, techyng *teaching*

techith, techyth *teaches*

tempest *trouble, agitation; (v.) trouble, tempt, upset*

thai, thei *they*

than *then, than*

the *the; thee, you*

ther *there; where; their*

tho *the; those; though*

thornys *thorns*

th(o)row *through*

thow(e) *although*

thowte *thought*

thred, thrid *third*

thre(i)st(e), thrist *thirst; (v.) thirsts*

throw see **th(o)row**

to *to; two*

togeder *together*

tokyn *take; taken; (n.) token, sign*

travel(le), trevell *trouble, work, travail*

travelled, travellid, traveylid *worked; to be troubled, harassed*

tresor, tresure *treasure*

tresur(i)d *treasured, cherished*

treuth, trewth, trueth *truth*

trevell see **travel**

trewth See **treuth**

trost(e), trosten, trostyn *trust; (v.) trust, trusts*

trosting, trostyng *trusting*

trowe(n) *believe*

trueth see **treuth**

tyme *time*

uggely *ugly*

underfongyn *to receive*

understonden *understand, understood*

unyd *joined, united, merged with*

vanyshid *vanished*

very *very; true*

vexin *perturb, trouble, afflict*

waxen, wexen *grow, become*

wele *well; well-being, joy, happiness; satisfactory, good*

wened *supposed, thought, assumed*

weste, wist(e), wisten *suppose, think, believe; know*

wete(n), wetyn, witt(en); wot(e), wott *know, understand, apprehend; knows, knew*

weyte *weight*

willen *intend, will, want, wish for*

wist(e), wisten see **weste**

witt(e), wittis *intelligence, wits; (v.) know*

witt(en) See **wete(n)**

wo *woe, grief*

wold(e) *would, would like, wish, wished; willed*

won(n)yng(e) *dwelling, home; (v.) dwelling*

wonyth *dwells, lives*

worshippe *honor, respect*

worship(p)ful(l), worship(p)fully *honorable, worthy; honorably, suitably*

wot(e), wott see **wete(n)**

wreth, wroth *wrath, anger; wrathful*

ya *yea, indeed, truly*

ye(e)r(e) *year*

yeme(n) *perceive, notice; govern, take care of*

Volumes in the Middle English Texts Series

To order please contact:

MEDIEVAL INSTITUTE PUBLICATIONS
Western Michigan University
Kalamazoo, MI 49008–3801
Phone (616) 387–8755
FAX (616) 387–8750

Other TEAMS Publications

Documents of Practice Series:

Love and Marriage in Late Medieval London, by Shannon McSheffrey (1995)

A Slice of Life: Selected Documents of Medieval English Peasant Experience, edited, translated, and with an introduction by Edwin Brezette DeWindt (1996)

Sources for the History of Medicine in Late Medieval London, by Carole Rawcliffe (1996)

Regular Life: Monastic, Canonical, and Mendicant Rules, selected with an introduction by Douglas J. McMillan and Kathryn Smith Fladenmuller (1997)

Commentary Series:

Commentary on the Book of Jonah, by Haimo of Auxere, translated with an introduction by Deborah Everhart (1993)

Medieval Exegesis in Translation: Commentaries on the Book of Ruth, translated with an introduction by Lesley Smith (1996)

Nicholas of Lyra's Apocalypse Commentary, translated with an introduction and notes by Philip D. W. Krey (1997)

To order please contact:

MEDIEVAL INSTITUTE PUBLICATIONS
Western Michigan University
Kalamazoo, MI 49008–3801
Phone (616) 387–8755
FAX (616) 387–8750